Baseball Research Journal

Volume 50, Number 1
Spring 2021

D1501776

Published by the Society for American Baseball Research

BASEBALL RESEARCH JOURNAL, Volume 50, Number 1

Edited by: Cecilia M. Tan
Assistant Editors: Keith DeCandido, King Kaufman
Design and Production: Lisa Hochstein
Cover Design and Front Cover Illustration: Gary Cieradkowski, Studio Gary C
Proofreading: Norman L. Macht
Fact Checking: Clifford Blau

Published by:
Society for American Baseball Research, Inc.
Cronkite School at ASU
555 N. Central Ave. #416
Phoenix, AZ 85004

Phone: (602) 496–1460
Web: www.sabr.org
Twitter: @sabr
Facebook: Society for American Baseball Research

Copyright © 2021 by The Society for American Baseball Research, Inc.
Printed in the United States of America
Distributed by the University of Nebraska Press

Paper: ISBN 978-1-970159-35-6
E-book: ISBN 978-1-970159-34-9

Contents

Note from the Editor

Welcome to the Spring 2021 issue of the *Baseball Research Journal*. It's been a banner year for baseball research and writing. Why? Because during the lockdown(s) of 2020, when folks couldn't go anywhere or do anything else, a lot of SABR members spent their time researching and writing. The result was a bumper crop of papers: so many that some that arrived in July 2020 aren't going to see print until November 2021 at the earliest. In the ten years that I've been editing the *Journal*—and I just realized it has been ten years!—we've never had a backlog quite like it. But we'll get through it, just like we're getting through the pandemic itself, with patience and taking things one step at a time.

One thing that I do with the submissions for each issue of the *BRJ* is categorize them into thematic groups. Almost never is there an article that can't be related to two or three others. Finding the threads of connection and coincidence between the articles is part of the puzzle of putting together an issue. Rarely does one article shed light directly on another, but they do sometimes seem to be in confluence, where a mode of thought or a passing mention in one article suddenly seems applicable in the next. No matter how specialized the subject, no baseball-related article sits entirely in its own silo. That's part of the fun.

This time around, by pure coincidence, we have three articles with a Babe Ruth connection, from exploring Ruth's path through Japan in 1934 with Steven Wisensale to Roberts Ehrgott debunking some "common wisdom" about the "called shot," plus Chadwick Award-winner Michael Haupert's fascinating piece on "The Business of Being the Babe." We also have more articles besides that one which go into baseball players' off-field business and media opportunities, as John Schwarz discusses Ted Williams's business agent, "Mr. Golf" Fred Corcoran, and Michael Hoenigmann recalls that not only was Mike Piazza a prodigious slugging catcher, his IMDB/Hollywood resume is nearly as impressive. When you add Mike Kaszuba's story of seeking out slugger Dave Nicholson, I felt we had a section that went beyond The Babe to encompass the way baseball hitters become heroes, and how these figures become part of the fabric of our culture and our lives.

Stories from the margins, of course, fascinate me, too. Bill Nowlin reveals how a barnstorming team of Black players brought the "Boston Red Sox" to Darby, Pennsylvania, for an exhibition in 1918, while Dan Schoenholz explores one of the wacky experiments Carl Zamloch exhibited about ten years later in California: "reversible baseball" in which the bases could be run counter-clockwise. Sounds like a wacky promotion that could have been run in the early 1990s in the Niagara area of Canada, where David Siegel reveled in the brief, shining moment when there were four pro ball teams within driving distance. As many of you know, the minor leagues as we knew them ceased to exist in 2020, not because of the pandemic, but by fiat of Major League Baseball. This means fewer teams in fewer places.

I don't think it means fewer stories, however. We're nowhere near knowing everything about this game. This issue honors the Chadwick Awardees for 2021: Robert W. Peterson, author of *Only the Ball Was White*, Gary Ashwill, the force behind Seamheads' Negro Leagues stats database, and Alan Nathan, the preeminent physicist studying baseball. Each of them, like the other authors in this issue, found no shortage of topics to explore. This thing we call "analytics" is not, in fact, "new," but the wholehearted embrace of analytics by teams and sports media, is. All manner of nerdery is mainstream now (not just in baseball) and, frankly, that's the future I want.

As usual, the STEM lens can be applied to looking at the past, the present, or the future (which will be the subject of this summer's issue of *The National Pastime: The Future According to Baseball*, being edited by Marty Resnick and me). I divided this issue's articles into those that re-evaluate historical data and those that could be applied to understanding of the game today. In the former group Gary Belleville ranks no-hitters, while Cam Gibson explores the alternative universe in which the teams with the highest Pythagorean winning average rather than the best record are the winners. Jay Wigley extends the research begun by David W. Smith of Retrosheet two decades ago asking "Do batters learn during a game?" to now look at whether hitters from the Deadball Era learned during the course of a game as well. And Doug Jordan once again finds a unique angle to look back at past greats, this time at the seemingly anomalous "black swan": a player who had never won an award before breaking out with an MVP season.

The latter section of research articles, meanwhile, is both the most academic and possibly of the most interest to professionals in the sport. A team of undergrads at Columbia University headed by Anthony Montes explores optimizing outfield positioning, a team of professors and researchers just northeast of them in Connecticut, headed by Paul Canavan, tests out a new form of full-body analysis using a body suit with embedded sensors rather than the camera-based motion-capture systems more commonly in use for biomechanical analysis. And another undergrad, Samuel Borgemenke, looks at how great players make championships teams...and how championship teams make great players. Come to think of it, Sam's article relates back to the theme of the first section, about heroes and star-making...And so it goes, around and around.

I hope this issue is a home run.

– Cecilia M. Tan
Cambridge, Massachusetts

The Business of Being the Babe

Michael Haupert

Babe Ruth is frequently lauded as the greatest player in Major League Baseball history, and arguably the first true superstar athlete. Ruth transcended the game of baseball, and with the aid of agent Christy Walsh, he profited tremendously from that transcendence. Beyond his salary and bonuses paid by the Yankees—which made him the highest-paid player in the game for a record thirteen consecutive years—Ruth was a financial juggernaut, earning substantial sums from endorsements, public appearances, and shrewd investments. He paved the way for generations of athletes to come, turning his baseball success into off-field fame and earning power on a scale never before seen in the sports world. Whether barnstorming, making movies, or modeling underwear, Ruth had a Midas touch that allowed his income to exceed even his famously outsized spending habits.

Ruth was already a superstar before he arrived in New York, and the most famous baseball transaction in the history of the sport only enhanced that image. But it was his arrival in New York that launched him beyond mere baseball fame to the icon he became. No stage other than New York could properly display the magnificence that was Babe Ruth.

His on field exploits are well known, and are not the focus of this study. Rather, I focus on the financial side of the Babe Ruth phenomenon. Using recently discovered documents made available through the generosity of author Jane Leavy, I construct a financial picture of Ruth that goes beyond his baseball career. With the aid of Walsh, Ruth leveraged his prodigious baseball talents into an impressive financial machine that allowed him to live large while he played, and survive comfortably when his career came to a sad and much more sudden end than he preferred. Despite his battles with Walsh, in fact because of Walsh's dogged determination, Ruth lived quite comfortably after retirement. While he never faded from the public eye, after retiring from baseball his income earning opportunities slowed. He was removed from the source of his greatest accomplishments, no longer enjoyed the shrewd guidance of baseball's first real agent, and suffered deteriorating health, all of which combined to reduce his income. But an income reduced from the lofty heights that Ruth enjoyed as a player still left him quite comfortable in his waning years, and allowed him to leave a substantial trust fund to his wife Claire after his death.

"I WANT TO REPRESENT YOU"

The story of how Walsh met Ruth is not well known, primarily because its main protagonist, Walsh himself, rarely repeated the same tale twice. The most entertaining (and least likely) version has Walsh climbing the fire escape outside Ruth's hotel, climbing in through the open window to his room, and disrupting Ruth, who at the time was "entertaining" a female associate. Walsh, in his telling, slapped Ruth's bare derriere and loudly proclaimed "Babe, I want to represent you!" The rest, as Walsh would say, was history.[1]

A more likely, though also never verified, tale of the joining of this pair was also told by Walsh. In this version, he discovered Ruth's favorite source of beer, a deli near his apartment. Walsh staked out the location, and opportunistically filled in for a missing delivery boy (or bribed said delivery boy, the version depending on the time, audience, and perhaps quantity of alcohol present at the time of its telling) when Ruth called in for a delivery. Gaining access to Ruth's apartment via a barrel of beer, Walsh then impressed upon him the riches he could deliver to Ruth as his representative (the word "agent" not yet being common).

Regardless of exactly how or when Ruth and Walsh first met, the results were stunning for both. Walsh guided Ruth to wealth and financial security, which allowed him to feed his outsized appetite for life. More importantly, Walsh was able to prepare Ruth for a very comfortable, if professionally unsatisfying, future. Ruth's talent on the field, his magnetic personality off it, and Walsh's persistence and shrewd planning benefitted both men for years to come.

Walsh's association with Ruth began with a simple one-year agreement to syndicate ghostwritten stories for the Babe, making a bit of easy money for the two of them. It grew into a life- and lifestyle-changing relationship that propelled Ruth off the field as much as Ruth propelled the game on the field.

Walsh was not the first person to represent Ruth in some way, but he consolidated all the job descriptions of the various predecessors into one, and then exceeded all of their accomplishments and expectations. Prior to Walsh, Ruth had variously employed a press agent, business manager, multiple barnstorming tour organizers, and a theatrical agent, with varying degrees of financial success.

Ultimately, Walsh formed two companies. The first, which existed before he landed Ruth, was the Christy Walsh Syndicate, which specialized in syndicating ghostwritten articles for celebrity athletes.[2] The second, Christy Walsh Management, was initially responsible for marketing and managing Ruth in all endeavors beyond the ghostwritten word. Both enterprises were buoyed primarily by Ruth, but did represent other high profile clients, including Lou Gehrig, Knute Rockne, Glenn "Pop" Warner, Ty Cobb, Dizzy Dean, Rogers Hornsby, and Walter Johnson, to name a few.[3]

BASEBALL'S BEST PLAYER…AND PAID LIKE IT!

Ruth was already a household name, a prodigious talent, and a well-paid player before he arrived in New York. On December 26, 1919, baseball's most famous sale was consummated between Harry Frazee, owner of the Red Sox, and Jacob Ruppert, co-owner (with Tillinghast L'Hommedieu Huston) of the Yankees, which sent Ruth to New York in return for $100,000 plus a loan in the amount of $300,000.[4] The sale was announced to the public on January 5, 1920, by which time Ruth had already informed the Yankees that he wanted a cut of the sale price and a new contract to replace the three-year $10,000 per season pact he had signed with Boston prior to the 1919 season.

Ruth had been publicly angling for a substantial salary increase for months before the sale was announced. In November, Ruth had threatened, "I deserve more money and I will not play unless I get it."[5] He repeated his demands a month later, saying, "If Frazee wants to give me $20,000 I'll play. But if the Red Sox don't want to pay that much…I won't play…Mrs. Ruth and myself won't have to worry over financial troubles for a few years and that's why we can be independent."[6]

He was well aware of his rising fame and box-office potential, even before Walsh's arrival. There were reports that Ruth had signed a film deal for $10,000, and the first cut was already finished. The script allegedly provided a small part for his wife, Helen.

"Ruth says he will stay in the movies indefinitely and play ball between times until Frazee comes through,"[7] reported one small-town newspaper. Ruth's cryptic comment about not needing baseball, and the fact that he was actually in Los Angeles at the time of the sale, helped lend credence to the rumors about his budding movie career.

For his part, Ruth had already sworn off the motion-picture business, claiming to have rejected Hollywood's siren song. "I told 'em what I wanted and they couldn't see the proposition that way, so it's all off as far as I am concerned…I have signed no contracts and I doubt if I will. I don't like the grease paint part anyway."[8] Ruth's resistance would not last. His first starring role was filmed the following summer, though in Haverstraw, New York, not Hollywood. *Headin' Home* was released in September 1920. It was his first, though certainly not last, credited acting role.[9] Ruth was promised $50,000, but only received $15,000 for his celluloid debut, the producers of the film having gone bankrupt.[10]

The Yankees dispatched Miller Huggins to California to reel in the Babe. While he did not get a cut of the sale price, the Yankees did agree to Ruth's demands for a new contract. The new deal doubled his pay for the two remaining years on the contract. While they did not raise his base salary, they did give him a $10,000 "signing bonus" for each of the two years left on the original three-year deal.[11] The renegotiated contract tied Ruth with Cobb and Tris Speaker as the highest-paid players in the game in 1920. The following year Cobb would pass Ruth for the top earner crown when the Tigers gave him a $25,000 contract. However, Ruth obliterated that record salary in 1922 when he signed a $52,000 deal. For the rest of his career, Ruth would stand alone as the highest paid player in baseball. (Table 1) Ruth's 14 years atop the salary mountain, and 13 consecutive years as the highest paid player in the game, have never been topped.[12]

The Yankees were aware of Ruth's reputation for being somewhat cantankerous and demanding when it came to matters fiscal. In fact, this was reported to be one of the reasons that Frazee was willing to part with one of baseball's rising stars.[13] But the Yankees were prepared. As part of the negotiation process, the Yankees secured a promise from the Red Sox that if Ruth held out for a salary increase, the Red Sox would pay 50% of any increase, up to $5000. So in the end, Ruth got $20,000 per year in 1920 and 1921, but it only cost the Yankees $15,000 each year. After a successful debut season in New York (he led the league in runs, RBIs, walks, OBP, slugging, OPS, and home runs—

smashing a heretofore unheard-of 54—while batting .376), Ruth again won a contract concession from the Yankees. This time, he got them to include a bonus clause that promised to pay him $50 per home run. Ruth did not disappoint, breaking the home-run record again, this time pounding 59, and adding $2950 to his Yankee paycheck in the process. This 29.5% addition to his base pay represented the last time the Yankees ever added a performance bonus to Ruth's contract.[14]

JUST HOW MUCH MONEY IS THAT ANYWAY

Table 2 indicates how rapidly Ruth's income increased from the Yankees, World Series shares, and, as will be discussed in more detail, from endorsement and investment earnings, almost all of which were due to Walsh. The significance of those dollar amounts is not easy to appreciate. After all, today we are bombarded with gaudy financial details of player salaries. And the average American household takes in more money today than most of Ruth's outsized paychecks of yesteryear. Inflation and a changing baseball labor market

Table 1. Highest Paid MLB Players 1920–34

Year	Ruth Salary	Average MLB Salary	Highest MLB Salary	Highest Paid Player	2nd Highest Salary	Player Earning 2nd Highest Salary
1920	$20,000	$3,877	$20,000	Babe Ruth, Ty Cobb, Tris Speaker	$15,000	Eddie Collins
1921	$20,000	$4,300	$25,000	Ty Cobb	$20,000	Babe Ruth
1922	$52,000	$4,957	$52,000	Babe Ruth	$35,000	Ty Cobb
1923	$52,000	$5,166	$52,000	Babe Ruth	$40,000	Ty Cobb
1924	$52,000	$5,548	$52,000	Babe Ruth	$40,000	Ty Cobb
1925	$52,000	$6,033	$52,000	Babe Ruth	$40,000	Ty Cobb
1926	$52,000	$6,434	$52,000	Babe Ruth	$40,000	Ty Cobb
1927	$70,000	$6,738	$70,000	Babe Ruth	$50,000	Ty Cobb
1928	$70,000	$6,971	$70,000	Babe Ruth	$35,000	Ty Cobb
1929	$70,000	$6,932	$70,000	Babe Ruth	$33,000	Rogers Hornsby
1930	$80,000	$7,175	$80,000	Babe Ruth	$33,000	Rogers Hornsby
1931	$80,000	$7,286	$80,000	Babe Ruth	$33,333	Al Simmons
1932	$75,000	$6,871	$75,000	Babe Ruth	$33,333	Al Simmons
1933	$52,000	$6,360	$52,000	Babe Ruth	$33,333	Al Simmons
1934	$35,000	$5,888	$35,000	Babe Ruth	$25,000	Al Simmons

SOURCE: Haupert Salary Data Base
NOTES: Ruth salary figures in 1920 and 1921 include signing bonus.

Table 2. Ruth Career Earnings

Year	Total Contract	World Series	Exhibition Games	Endorsement Income	Annuity	Trust Fund	Total Earnings
1920	$20,000						$20,000
1921	$22,950	$1,272		$4,247			$28,469
1922	$52,000	$2,104		$7,985			$62,089
1923	$52,000	$2,405		$11,509			$65,914
1924	$52,000			$33,362			$85,362
1925	$52,000			$13,219			$65,219
1926	$52,000	$3,872		$50,244			$106,116
1927	$70,000	$6,214		$73,247		$643.13	$150,104
1928	$70,000	$6,529		$44,233		$3,200.00	$123,962
1929	$70,000	$1,078		$34,225		$4,000.00	$109,303
1930	$80,000	$600	$4,098.33	$28,967		$5,295.00	$118,960
1931	$80,000	$890	$2,808.28	$33,367		$7,900.00	$124,965
1932	$75,000	$5,659	$2,969.82	$13,989		$8,500.00	$106,118
1933	$52,000	$791	$2,681.37	$15,365		$8,720.87	$79,558
1934	$35,000	$911	$1,696.81	$58,011	$527	$8,675.67	$104,821
Total	$834,950	$32,325	$14,255	$421,970	$527	$46,935	$1,350,961

SOURCE: American League Base Ball Club of New York Records; Audited Financial Reports of the Office of the Commissioner; Christy Walsh Records

have made direct salary comparisons meaningless. In order to truly appreciate Ruth's earnings accomplishments, a bit of context is necessary.

The most obvious way to put Ruth's salary in context is to simply adjust it for inflation. When we do this by using the standard CPI deflator, his peak salary of $80,000 in 1930 and 1931 translates into a rather pedestrian (by MLB standards) $1,220,000 in 2019 dollars. This is only 27% of the average MLB salary, and $20,000 more than what the Padres paid Aaron Loup that year. Loup appeared in four games for San Diego, pitching a total of three innings and generating a WAR of 0.2. Ruth certainly did not have his best year in 1930, but he did bat .359 and led the league with 49 home runs, a .493 OBA, .732 SLG, 1.225 OPS, and 136 walks. He also drove in 153 runs, and just for good measure, picked up a complete game victory in his first mound appearance in nine years. His season was good for 10.5 WAR, 53 times higher than Loup.[15]

Another way to appreciate the spending power of Ruth's income is to compare it to the average American income instead of simply adjusting for inflation. What would Ruth earn today if his salary was the same multiple of the average American income as it was during his Yankee career? Figure 1 exhibits this relationship, comparing Ruth's career earnings to the 15 most recent years of currently available US household income data. For example, in 1920 Ruth earned 13.5 times what the average American earned. If he earned that much in 2004, he would have earned $777,379. His salary using this comparison peaks at $5.7 million in 2018, far better than the simple inflation adjusted value of $1.2 million, but still not particularly impressive. For example,

it would have made him only the 16th highest paid player on the 2019 Yankees.

For another perspective, Figure 2 compares Ruth's adjusted salary, using the same method of multiple of average income, to the actual earnings of Barry Bonds during his career. As we can see, each year Bonds earned between two and six times Ruth's calculated modern day salary. In fact, Ruth's calculated modern day salary more closely resembles the career salary path of Billy Hamilton than it does Bonds. So the obvious question is why does Ruth look like Hamilton? Surely that cannot be the modern day equivalent of Babe Ruth's earning power.

The answer to this lies not in the relative abilities of players today versus yesteryear, nor in simple multiples of older salaries to account for inflation or average incomes. Rather, it is a function of how the business of baseball has changed. In Ruth's day, there was one primary source of income for a team: ticket sales. During Ruth's career, the Yankees regularly earned 50–60% of their total income from the sale of tickets each year. Compare that to today, where the average team gets only a third of its earnings from gate revenue. Television is the major source of income for MLB, though it does vary considerably across teams. Concession revenues are much higher, and advertising has become much more sophisticated and pays more than it ever did. In 1930, no MLB team earned stadium naming rights. Today almost every team does. Luxury boxes and parking are other significant revenue sources that did not exist in Ruth's day. Players today earn much more than they did in Ruth's day however, mostly because of free agency. Ruth had two

Figure 1. The Value of Ruth's Salary from a Modern Perspective

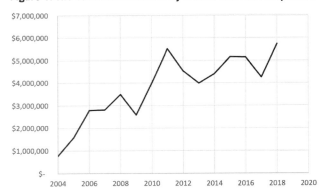

NOTES: Modern day Ruth earnings calculated by taking Ruth's actual multiple of average US household income and multiplying it by current values of average US household income over the past 15 years (the length of Ruth's Yankee career).

SOURCES: American League Base Ball Club of New York Records; Federal Reserve Bank of St. Louis

Figure 2. Babe Ruth and Barry Bonds Career Earnings Profiles

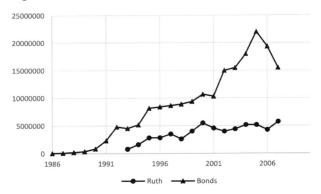

NOTES: Annual earnings for Bonds compared to Ruth's modern day calculated salary for the years he played with the Yankees. Ruth modern salaries are calculated by taking Ruth's actual multiple of average US household income and multiplying it by current values of average US household income over the last 15 years (the length of Ruth's Yankee career) of Barry Bonds's career.

SOURCES: American League Base Ball Club of New York Records; Federal Reserve Bank of St. Louis

options: play for the Yankees, or find a different line of work. The ability of a player to sell his services to the highest bidder, and the far greater amount of revenue those bidders now generate, explains why Hamilton earns more than Ruth's projected modern income.

To get a true sense of how audacious Ruth's salaries were in modern terms, we need to think of his salary in a different way. During his tenure with the Yankees (1920–34), the team signed 238 different players to contracts. At no time was *anyone* affiliated with the Yankees paid more than Ruth.[16] These contracts called for a total salary of $3,529,159, of which $867,275 was paid to Ruth. In other words, over the course of his career Ruth took home 24.6% of the total payroll doled out by the Yankees, while the other 237 players split the remaining 75.4%. Ruth's annual take of the Yankee player payroll ranged between a low of 14.5% in 1920 to a high of 27.8% in 1931 (Figure 3). In five different seasons Ruth alone was paid more than a quarter of the team's total payroll. That kind of share of team payroll is more common today in the free agent era. For example, in 2019 Zack Greinke, who was paid $34.5 million, accounted for 30.2% of the Diamondbacks payroll, and the average team allocated 18.8% of its player payroll to its highest paid player. Viewing this from the other direction, if Ruth were paid 24.6% of the 2019 Yankee payroll, he would earn $58.5 million, which would make him the highest paid player in the history of the game.

Ruth's pay relative to the average American household and the average MLB player was also quite impressive (Figure 4). He often earned ten times the average player, peaking at 11.2 times the average MLB salary in 1930. Putting a modern spin on that, if Stephen Strasburg, the highest paid player in 2019 at $38.3 million, had earned 11.2 times as much as the average major leaguer, he would have taken home a tidy $49.8 million. Ruth also dwarfed his fellow Americans in the income category, taking home 83 times as much as the average American household in 1932. That kind of ratio relative to average Americans is commonplace today. The average MLB player earns 70 times what the average American household took home in 2019. Steven Strasburg earned more than six hundred times the average American household income. And note here the difference between household and individual. In 2018 the average American earned slightly more than $43,000, but the average American household, which oftentimes features two full time income earners, brought in $63,179.[17]

In 1934, Ruth made more from Quaker Oats than he did from the New York Yankees.

Figure 3. Ruth's Share of Yankee Player Payroll

SOURCE: American League Base Ball Club of New York Records

Figure 4. Ruth's Income Relative to Average MLB and US Household

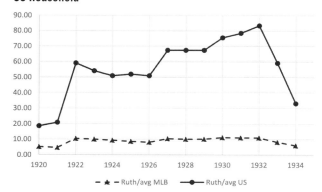

SOURCE: American League Base Ball Club of New York Records; Federal Reserve Bank of St. Louis

THERE IS ONLY ONE BABE RUTH!

But Ruth earned far more than just his contracted salary (Table 2). In addition to the aforementioned bonuses, he earned player shares of the World Series receipts in most every season.[18] Toward the end of his career he was also paid a percentage of the gate for exhibition games in which he participated. But most significantly, there was the endorsement income (Table 3), most of which was thanks to Walsh. The Yankees paid Ruth a total of $867,275 during his

Table 3. Source of Ruth's Endorsement Income

Year	Christy Walsh Syndicate	Spalding	McLoughlin Mfg Co (underwear)	Candy	Barnstorming	Adolph Kastor (knife)	Diamond Point Pen
1921	$4,247						
1922	$7,985						
1923	$11,509						
1924	$13,093				$19,019		
1925	$13,219						
1926	$12,607		$1,250	$4,914	$11,081		
1927	$12,808	$3,235	$2,250	$577	$28,282		
1928	$13,736	$5,459	$1,464	$775	$15,955		
1929	$20,485	$5,782	$2,195		$1,695		
1930	$15,190	$3,337	$1,750	$120	$4,196	$342	
1931	$13,132	$2,076	$989		$10,887	$308	
1932	$8,715	$1,703	$1,891			$117	
1933	$4,892	$517	$187			$38	
1934	$3,109	$1,600	$366			$4	$1,125
1935	$1,200	$1,062	$417		$2,912		$233
1936	$1,070	$778	$213			$3	$168
1937	$34	$588	$327				
1938		$244	$144				
Total	$157,030	$26,382	$13,443	$6,385	$94,027	$812	$1,525

Year	Quaker Oats	Esso and Sinclair Oil	Benrus Watch	Milton Bradley	Vaudeville, radio, and movies	Putnam (book)	Misc
1921							
1922							
1923							
1924					$1,250		
1925							
1926					$18,641		$1,750
1927			$500		$22,488		$3,108
1928				$975	$1,500	$1,000	$3,370
1929					$1,500		$2,568
1930					$1,875	$183	$1,975
1931				$2	$5,625	$23	$325
1932				$65			$1,499
1933				$38	$1,125		$8,568
1934	$38,625	$12,375	$188	$30			$589
1935	$18,750		$614		$1,479		$725
1936	$5,413				$750		$675
1937		$14,625			$1,875		$375
1938							$750
Total	$62,788	$27,000	$1,302	$1,086	$58,108	$1,207	$26,275

SOURCE: Christy Walsh Records

career, and during that same time he earned an additional $469,432 in endorsement and investment (annuity and trust fund) income. Actually, he earned more, as the only endorsement income records we have are from Walsh's records, and he did not begin to represent Ruth until 1921. In addition, even when represented by Walsh, Ruth occasionally negotiated some deals on his own, and he had preexisting contracts for vaudeville appearances and barnstorming tours that ran as late as 1923.

Walsh used the Rod Tidwell rule for choosing endorsement opportunities for Ruth: "Show me the money."[19] Babe hawked everything from underwear to annuities, and put the earning power of his baseball peers to shame while doing it. He earned $3000 for a print ad for Whizit coveralls. This was what the average major leaguer earned in an entire year in 1920, and was 30% of his base salary that year. He got $1302 for a similar type ad for Benrus watches. That is how much the average American earned in 1921.

His most lucrative deal was a three-year contract Walsh negotiated with Quaker Oats that netted Ruth $62,788, not to mention all the Puffed Wheat and oatmeal he cared to eat. That amount was about what the entire Yankees pitching staff took home in 1921.

Babe also sold underwear, earning $13,433 for lending his name to Babe Ruth's All America Athletic Underwear line. It was his longest lasting commercial relationship, covering 13 years, one year longer than the deal he had with Spalding Brothers. "There is Only One Babe Ruth," crowed the tag line in one of his underwear ads. And apparently that was worth a lot to both Ruth and the proprietor of said undergarments. Ruth once negotiated a $1000 appearance fee for spending an hour with a pile of underwear in one of Chicago's leading department stores.[20]

Ruth was also a popular addition to vaudeville programs, earning $19,890 for his brief appearances telling corny jokes and performing kitschy songs. It took the average major leaguer more than three years to take home the amount that Ruth got for a few weeks of appearances.

His biggest paychecks were cashed selling himself: $157,030 earned from his ghostwritten syndications and another $94,027 from barnstorming tours, the most famous of which was the 1927 tour he and Lou Gehrig took across America. During Ruth's career, the Yankees signed 238 total players to big-league contracts, one of whom was Ruth. Only nine of them earned as much over their entire careers as Ruth did barnstorming.

Ruth earned $6,835 shilling his Ruth's Home Run candy bars for a nickel apiece, but not a cent from the sale of the Baby Ruth bar. You can still get a Baby Ruth (which was *not* named after President Grover Cleveland's daughter), but good luck finding a Ruth's Home Run bar. Curtiss Candy, shamelessly capitalizing on the popularity of Ruth, was selling one billion bars each year by 1925 when Ruth and Walsh began a fruitless six-year court battle to gain a bite of the sweet proceeds.[21]

Walsh ended his relationship with Ruth in 1935. The confluence of Ruth's retirement and the dissolution of Walsh's marriage led to his severing ties with both the Babe and the Christy Walsh Syndicate. The final contract he negotiated for Ruth expired on May 1, 1938, thus ending their financial relationship. He sent Ruth an itemized accounting of their financial relationship over "17 years of congenial and mutually profitable relations."[22] Walsh did make one brief, final appearance on behalf of Ruth when he negotiated his coaching contract with the Brooklyn Dodgers three years later.

PRIVATE CITIZEN RUTH

Ruth's career came to an inglorious end, back in Boston where it had begun. He was unceremoniously released by the Yankees on February 26, 1935, and signed that same day by the Braves. He did enjoy one last hurrah, banging out the final three home runs of his career in a game at Forbes Field on May 25. But the sizzle was gone, and when Ruth realized he had been misled, and the Braves really did not have any plans to make him a manager or front-office executive, he retired shortly thereafter. He did appear in uniform again, signing a one-year deal for $15,000 to coach first base for the Brooklyn Dodgers. He had been talked into this position under the pretense of being given a shot at managing. The offer was not serious, and once again, when Ruth realized he was merely a sideshow, he walked away, this time for good.

It didn't really get much better for Ruth. He did negotiate numerous appearances, both grand (visiting children in the hospital) and garish (dressing in costume for a country club softball game). While his post-career life did not live up to his career accomplishments, he did not suffer financially, thanks to the perseverance and shrewd investments made by Walsh.

When Walsh was squirreling money away for the Babe during his fattest career earning years, Ruth protested, preferring the instant gratification that came from faster cars, more booze, and more women to share it with. But ultimately, Walsh prevailed. This allowed Ruth to live a very comfortable, if not lavish, lifestyle during his retirement (Table 4).

Table 4. Ruth's Post-Career Earnings

Year	Endorsements	Annuity	Trust Fund	Sale of Securities	Total	Average US Non-Farm Wage
1935	$27,391		$8,000		$35,391	$1,096
1936	$9,069		$8,000		$17,069	$1,117
1937	$17,824		$8,000		$25,824	$1,279
1938	$1,139		$8,000		$9,139	$1,299
1939			$8,000		$8,000	$1,299
1940			$8,000		$8,000	$1,424
1941			$8,098	$17,000	$25,098	$1,613
1942			$6,800	$11,000	$17,800	$1,922
1943		$3,910	$6,800		$10,710	$2,391
1944		$4,265	$6,800		$11,065	$2,462
1945		$4,265	$6,800		$11,065	$2,486
1946		$4,265	$6,800		$11,065	$2,396
1947		$4,265	$6,800		$11,065	$2,756
1948		$2,843	$5,100		$7,943	$2,989

SOURCE: Christy Walsh records

Though Ruth's annual earnings decreased during his retirement as a result of diminishing endorsement income, it still afforded him a very comfortable standard of living relative to the average American (Figure 5). Ruth's deteriorating health slowed down his activities and his spending, so the fact that he was earning only 6% of his peak career earnings by the end still left him far from destitute. In fact, since his first full season in 1915, he never earned less than two and a half times more than the average American for the rest of his life. Not bad for a kid who grew up in a boys' home.

Walsh worked wonders for the Babe, and he didn't do so badly for himself either, taking a cool 25% of Ruth's endorsement earnings as his commission. In case you are wondering, that is about five times what the modern sports agent earns—though as previously indicated, on a much higher base. Walsh's annual earnings from Ruth alone were five to ten times the average American paycheck of the day, and Ruth was not his only source of income, though he was his most lucrative.

And the Yankees did all right as well. Figure 6 shows their earnings due solely to Ruth and compares them to alternate investments that they could have made with the $100,000 they paid for Ruth.[23] Of course, as recent research has shown,[24] the Yankees actually paid far less than that for Ruth, which makes the deal even sweeter…if you're a Yankees fan. ■

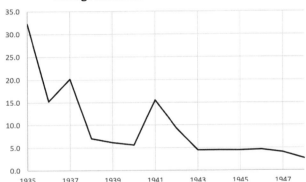

Figure 5. Ruth's Retirement Earnings Relative to the Average American

NOTE: Ruth's post-retirement earnings from all sources (see Table 3) relative to the average US non-farm wage.

SOURCES: Christy Walsh Records; Federal Reserve Bank of St. Louis

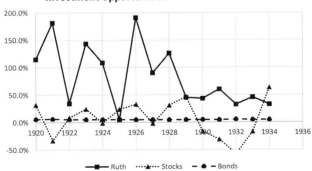

Figure 6. Yankee Earnings Due to Ruth vs Alternate Investment Opportunities

NOTES: Alternate annual returns calculated based on $100,000 investment in the Dow Jones Industrial Average and AAA bonds from January 1, 1920 through December 31, 1934. Yankee return on Ruth investment from Haupert 2015.

SOURCE: Haupert 2015

Bibliography

Ahrens, Mark, "Christy Walsh, Baseball's First Agent," August 4, 2010, https://www.booksonbaseball.com/2010/08/christy-walsh-baseballs-first-agent.

American League Base Ball Club of New York Records 1913–1950, National Baseball Hall of Fame Library, Cooperstown, NY.

Audited Financial Reports of the Office of the Commissioner, National Baseball Hall of Fame Library, Cooperstown, NY.

Baseball-Reference.com.

Boston Globe, various issues.

Christy Walsh Records, private collection.

The Daily Times (Davenport), various issues.

Federal Reserve Bank of St. Louis, Economic Data, https://fred.stlouisfed.org.

Haupert Baseball Salary Database, private collection, 2020.

Haupert, Michael, "The Sultan of Swag: Babe Ruth as a Financial Investment," *The Baseball Research Journal* 44 no. 2, (Fall 2015), pp 100–07.

Haupert, Michael, "Sale of the Century: The Yankees Bought Babe Ruth for Nothing," in Bill Nowlin, ed., *The Babe*, Phoenix: SABR, 2019, pp 79–82.

Internet Movie Data Base, https://www.imdb.com/name/nm0751899/?ref_=fn_al_nm_1.

Leavy, Jane, *The Big Fella: Babe Ruth and the World He Created*, New York: Doubleday and Co., 2018.

Los Angeles Times, various issues.

Lynch Jr., Michael T., Harry Frazee, *Ban Johnson and the Feud That Nearly Destroyed the American League*, Jefferson, NC: McFarland & Company, Inc., 2008.

The New York Times, various issues.

Stout, Glenn, *The Selling of the Babe*, New York: Thomas Dunne Books, 2016.

Voigt, David Quentin, *American Baseball: From the Commissioners to Continental Expansion*, Lincoln, NE: University of Nebraska Press, 1983.

Notes

1. For more detail on the alleged stories of the meeting between Ruth and Walsh, see Leavy.
2. At its peak, Walsh employed 34 writers, including Ford Frick and Damon Runyon. See Voigt.
3. Ahrens; See Leavy for a more detailed discussion of Walsh's business affairs.
4. Haupert, "Sale of the Century."
5. "Ruth Sends Back Contract to Frazee," *Boston Globe*, November 4, 1919.
6. "Renounces Films and May Give Up Baseball," *Los Angeles Times*, December 2, 1919.
7. "Babe Ruth Moves to Film Headquarters," *The Daily Times* (Davenport, IA), November 4, 1919.
8. "Renounces Films and May Give Up Baseball," *Los Angeles Times*, December 2, 1919.
9. Ruth appeared in nine more films between 1927 and 1932, and appeared as himself in an additional 20 films, shorts, and documentaries. He is also credited with three soundtrack appearances (though two came after his death), and as a writer for *The Babe Ruth Story*. See imdb.com for complete details.
10. Leavy, 228.
11. Giving a player a raise by adding a signing bonus to his contract was a common tool used by owners to mollify players who demanded a raise (and were talented enough to have some bargaining leverage). This gave the player the money they desired, but preserved a lower base salary for future bargaining purposes. If the team and player negotiated a percentage raise in the future, it was based on the salary, not the total pay in the contract.
12. The closest challengers have been Alex Rodriguez (12-time salary leader, six consecutive years) and Willie Mays (11-time salary leader, seven consecutive years), see Haupert Baseball Salary Database.
13. "Red Sox Sell Ruth for $100,000 Cash," *Boston Globe*, January 6, 1920, 1,5.
14. Later in his career, the Yankees added an exhibition-game clause to Ruth's contract, giving him a percentage of the gate for exhibition games in which he played for the Yankees.
15. Performance data measures from Baseball-Reference.com.
16. This includes all employees, even owners Ruppert and Huston, who did not take salaries from the team. Note that taking a salary and collecting team profits are different. AL Base Ball Club of New York Records.
17. Federal Reserve Bank of St. Louis.
18. Participants in the World Series earned substantial shares of the receipts, while teams finishing in second through fourth in each league earned progressively smaller shares. Audited Financial Reports of the Office of the Commissioner.
19. Cuba Gooding, Jr., playing the character Rod Tidwell, uses this line in a conversation with his agent, in *Jerry Maguire*, Tri Star Pictures, 1996.
20. Leavy, 223
21. See Leavy, p. 223–36 for a thorough account of the legal battle between Ruth and Curtiss Candy Co.
22. Leavy, 419.
23. Haupert, "The Sultan of Swag."
24. Haupert, "Sale of the Century."

Playing Dominoes with the Called Shot

Did Violet Popovich Really Set the Whole Thing Off?

Roberts Ehrgott

Post hoc, ergo propter hoc: used in logic to describe the fallacy of thinking that a happening which follows another must be its result.
— *Webster's New World Dictionary,* Second College Edition

When the legend becomes fact, print the legend.
— *The Man Who Shot Liberty Valance* (1962)[1]

By long-standing consensus, a 21-year-old show girl named Violet Popovich "opened the door for [Mark] Koenig to become a Cub and baseball legend" when she shot Bill Jurges of the Chicago Cubs in July 1932. Three decades later, Bill Veeck Jr., whose father ran the Cubs franchise in that era, vividly remembered the sensational impact of Popovich's deed: "Turmoil! Sirens! Police! Doctors! Newspapermen! Scandal!"[2] One effect of Popovich's resulting notoriety has been to furnish innumerable baseball writers with an all-but-irresistible opening act for the saga that culminated in Ruth's called shot.

In more nuts-and-bolts fashion, the shooting invariably serves to explain Mark Koenig's arrival in Chicago—namely, that the Cubs had to rush out and replace the wounded Jurges with another shortstop, a former Yankee whose mistreatment by the Cubs would later rouse Ruth's (probably feigned) ire. This conventional wisdom regarding Koenig's path to Chicago began taking shape as early as September 1932, when Murray Tynan of the *New York Herald-Tribune* noted that the Cubs had bought Koenig "**to take care of the emergency that existed when Jurges was shot and wounded**" (emphasis added).[3] Since then, a legion of baseball voices, whether or not privy to Tynan's pioneering effort, has reached near unanimity on this point (Table 1).

Table 1. "Koenig Replaced Jurges After He Was Shot"

"After casting around for a replacement for Jurges the Cubs came up with one-time Yankee Mark Koenig."	Sugar 1986[4]
"[Koenig] was called up by the Cubs in August when Billy Jurges was shot."	Shatzkin 1990[5]
"[Koenig] was tapped to replace regular shortstop Billy Jurges, who had been shot by a showgirl in his hotel."	Seaver & Appel 1992[6]
"By the time Jurges returned [Koenig was playing shortstop]."	Golenbock 1995[7]
"The Cubs signed shortstop Mark Koenig to substitute [for Jurges]."	Johnson & Ward 1995[8]
"Jurges had been shot. ...Chicago looked to San Francisco. ... 'Grab [Koenig],' ordered Cub president Bill Veeck, Sr."	Trachtenberg 1995[9]
"[E]x-Yankee Mark Koenig was [bought] to play shortstop after Billy Jurges had been shot in the hand by a girl in Chicago."	Neft & Cohen 1996[10]
"The Cubs picked [Koenig] up when their own shortstop [Jurges] got injured."	Lally 2003[11]
"Koenig was brought to Chicago to fill in for Jurges."	Santo & Pepe 2005[12]
"[T]he Cubs...needed a shortstop to replace Jurges while his injuries healed. They settled on Mark Koenig."	Montville 2006[13]
"The Cubs picked up [Koenig] as a replacement for... Jurges, who had been wounded by a Chicago showgirl."	Frommer 2008/2015[14]
"The Cubs...needed a shortstop without a bullet wound. So they signed Mark Koenig."	Will 2014[15]
"Koenig...had joined the team in August (after a showgirl shot Cubs' starter Billy Jurges in the hand)."	Wehrle 2018[16]

Contrary to the hypothesis of Tynan et al., however, Koenig absolutely, positively did not fill in for or replace Jurges while he recovered from his gunshot wounds. Two points bear emphasis: 1) for the entire span of Jurges's absence in July, Koenig was gainfully employed as a shortstop in the Pacific Coast League, and 2) he did not make a start for the Cubs until six weeks after the shooting. Every inning Jurges missed while recuperating was covered by the Cubs' incumbent starting third baseman, Woody English. You can look it up. Nonetheless, casual as well as more-attentive students of the called shot can be forgiven for believing that Koenig (who did take Jurges's place by the second half of August) all but stepped over Jurges's prostrate form to take up his new position at shortstop. Popovich may go unnamed, but one way or another her bullets invariably seem to be the catalyst for the called shot.

The Internet era seems to have provided renewed opportunities for mischief-making about Jurges's and Koenig's status at various points in summer 1932. A biography commissioned by the Society for American Baseball Research asserts that Koenig was already starting for the Cubs at "the end of July"—while the National Baseball Hall of Fame website places Koenig's arrival in "late August."[17] Koenig's purchase date of August 5 and arrival on August 11 render both statements inaccurate. As for Jurges, an item at Baseball-Reference.com ignores the site's sizable databases in order to claim that the wounded Cubs shortstop missed "three weeks," nearly a week longer than the actual 15 days.[18] That's a rounding error compared to the calculations of another site, which extends Jurges's absence through "the end of the season"—a fivefold increase in the period involved.[19]

One result of the Internet era's free-form approach to the story is to obscure the exact nature of Koenig's acquisition—not only *when* but, more important, *why* this essential figure in the chain of events actually became a Cub. One means of investigating the problem begins with a seemingly innocuous question: If the Cubs needed Koenig urgently after Popovich shot Jurges, why did they take another month—until August 5—to acquire him?

The inclination to ignore Jurges's and Koenig's whereabouts during the missing month probably has more than one point of origin. Confirmation bias provides one plausible source: after all, Koenig took over after the Cubs' original shortstop was almost killed, didn't he? Then too, tracking the Cubs' personnel maneuvers in July and August 1932 can prove daunting without a scorecard—and there's the ever-present lure

of adding a dash of sex and violence to one of the most memorable baseball stories ever told.

Table 2. Basic Jurges–Koenig Timeline, 1932

1.	July 6	Jurges shot
2.	July 6–23	English takes over as Cubs' shortstop
3.	July 24	Jurges reinstated as starting shortstop
4.	August 5	Koenig acquired (Jurges continues starting)
5.	August 11	Koenig joins ballclub (Jurges continues starting)
6.	August 14–18	Koenig makes three late-inning appearances as pinch-hitter or defensive replacement (Jurges continues starting)
7.	August 19	Jurges sits down Koenig begins 22 consecutive starts at shortstop

Besides the date of Jurges's shooting, few accounts of Mark Koenig's arrival in Chicago include the dates or events listed above. (Courtesy Baseball-Reference.com)

In recent years, several efforts have substantiated the Jurges-Koenig timeline in more accurate detail. In 2013, this writer's *Mr. Wrigley's Ball Club* traced the dates of Koenig's acquisition and his progress into the Cubs' lineup; since then, *Babe Ruth's Called Shot: The Myth and Mystery of Baseball's Greatest Home Run* (2014); "The Show Girl and the Shortstop" (*Baseball Research Journal*, Fall 2016); and *The Called Shot: Babe Ruth, the Chicago Cubs, and the Unforgettable Major League Season of 1932* (2020) have likewise mapped the same basic timeline.[20] These efforts concur that Koenig did not appear on the field for the Cubs until mid-August 1932—a common framework that, at a minimum, rules out the long-held consensus that Koenig arrived under emergency circumstances.

That's progress, yet both *Ruth's Called Shot* and "Show Girl" afford Popovich at least some role, however tenuous, in facilitating Koenig's arrival in Chicago. "Show Girl" in particular stresses the far-reaching, historic importance of being Violet Popovich, a woman who left no domino standing:

When Violet [Popovich] recklessly pulled the trigger in the Hotel Carlos, her bullets not only **struck Jurges** but had a ***domino effect*** on the **Cubs**, Mark **Koenig**, the 1932 **pennant race**, the division of the World Series **money**, and Babe Ruth's arguable "***called shot***." ("The Show Girl and the Shortstop," page 74; emphasis added.)[21]

Popovich did it with her .22 on the fifth floor of the Carlos, and from there the entire strand fell cleanly to the legendary finale starring Babe Ruth, not a miss or even a wobble on the way. As in the oft-told stories of decades past, Popovich bears ultimate responsibility for the drama that continues to fire the imagination of baseball fans everywhere. Search engine optimization, Google Books, and the ubiquitous Wikipedia should ensure a long life for this version of Popovich's impact on baseball history.[22]

MAKING A DIFFERENT CASE

Or maybe not. The narrative of *Mr. Wrigley's Ball Club* plainly tied Koenig's purchase on August 5 to Rogers Hornsby's removal from the roster on August 3, and in 2020, *The Called Shot* confirmed that Koenig was indeed Hornsby's direct replacement. In between those two efforts, "Show Girl" also lowered its pro-Popovich stance momentarily to concede offhandedly that there just might be something to the Hornsby-replacement case:

> **One could make a case that the Cubs hired Koenig to replace Rogers Hornsby**…[b]ut sportswriters observed that [William] Veeck had been concerned about Jurges's recovery. ("The Show Girl and the Shortstop," page 71; emphasis added.)

However, no investigation ensued concerning the possibility that the Cubs "hired Koenig to replace Rogers Hornsby." Nonetheless, if there's any credible case that Koenig was acquired to replace Hornsby, an associated inference arises: *Perhaps Popovich toppled nothing but the Jurges domino and missed the rest of the line completely.* Hornsby's woes would replace Jurges's as the Cubs' main incentive for obtaining Koenig.

With the disposition of so many dominoes at stake in some of baseball history's best-known outlets, it seems only sporting to look at both cases (including variant versions) in greater depth. There's really no lack of raw material to sift through: to begin with, Bill Veeck Sr. and more than a few sportswriters (more precisely, *baseball* writers, a distinction that makes a difference) addressed the point repeatedly in August 1932. Such standard research tools as statistics, box scores, and specific recorded events are also readily available. (See Table 3.)

The idea that Koenig stepped into Rogers Hornsby's shoes rather than Bill Jurges's may strike many students of the game, schooled to accept Jurges as the weak link and Koenig as the solution, as downright outlandish: "Koenig replaced Jurges, didn't he?" Well, yes and no; in a way; something like that. Perhaps a more systematic airing of the Hornsby-replacement case and other forgotten voices from the past can begin to peel away decades of misunderstandings and establish a better platform for future discussions.

1. The Roster Opening. The process begins by revisiting the unremarkable but necessary underpinning of the Koenig transaction: that is, on August 3 the Chicago Cubs officially released a reserve infielder named Hornsby and, two business days later, purchased a Pacific Coast League infielder named Koenig. In the narrowest, most elementary sense, then, the ball club certainly did "[hire] Koenig to replace Hornsby."

2. Hornsby: A Two-for-One Package. Merely reciting the bare bones of the roster transaction, though, does not explore additional factors that might have led to the release of this particular reserve infielder. Bad bat? Bad glove? Bad influence in the clubhouse? All of the above, yes—but more important, the evening before releasing reserve infielder Hornsby, Bill Veeck Sr. convened a press conference at Philadelphia's Ben Franklin Hotel to announce a non-roster transaction: he had just fired infielder Hornsby's inseparable twin, *manager* Rogers Hornsby.[23] The managerial firing left infielder Hornsby technically still a Cub until the league offices opened the next morning, Tuesday, August 3, the official date on which infielder Hornsby is recorded as following manager Hornsby out the door. Hornsby's vacated roster spot lay open until Thursday, August 5, when the Cubs acquired a replacement infielder, Koenig (although he did not join the club in person until the next week).

Veeck had fired an executive for cause: that was the main thing, on its face nothing to do with Jurges's performance or anything Popovich had done, and that action also automatically involved cutting a reserve infielder. (Admittedly, the opportunity to upgrade the infield in the bargain must have been the cherry atop Veeck's sundae.) Whether or not Veeck was simultaneously concerned about Jurges's continued viability as a starter, the firing of Hornsby was what set things off—pushed over the next domino, if you will. The demonstrable elements of the firing and its context merit a thorough, good-faith evaluation before plunging into more-nebulous considerations. In short, it is no stretch to suggest that Veeck's overriding concern in early August was ridding the club

Table 3. Mark Koenig's Projected Role with the Cubs: Press Comments Appearing in August–September, 1932

KOENIG'S PROJECTED ROLE	PUBLICATION
• BILL VEECK SR.'S STATEMENTS IN THE PRESS	
"We already have added Mark Koenig, the former Yankee shortstop, for **utility purposes**."	Associated Press report in *St. Louis Post-Dispatch* August 9, 1932
"We have acquired Mark Koenig from the Missions as a utility infielder **to replace Hornsby**."	*New York World-Telegram* September 24, 1932
• NEXT-DAY REPORTS OF KOENIG'S ACQUISITION	
"**Infielder**"	*Chicago Tribune*, August 6, 1932
"**Extra infielder**"	Associated Press report in *The New York Times* August 6, 1932
"**Utility infielder**"	*South Bend Tribune*, August 6, 1932
"Koenig was purchased by the Cubs for **utility purposes** as Mark stands **little chance to displace** such sterling performers as Herman, English or **Jurges**."	*San Francisco Examiner,* August 6, 1932
"Koenig will **replace Stan Hack** on third base in all probability."	*Santa Cruz Sentinel*, August 6, 1932
• POST-ACQUISITION COMMENTS IN CHICAGO NEWSPAPERS	
"[Koenig's] addition means the Bruins are well equipped for **any infield eventuality**, such as illness of the regulars, or injuries."	*Chicago Herald-Examiner*, August 13, 1932
"Koenig **inherited Hornsby's utility role**" and uniform number.	*Chicago Times*, August 16, 1932
"[W]hen Hornsby was removed, the imperative need for a **utility infielder** prompted the Cubs to purchase [Koenig]."	*Chicago Herald-Examiner*, August 21, 1932
"**Utility infielder**"	*Chicago Tribune*, August 21, 1932
"The Cubs sent out a call for a young **infielder**, and Scout Jack Doyle recommended Koenig."	*Chicago Daily News*, August 24, 1932
"The Cubs began to worry about the **reserve strength** of their infield."	*Chicago Tribune*, August 31, 1932
"[Koenig] was brought back as a possible **utility infielder**."… [T]he Cubs needed a man to fill the Rajah's dual role as **utility infielder**."	*Chicago Times*, c. September 11, 1932
• POST-ACQUISITION COMMENTS IN WIRE SERVICE REPORTS	
"**Utility infielder**"	United Press report in *Wisconsin State Journal* August 9, 1932
"**Reserve role**"	United Press report in *Ames Daily Tribune* August 24, 1932
"**Relief duty**"	United Press report in *Indianapolis News* August 26, 1932
"[The Cubs selected Koenig as an] **infielder**."	Consolidated Press Association (CPA) report in *Oakland Tribune*, September 2, 1932
"**Reserve infield material**"	Newspaper Enterprise Association (NEA) report in *Gloversville* [NY] *Morning Herald*, September 8, 1932
• ADDITIONAL POST-ACQUISITION COMMENTS	
"**Utility man…utility duty**"	*Los Angeles Times*, September 5, 1932
"[Charlie] Grimm suggested to President Veeck that a veteran player would be highly desirable as a **safeguard at shortstop**"	*The Sporting News*, September 15, 1932

In the weeks following Mark Koenig's acquisition on August 5, 1932, sportswriters consistently noted that the Cubs had purchased Koenig with a reserve role in mind. (Two possibly dissenting observations are shaded gray.) Several items mentioned that Koenig directly replaced Rogers Hornsby, the former player-manager whose role from mid-June on had been confined to pinch hittng or playing third base.

of manager Hornsby and that Koenig's acquisition was simply a byproduct of the firing. If that case can be assembled coherently, the consequences of Hornsby's behavior, not Violet Popovich's, could be considered the driver of events toward the called shot.

3. Filling Hornsby's Cleats. Reviewing the construction of the Cubs roster at the time of the firing provides one means of evaluating what Veeck's plans for Koenig might have been. Koenig, at least technically, simply filled the void that had been created by terminating the player portion of a player-manager arrangement: so far, so good, but did the Cubs president have any expanded role in mind for the new man beyond merely inheriting Hornsby's limited playing duties—such as, say, taking over shortstopping duties for a recently injured player?

A fair question—but at the time, Veeck explained that Koenig had been acquired for "utility purposes" and as a "utility infielder," both terms closely matching the common understanding of Hornsby's previous role on the squad.[24] In the following weeks, describing Koenig's role in Veeck's terms (not to mention a dearth of references to any faltering or inadequacy on Jurges's part) was echoed in a score of comments from more than a dozen contemporary writers, several of them assigned to cover the Cubs daily. (It was also noted

When the Cubs acquired Mark Koenig, he was projected as a backup infielder, not as a replacement for Bill Jurges.

that Koenig received Hornsby's old jersey number.) Intimations that the former Yankee might have been brought in with another role in mind began to appear only weeks later, after Koenig had established himself as the new star of the Cubs' pennant drive.

4. The Shortage of Shortstops. Why did Veeck settle on shortstop Koenig in particular? No doubt, Koenig's remarkable comeback in the Pacific Coast League had caught his eye, and it's been suggested that Jurges's health was still in question. But were there any demonstrable reasons beyond concern about Jurges to focus on acquiring another shortstop? Examining the available records can shed additional light here as well.

In the immediate aftermath of the shooting, Woody English had manned shortstop for more than two weeks with no realistic backup should he sprain a finger. It was by no means the first time in 1932 that the Cubs found themselves in such a predicament: both Jurges and English had already spent extended stretches of the season soloing at short without a net when one or the other was injured. Aggravating the situation, English was the team's regular starting third baseman: each time he had to slide over to short, the Cubs were forced to call upon a couple of less than satisfactory reserves (one named Hornsby) at third. In sum, most fantasy-baseball managers would appraise the left side of the 1932 Cubs infield as in urgent need of an upgrade. It's not unreasonable to suggest that this long-festering problem was Veeck's primary concern as he mulled over a potential replacement for infielder Hornsby, all the more so if evidence of Jurges's unsatisfactory performance should prove less than convincing.

5. Jurges's Condition. Was Jurges's performance during his comeback unsatisfactory? The same record book that establishes the precise dates of his absence also demonstrates that in the month after Jurges returned to action July 22, he outwardly displayed the stamina of a healthy, fully recovered ballplayer: starting 26 consecutive games, departing only occasionally for late-inning pinch hitters, and playing anywhere between 14 and 19 innings on eight different days (six double headers plus two extra-inning games). None of that seems to raise the kind of red flags that ordinarily trigger a search for a healthier replacement. Nor does scrutinizing such benchmarks as batting average and various fielding metrics reveal measurable declines in Jurges's performance during his comeback. Jurges maintained his starting role without a pause through a historic, wrenching change of managers, soon followed by the acquisition and arrival of the better-known and much more experienced Koenig.

6. The unexplored country. The Cubs' pace in acquiring and using Koenig is another factor in evaluating the narrative that Jurges's incapacity or diminished performance provoked Koenig's acquisition. The weeks that elapsed between the shooting and Koenig's purchase were followed by a further two unhurried weeks of arrival and deployment. Upon joining the Cubs on August 11, Koenig was immediately consigned to the bench; not until August 19—six weeks after the shooting, nearly a month after Jurges returned to the lineup, and more than a week after Koenig's arrival—did the signal suddenly switch to "go" for the ex-Yankee. In an abrupt reversal that began on that date, the Cubs quickly made Koenig their exclusive starting shortstop and just as swiftly demoted Jurges to the role of reserve infielder previously occupied by Hornsby and Koenig himself.

The reasons the Cubs chose one particular day in mid-August for their about-face regarding Koenig are among the most intriguing and problematic factors in the Hornsby-replacement case, yet that day has been decidedly underreported in nearly all quarters, even though you can look that up, too. To believe the reports of the Chicago dailies—two of them appearing the next morning—Koenig's first start on August 19 amounted to an unanticipated happenstance, not the fulfillment of a front-office plan.[25]

The idea that Mark Koenig owed his opportunity to Violet Popovich began to gain traction in the press only after Koenig had established himself as the Cubs' regular shortstop. The sources for such reassessments, however, tend to be unclear, and details that can be confirmed are scarce or fuzzy—even down to what the exact problem with Jurges or shortstop was supposed to have been. Beginning with that shaky foundation, the accounts often contradicted one another, forgot to remember what their own papers had reported about the Koenig transaction, and avoided addressing the 14-day gap between Koenig's purchase and his first start.

Those are sizable, though not insurmountable, hurdles in the way of the idea that the Cubs needed Koenig because Violet Popovich hurt Bill Jurges. To be sure, the *ex post facto* accounts, if shy on verifiable details,

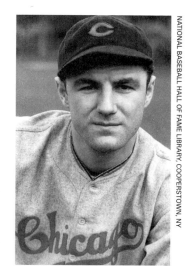

After being shot, Bill Jurges returned to action July 22 and started in 26 consecutive games, including six double-headers and two extra-inning games.

originated with veteran, well-situated writers: the two most congruent versions evidently originated with the sports desk of none other than the *Chicago Tribune*.[26] That itself is a clue worthy of its own full airing as the main portal to link Violet Popovich and Mark Koenig.

DOES IT MATTER?

For reasons large and small, scrutinizing Popovich's relevance to the called shot impacts more than quibbles and gotchas over fine points of particular comments, or guesswork about the Cubs' personnel decisions.

The Credibly Shrinking Violet. To begin with, if credible evidence lessening or removing Popovich's effect on the Koenig domino gains a foothold in the literature, her role in the big story of 1932 shrinks to that of a mere bystander whose misadventures affected the field of play only briefly; she becomes a meddlesome if dangerous hanger-on whose legacy ultimately differs little from that of another well-known gun-toting Chicago woman, Ruth Ann Steinhagen.[27]

Who Pushed Over the First Domino, and When? Subtracting Popovich from the equation would also shorten the line of dominoes, which would not begin toppling toward the called shot until a different and later point. A brand-new, unwitting author of the Cubs' eventual debacle would take Popovich's place at the head of the downsized line: Rogers Hornsby, the man who provoked Bill Veeck into taking drastic action.

What Was the Plan? Mischaracterizing or exaggerating Popovich's continued responsibility for Jurges's condition also tends to equate Koenig's acquisition with the modern era's late-summer roster moves designed to put contenders over the top. But if all the 1932 Cubs originally intended was to shore up their bench—and as suggested earlier, credible evidence exists to support that case—Koenig's acquisition originally amounted to no more than adding a journeyman.

Whether or not the eventual World Series controversy had anything to do with Popovich, it's still undeniably true that Koenig starred at shortstop, the Cubs halved his Series share, the feud commenced, and Ruth eventually turned Wrigley Field into his personal playground. Students of the called shot remain hopelessly divided on the question of Ruth's gesture to center field on October 1, yet on either side of the great divide it remains a truism that the show opened on July 6, with Popovich setting the cascade of dominoes on its way. Generations of insistent repetition in that regard have grafted the show girl's sad tale into the permanent narrative.

Should it develop that there's no Popovich to kick around anymore, the lodestar that the young woman "opened the door for Koenig to become a Cub and baseball legend" will no longer provide a convenient, safe shortcut through the dog days of the 1932 pennant race and the fabled postseason that followed. Before diving deeper into a swirl of contrarian evidence, counterevidence, and rebuttals, a couple of preliminary spoilers may be in order: Mark Koenig's famous starring role in the pennant race did not unfold in the manner repeated by generations of writers and fans, and as a result, the importance of being Violet Popovich just may have been oversold. ■

Notes

1. *Second epigraph* ("When the legend becomes fact..."): Carleton Young, playing a newspaper editor in the motion picture *The Man Who Shot Liberty Valance* (1962), uttered these words near the end of the film. Director: John Ford. Screenplay: James Warner Bellah and Willis Goldbeck.
2. Bill Veeck, Jr., with Ed Linn, *The Hustler's Handbook* (New York: G. P. Putnam's Sons, 1965), 164.
3. Murray Tynan, "Koenig Comes Back to Dazzle Those Who Counted Him Done," *New York Herald-Tribune*, September 4, 1932.
4. Bert Randolph Sugar, *Baseball's 50 Greatest Games* (New York: Exeter Books, 1986), 70.
5. Mike Shatzkin, *The Ballplayers: Baseball's Ultimate Biographical Reference* (New York: Arbor House Publishing, 1990), 581.
6. Tom Seaver and Martin Appel, *Great Moments in Baseball* (New York: Carol Publishing Group, 1992), 102.
7. Peter Golenbock, *Wrigleyville: A Magical History Tour of the Chicago Cubs* (New York: St. Martin's Press, 1996), 232.
8. Lloyd Johnson and Brenda Ward, *Who's Who in Baseball History* (New York: Barnes & Noble Books, 1994), 226.
9. Leo Trachtenberg, *The Wonder Team: The True Story of the Incomparable 1927 New York Yankees* (Bowling Green, OH: Bowling Green State University Popular Press, 1995), 17.
10. David S. Neft and Richard M. Cohen, *The Sports Encyclopedia: Baseball*, 16th edition (New York: St. Martin's, 1996), 172. This wording from the long-running annual series can be found on Google Books; it also appears in this writer's well-thumbed hard-copy version of the 16th edition (1996). However, the 1981 edition, also present on Google Books as of February 23, 2021, says only: "A sore spot was eased late in the year when ex-Yankee Mark Koenig was brought [*sic*] to play shortstop," without the additional "after Billy Jurges had been shot . . ." phrasing. Word searches in the 1981 edition for "Jurges" produced only a table with his batting statistics. Evidently, sometime between 1981 and 1996, one of the authors (Neft died in 1991) must have come across some plausible secondary information and added it to the annual's ongoing 1932 season recap.
11. Frank Crosetti, quoted in Richard Lally, *Bombers: An Oral History of the New York Yankees* (New York: Three Rivers Press, 2003), 4. Crosetti's statement is interesting on several accounts. Although Crosetti was a starter for the 1932 Yankees throughout the season and the World Series, what did he know, and when did he know it? A couple of assumptions: a) everyone in professional baseball had heard about Jurges's shooting on July 6, but b) Koenig's acquisition on August 5 necessarily received much attention. However, c) surely someone on the Yankees had been following their former teammate's remarkable comeback in the P.C.L. and his re-entry into the major leagues. The Yankees, then, d) must have known at the start of the Series that the Cubs had not picked up Koenig to replace the injured Jurges. Perhaps the overwhelming nature of the developing Cubs-Yankees feud and its famous consequences more or less blurred this less-critical distinction from their consciousness. Alternatively, the Yankees possessed closely guarded inside information about the Koenig transaction—or more likely, with the passage of decades and the inexorable pull of "Koenig at shortstop, replacing the injured Jurges" (perhaps aided by some less-than-thorough baseball history methodology in the pre-Seymour era), Crosetti came to believe a point that might have struck him as absurd in August 1932.
12. Ron Santo and Phil Pepe, *Few and Chosen: Defining Cubs Greatness Across the Eras* (Chicago: Triumph Books, 2005), 46.
13. Leigh Montville, *The Big Bam: The Life and Times of Babe Ruth* (New York: Doubleday, 2006), 309.
14. Harvey Frommer, *Five O'Clock Lightning: Babe Ruth, Lou Gehrig, and the Greatest Baseball Team in History, the 1927 New York Yankees* (Hoboken, NJ: John Wiley & Sons, 2008), 227.
15. George F. Will, *A Nice Little Place on the North Side: Wrigley Field at One Hundred* (New York: Crown Archetype, 2014), 57.
16. Edmund F. Wehrle, *Breaking Babe Ruth: Baseball's Campaign Against Its Biggest Star* (Columbia: University of Missouri Press, 2018), 199.
17. "End of July": Paul Geisler Jr., "Billy Jurges," accessed February 23, 2021, https://sabr.org/bioproj/person/aada6293. "Late August": Scott Pitoniak, "He Called It," accessed February 23, 2021, https://baseballhall.org/discover-more/stories/baseball-history/ruth-called-it.
18. Anonymous, "Billy Jurges," accessed February 23, 2021, https://www.baseball-reference.com/bullpen/Billy_Jurges.
19. Anonymous, "1932: The So-Called Shot," accessed February 23, 2021, http://www.thisgreatgame.com/1932-baseball-history.html.
20. Roberts Ehrgott, *Mr. Wrigley's Ball Club: Chicago and the Cubs during the Jazz Age* (University of Nebraska Press, 2013); Ed Sherman, *Babe Ruth's Called Shot: The Myth and Mystery of Baseball's Greatest Home Run* (Guilford, CT: Lyons Press, 2014); Jack Bales, "The Show Girl and the Shortstop" (*Baseball Research Journal* 45, no. 2, Winter 2016); Thomas Wolf, *The Called Shot: Babe Ruth, the Chicago Cubs, and the Unforgettable Major League Season of 1932* (University of Nebraska Press, 2020).
21. Although the author's name appears on page 74 as providing assistance with the article, the quoted passages from pages 71 and 74 of "Show Girl" do not represent any input he provided in the course of several prepublication email exchanges.
22. On January 30, 2019, such conclusions dominated the first pages of Google, DuckDuckGo, and StartPage after the phrase "Jurges Popovich" was entered into each search engine.
23. See *Mr. Wrigley's Ball Club*, 303–304. According to various newspaper accounts of the time, Hornsby had two contracts with the Cubs—one as a manager and one as a player.

24. "Utility purposes": Associated Press report in *St. Louis Post-Dispatch*, August 9, 1932. "Utility infielder": Veeck as quoted by Dan Daniel in "Dan's Series Dope," *New York World-Telegram*, September 24, 1932.

25. For instance, an unsigned item in the August 20 *Chicago Tribune* reported that Jurges had taken the bench due to "*a misery in his stomach* [emphasis added], but there have been complications involving his batting average." Hence, the city's major daily reported that Jurges was out sick, but the back half of the item also illustrates the problems involved in evaluating other possibilities involving Jurges's benching: his batting average had actually risen a tick since he was shot six weeks earlier, and he was also, for him, on something of a batting tear—7 hits in his last 21 plate appearances, a walk-off RBI single a few days earlier, and the next day, a 19-inning, 2-for-7 stint along with one of the Cubs' three RBI. The author hopes to publish a longer monograph that attempts to demonstrate just how elusive and murky the Popovich-Jurges-Koenig scenario continues to be, even after removing the most-glaring misconceptions—an area that, barring the discovery of some rock-solid primary source, is probably no more likely to reach final resolution than the called shot itself.

26. Arch Ward, "Talking It Over," *Chicago Tribune*, August 31, 1932, 17; "Series May Cast Old Pals in Role of Foes" (no byline), *The Sporting News*, September 15, 1932, 3. The author's understanding is that *Tribune* reporters contributed the Cubs (and White Sox) reports in *The Sporting News*. Because Edward Burns covered the Cubs for the *Tribune* during the second half of the 1932 season, he would thus be the presumed writer of "Series May Cast Old Pals." As stressed in the current article, there is substantial reason to question whether either the *Tribune* or *The Sporting News* piece can be regarded as definitive or—particularly in Ward's case—accurate.

27. In June 1949, Steinhagen, like the Popovich of 1932 a young, single Chicagoan, shot Eddie Waitkus of the Philadelphia Phillies in a Chicago hotel room. Steinhagen had become infatuated with her future victim during his previous tour of duty with the Cubs. Waitkus's injuries caused him to miss the last 3½ months of the season. (One measure of the relative notoriety of these would-be *femmes fatale*: an Internet search for "Violet Popovich" on February 12, 2019, resulted in 271,000 Google hits, compared to 65,000 for "Ruth Ann Steinhagen." Evidently, the grip of the Bambino, his called shot, and possible related events has maintained a greater hold on the public imagination than a well-regarded novel that was adapted as a successful and memorable movie.)

"This compilation, a distillation of all that is important to the society's members . . . showcases the SABRite at his or her baseball-loving, stat-obsessed best."
—Paul Dickson, *Wall Street Journal*

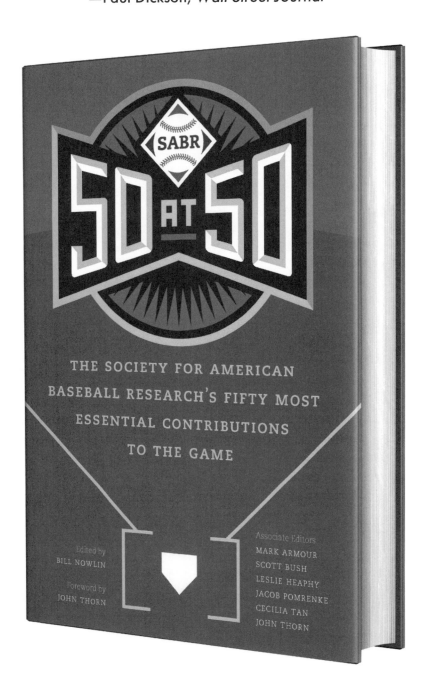

UNIVERSITY OF NEBRASKA PRESS   nebraskapress.unl.edu

In Search of Babe Ruth's Statue in a Japanese Zoo

Steven K. Wisensale, PhD

Though war clouds were gathering, it dropped peacefully out of the sky of Japan, seven years before bombs fell on Pearl Harbor and eleven years before atomic blasts destroyed Hiroshima and Nagasaki. It landed softly on the other side of the fence in right center field at a ballpark in Sendai, a city on the northeast coast of Japan, 187 miles from Tokyo. It was November 9, 1934, and Babe Ruth had just connected for the first of his 13 home runs during an eighteen-game, 12-city goodwill tour of Japan.[1]

The team of all-stars came by ship, the *Empress of Japan*, that departed Vancouver, British Columbia, on October 20 and arrived in Yokohama 10 days later.[2] The All-Americans represented the best of the best. Managed by the legendary Connie Mack, the team included future Hall of Famers Babe Ruth, Lou Gehrig, Jimmie Foxx, Charlie Gehringer, Lefty Gomez, and Earl Averill. Also on the tour was Moe Berg, a mediocre journeyman catcher who secretly filmed Tokyo Bay. According to some accounts, Jimmy Doolittle later used Berg's film, among others, to plan his famous attack on Tokyo in 1942.[3]

After receiving a warm welcome in Yokohama, the team journeyed by train to Tokyo where hundreds of thousands lined the streets to greet the All-Americans as they rode in a caravan of open-air cars. Babe Ruth was in the lead car, perched atop the back seat and smiling broadly while he waved an American flag in one hand and a Japanese flag in the other. Parades and banquets would follow in other cities, including Osaka, Nagoya, Kokura, Kyoto, Omiya, Sendai, and Yokohama.[4]

For Ruth, it was the beginning of the end. Mere weeks before he and his teammates departed for Japan, he had played his final game for his beloved New York Yankees. Rotund at age 39 and uncertain about his future, he would retire from baseball as a Boston Brave only two months into the 1935 season. But in Japan he had one grand hurrah. Adored by millions of Japanese, he often posed for photos with dignitaries, ordinary citizens, and children. He wore a kimono while posing with schoolgirls and he borrowed a fan's umbrella while playing the outfield during a downpour.[5] He was truly loved by the Japanese.

During the tour in which the team went 18–0 against Japanese All-Stars, Ambassador Joseph Grew proudly stated that "Babe Ruth is a more effective Ambassador than I could ever be."[6] After returning to the United States and during a celebratory banquet, manager Connie Mack concluded that the tour was one of the greatest peace measures in the history of nations and "there will be no war between the United States and Japan."[7] Simultaneously, *The New York Times* reported that "The Babe's big bulk blotted out such unimportant things as international squabbles over oil and navies."[8]

The now famous tour also benefitted the Japanese. Wealthy newspaper owner Matsutara Shoriki, who sponsored the tour and was greatly disappointed in his team's performance, elected to keep his squad together and create Japan's first professional baseball team, the Greater Japan Tokyo Baseball Club, in December 1934. It was the beginning of professional baseball in Japan. A year later Shoriki's club completed its own goodwill tour in the US, playing 90 games, mostly against minor league, college, and amateur teams. That team consisted of 11 future Japanese Hall of Famers and would later become the Tokyo Yomiuri Giants, as the team is known today.[9]

NATIONAL BASEBALL HALL OF FAME LIBRARY, COOPERSTOWN, NY

Ruth was at the tail-end of his baseball career, but his home-run hitting and boisterous character during the 1934 tour made him a beloved figure in Japan.

The outline of the ballpark as it existed in 1934, shown overlaid on a photo of the zoo. The small circle is where Babe Ruth's first home run in Japan landed and where his statue stands today.

But the goodwill tours of 1934 and 1935 could not stave off war. Learning that the Japanese had attacked Pearl Harbor, Ruth reportedly tossed many of his Japanese gifts out the window of his New York City apartment.[10] Japanese soldiers would shout "Go to hell Babe Ruth" while engaged in battle with Americans.[11] The war was particularly devastating for professional baseball in Japan. They lost 69 Japanese Baseball League players in combat, five of whom had competed against Ruth and his teammates during the 1934 tour. The US, on the other hand, lost two former major league players in combat and another to illness during the war.[12]

Following the bombings of Hiroshima and Nagasaki that brought an end to the war, the healing process began. Lefty O'Doul and his San Francisco Seals arrived in Japan in 1949 for a national tour, the first in 15 years. Other tours would follow and so would the exchange of players between nations. By 2020, more than 600 Americans had gone to Japan to play professionally. Fifty-eight Japanese players have been on the rosters of MLB teams. And, not to be overlooked, eight Americans have managed Japanese teams, most notably Don Blasingame, Bobby Valentine, Trey Hillman, Marty Brown, and Terry Collins.[13]

Although the old ballpark in Sendai where Ruth hit his first home run of the 1934 tour was dismantled and replaced with the city's first zoo, the very spot where Ruth's home run ball landed was permanently marked and recognized as sacred ground. In 2002, a statue of Babe Ruth was erected on the very spot in Yagiyama

Zoological Park in Sendai City, formerly the Miyagi Prefecture Yagiyama Baseball Stadium. The statue was funded by donations from local citizens who had formed the "Let's Build a Babe Ruth Statue in Former Yagiyama Field" committee.[14]

In the Summer of 2006, and on the eve of the first World Baseball Classic, Japanese Ambassador to the US, Ryozo Kato, spoke about the Babe's continued popularity in Japan today: "Concerning the sport of baseball, most knowledgeable Japanese fans are familiar with Joe DiMaggio, Ted Williams, Hank Aaron, and Willie Mays among others. Many of the current MLB stars are also popular in Japan. In other sports, some boxing champions are popular along with golfers such as Jack Nicklaus, Arnold Palmer, and Tiger Woods, and sumo wrestlers, Akebono, Musashimaru, and Konishiki (all of Hawaiian descent) can be mentioned. However, over the last century, baseball remains the most popular game in Japan and Babe Ruth is still considered the 'King.' That fact alone is an amazing feat."[15] (Kato later became the Commissioner of Nippon Professional Baseball, serving from 2008 to 2013. However, he resigned after it was disclosed that the baseballs were secretly juiced during the 2013 season, although Kato claimed he had no knowledge of it.[16])

But finding the Babe's statue is not easy. In the summer of 2017, as I was completing a Fulbright Fellowship in Japan where I taught a course titled "Baseball Diplomacy in Japan-US Relations" at two universities, I began my quest to visit each of Nippon Professional Baseball's stadiums. Riding the shinkansen (bullet trains) from north to south, east to west, I not only took in lots of ballgames and absorbed and observed Japanese culture in its various regional forms, I often imagined myself as a member of that 1934 tour. I deliberately stayed in several hotels where the '34 team stayed, including the Hotel New Grand in Yokohama and the Imperial Hotel in Tokyo. I walked the streets of Ginza, the shopping district of Tokyo where the caravan of the American All-Stars maneuvered its way through thousands of adoring fans, and I visited Hibiya Park where the team was formally welcomed by Japanese officials. And I also sat in two stadiums where the Babe played in 1934: Hanshin Koshein Stadium (built in 1924) and home to the Hanshin Tigers, and Meiji Jingu Stadium (built in 1926), home of the Tokyo Yakult Swallows.

The trip from Tokyo to Sendai to the north can be completed in less than two hours by bullet train. My room at the Mitsui Garden Hotel was a welcome refuge from a hot and humid August night. The next morning I arose early and took a 25-minute subway ride from my hotel to the Yagiyama Zoological Park. According to its website, the zoo opened in 1965 and 144 different species of animals are housed there, including monkeys, elephants, penguins, and tigers.[17] After paying a small admission fee, I entered the zoo and immediately got lost somewhere between the monkey and penguin exhibits. Backtracking to the entrance as best I could, I found a very kind guide who assisted me with my quest to find Babe Ruth's statue. Confronted with a language barrier, I imitated a batter's swing. The guide smiled and then laughed as she motioned for me to follow her. We moved through a winding maze of animal exhibits and finally, as we emerged from a blind curve, there was the Babe, completing his powerful swing that produced his first home run in Japan. No more than twenty feet away was his roommate, a powerful rhinoceros. How appropriate!

I handed the guide my iPhone and politely motioned for her to take my photo as I climbed up to assume a position next to the Babe. Wrapping my arm around his broad back, I thanked him for his contribution to baseball and I thanked Japan for acknowledging the

important role he has played in cultivating wholesome Japanese-American relations.

That evening I saw the Tohoku Rakuten Eagles win a home game at Rakuten Seimei Park Miyagi. Two days later and further north I saw Shohei Ohtani and his Nippon Ham Fighters win in Sapporo, and two days after that I was in Osaka for the opening ceremonies of the famous Koshien high school baseball tournament.[18] My journey through Japanese baseball was complete. I circled the bases with the Babe by my side.

A few months after my return to the United States I found time to reflect on my many wonderful experiences in Japan, not the least of which was my special side trip to visit Babe Ruth's statue in Sendai's Yagiyama Zoo. I compared my journey to Japan to the journey of the 1934 All-Stars. They came by ship; I came by plane. They came during peacetime and so had I. They came to teach and learn as baseball players, and I came to teach and learn as a Fulbright Scholar. They were Americans who played baseball in Japan; I was an American who taught a course about baseball in Japan. They traveled to 12 cities to play baseball; I traveled to 12 cities to see baseball. And they practiced the art of soft power diplomacy and so did I. We played the same game on the same field 83 years apart. We were all teammates acting as goodwill ambassadors doing our best to make the world a better place. The Babe was our captain. ■

Acknowledgments

The author would like to thank Yoichi Nagata, Satomi Mitani, and the members of Tokyo SABR for their assistance in conducting his research.

Notes

1. Robert Fitts, *Banzai Babe Ruth: Baseball, Espionage & Assassination During the 1934 Tour of Japan* (Lincoln: University of Nebraska Press, 2012), 130. Also refer to the game's line score on page 277. Ruth hit two home runs that day.

2. From 1930 to 1939 the *Empress of Japan* served as the luxurious flagship of the Canadian Pacific Steamship Company. Capable of accommodating 1,260 passengers, it made the roundtrip journey between Vancouver and Yokohama 58 times in nine years before being converted to a troop transport ship at the beginning of World War II. More information about the *Empress of Japan*, including photos, can be accessed at the CruiseLine-History.com site: https://www.cruiselinehistory.com/cruise-line-history-the-empress-of-japan-10-days-from-Vancouver-to-japan.

3. Fitts, 254. If Doolittle used Berg's 22-second film at all, its overall contribution to planning the raid was probably very minor. Doolittle relied heavily on Captain Steve Jurika who lived in Tokyo between 1939 and 1941 where he identified and mapped potential bombing targets for future raids if there was a war. According to Amazon.com, there have been sixteen books written about Berg's espionage exploits and two films have been produced: The Hollywood version, *The Catcher Was a Spy*, starring Paul Rudd, was released in 2018. Aviva Kempner's documentary, *The Spy Behind Home Plate*, was released in 2019. (Kempner also did a documentary on Hank Greenberg.)

Ruth's statue, with the author.

4. The National Baseball Hall of Fame and Museum, along with its library, offers many resources for researchers interested in studying the 1934 tour in more detail. The six-minute video, "The 1934 Japan Tour Footage" (filmed by Jimmie Foxx) and the accompanying article, provide an excellent summary of the tour. (See https://baseballhall.org/discover-more/stories/baseball-history/1934-japan-tour-footage-uncovered) Still photos from the tour, including one of Ruth waving an American flag in one hand and a Japanese flag in the other during the welcoming parade in Tokyo, along with another picture of him using an umbrella while playing the outfield during a game in rainy Kokura in late November, can be found in Fitts' *Banzai Babe Ruth* photo gallery between pages 146 and 147.

5. Many images of Ruth in Japan, including one of him wearing a kimono, can be accessed via online image search. See https://www.bing.com/images/search?q=Images+of+Babe+Ruth+in+Japan&qs=n&form=QBIDMH&sp=-1&pq=images+of+babe+ruth+in+japan&c=0-28&cvid=F8169EE6DC68468CB3AB3862F7BBF328&first-&scenario=ImageBasicHover&cw=1349&ch=751.

6. Fitts, 83.

7. Fitts, 193.

8. *The New York Times*, November 3, 1934.

9. Sayuri Guthrie-Shimizu, *Transpacific Field of Dreams: How Baseball Linked the United States and Japan in Peace and War* (University of North Carolina Press, 2012). Refer to chapter 5 for more details about the 1935 goodwill tour in the United States.

10. Patrick Parr, "The Sultan of Swat Babe Ruth Visits Japan." *Japan Today*, November 8, 2018, https://japantoday.com/category/features/lifestyle/babe-ruth-the-sultan-of-swat-visits-japan. The incident of Ruth destroying his Japanese gifts after hearing about the attack on Pearl Harbor has been confirmed in several interviews with his daughter, Julia Ruth Stevens, who witnessed the event. See *Banzai Babe Ruth*, page 255, where Fitts references his interview with Stevens on November 7, 2007. She died at age 102 in March 2019.

11. Jeremiah A. O'Leary, "To Hell with Babe Ruth, Yell Charging Japanese." *The New York Times*, March 3, 1944. Staff Sergeant O'Leary, a Marine Corps combat correspondent filed his story from Cape Gloucester in New Guinea in March 1944. However, in May 2011, Bonnie Taylor Blake, a freelance writer and blogger challenged this story and other similar war stories. See her blog entry "To Hell with Babe Ruth," at https://btaylorblake.com/2011/05/29/to-hell-with-babe-ruth.

12. *Baseball's Greatest Sacrifice: World War II Deaths* is part of Gary Bedingfield's "Baseball in Wartime" network. https://www.baseballsgreatestsacrifice.com/world_war_ii.html; See also Robert Weintrob, "Two Who Did Not Return," The *New York Times*, May 25, 2013. https://www.nytimes.com/2013/05/26/sports/baseball/remembering-the-major-leaguers-who-died-in-world-war-ii.html?.

13. Brad Lefton, "Japan Shifting Views on Managers," *The New York Times*, August 24, 2010. https://www.nytimes.com/2010/08/25/sports/baseball/25managers.html.

14. Babe Ruth Central, "Babe's 1934 Barnstorming Trip to Japan." This site is devoted to cultivating and preserving the legacy of Babe Ruth. This story can be accessed at http://www.baberuthcentral.com/babesimpact/babe-ruths-legacy/babes-1934-barnstorming-trip-to-japan.

15. Babe Ruth Central, 2.

16. ESPN.com News Services, "Ryozo Kato Resigns as Commish." September 19, 2013. Kato resigned just days after former major leaguer Wladimir Balentien, a gaijin (foreigner), hit home runs 56 and 57, breaking the Japanese season record held by legendary slugger Sadaharu Oh for 49 years. https://www.espn.com/mlb/story/_/id/9692461/japanese-commissioner-ryozo-kato-resigns-juiced-ball.

17. Interested readers can visit the Zoo's website at http://www.city.sendai.jp/zoo/index.html where a translator option will provide the information in English. Babe Ruth's next-door neighbor is a very large rhinoceros.

18. The Koshien high school tournament is 100 years old. Each year 49 teams from 47 prefectures compete over a two-week period in August in legendary Koshien Stadium, home of the Hanshin Tigers. Each day 50,000 fans pack the stadium to watch teams compete in the single elimination tournament. A major TV network provides national coverage for those who cannot get tickets to the games. More information about a recent documentary on Koshien can be accessed at https://www.mlb.com/news/japan-s-koshien-tournament-featured-in-documentary.

Fred Corcoran, Mr. Golf's Turn at Bat

John H. Schwarz

Fred Corcoran was the go-to guy in golf circles, starting in the late 1930s. He had successfully helped promote and sustain the fledgling PGA tour and not only had applied his business acumen to the game but had also helped guide the career of the incomparable Sam Snead. Already one of golf's greatest players, Snead had become, with Corcoran's help, one of the most sought-after golf celebrities of the 1940s.

But Corcoran's sports knowledge and internal Rolodex went way beyond professional golf and golfers. During World War II, he took former boxing champion Jack Sharkey and New York Yankees pitcher Lefty Gomez on a tour of US Army bases in England and Italy. There he conducted a combination pep talk and sports nostalgia discussion to help raise the morale of the troops and bring them a part of American life that most GIs easily and fondly related to.

Known as "Mr. Golf," Corcoran befriended almost everybody who was anybody in sports and entertainment. Among his friends were Bing Crosby, Bob Hope, Johnny Weissmuller, Jim Thorpe, Walter Hagen, Babe Ruth, and Ty Cobb, as well as most members of the sports press. His ties to most of these people came from the emerging popularity of golf, his engaging personality and encyclopedic recall of sports statistics, and some of the promotions he directed. But Corcoran's influence in the sports world broadened into the game of baseball when he met Ted Williams in 1946.

Life was a lot more casual in the late forties and Williams, a fixture on the Boston sports scene, was much more of a "regular" person in his daily life than the sports superstars of today. He lived in the heart of the community and he had to take care of his basic needs just like everyone else did. When he needed to buy a car, Ted ended up favoring a car dealership in Wellesley, Massachusetts, that sold Fords. The manager of the dealership was John Corcoran, Fred's brother. The Corcoran boys had grown up in Cambridge and all got their start in golf as caddies at the Belmont Golf Club.

Stopping at the dealership to see John one day, Williams complained bitterly about all the demands people put on his time and the distractions it created from his main focus—hitting a baseball. As he put it in his inimitable Ted Williams style, "These goddam guys won't leave me alone and I don't want them bothering me. I'd like somebody who could deal with these sons of bitches and get 'em off my back."[1]

In the mid-forties, athletes were pretty much on their own. Ted had an accountant/business manager named James Silin, whom he later replaced with Corcoran, but no one before Corcoran proactively thought about how to capitalize on the demand for Williams's charisma.[2] Negotiating player contracts before 1975, when the renewal clause was limited to one year, was pretty much a one-way street. The team made you an offer; if you didn't like it you could bellyache, but in the end, you signed the deal and got paid, or you didn't sign, held out as long as you could, and didn't get paid. But for a select few, like Williams, their stardom surpassed the baseball diamond and led to potential value from their name and face off the field.

John Corcoran suggested to Williams that he meet his brother. Fred was handling a lot of these "distractions" for Snead and others in the golf world, and Corcoran knew everyone and everything that was going on in the sports world. It would be a perfect marriage. Williams was game, maybe even desperate at the time, and a meeting was arranged.

Corcoran and Williams hit it off right away. Corcoran had clout in his field that matched that of Williams on the baseball field. To solidify their arrangement, Corcoran suggested a short letter of agreement, but Williams preferred just a handshake. As was proven later in his life when his son blatantly took advantage of his father, Williams could be too trusting. But in 1946, it was a good thing he was dealing with Corcoran, who did get a short agreement typed up. The conversation around their first agreement went something like this:

"I'll take fifteen percent," Corcoran said.

"Fifty, okay," Williams replied.

"No, not fifty," Corcoran corrected him, "Fifteen."

"Whatever you say. If you want to make it fifty, it is all right with me," responded Williams.

"I assure you that fifteen percent is a generous working margin," repeated Corcoran.[3]

The two shook on it, and when the understanding came up for renewal, Williams insisted on giving Corcoran a raise and memorialized the deal in Williams fashion. He provided a letter to Fred outlining the terms and signed by each. It was a simple note which read as follows and was signed by both men:

Dear Fred:

This will confirm that we extend our agreement of management made in 1946 which was for a five year period for an additional period of five years for the same terms and conditions except you are to receive 30 percent.

– Theodore S. Williams

Agreed Fred Corcoran

A far cry from a player-agent contract in today's world.

At the time Williams forged this relationship with Corcoran, there was very little history of baseball players or any sports figure employing an agent. When Red Grange decided to play pro football in the twenties, he did employ an agent named Charles "CC" Pyle (CC appropriately stood for Cash and Carry), and later Babe Ruth and several other baseball greats used Christy Walsh, a super promoter, to garner them some additional money using their names and/or appearances. Walsh's specialty was employing professional writers to author newspaper columns under the name of the star. Most of the articles were ghostwritten to present a "you were there" kind of column as though the player were taking you into his thoughts on the events. Walsh served as both a PR agent and a financial advisor for Ruth, which did create a model for later agents, but following his representation of Ruth and others including many non-baseball celebrities, there was a long hiatus before the modern agent as represented by Corcoran's relationship with Williams developed.[4]

Frank Scott, another agent, began helping baseball players shortly after Corcoran began working for Williams. Many baseball historians have incorrectly assigned Scott the role of first player agent. While Scott expanded his roster to a far greater number of ballplayers than Corcoran (who still had golf responsibilities), his representation was based on Corcoran's model with Williams. Scott was a traveling secretary for the Yankees, but was fired when he sided with the players over management when it came to spying on their road goings-on. From a friendship with Yogi Berra, Scott realized both what a distraction various side requests were to players and how they were often rewarded for their time with only token gifts.[5] His early work with Yankee greats began in 1950, four years after Corcoran and Williams were together.

Corcoran, who was the first non-player enshrined in the World Golf Hall of Fame, didn't receive his due in some circles. When you ask, "Who was the first person to represent golfers?" the answer 99% of the time is Mark McCormick. And when you ask about baseball, if anyone hazards a guess at all, they name Scott. In reality, Corcoran preceded both.

Prior to meeting Williams, Corcoran's main connection to baseball was his friendships with the retired Ty Cobb and Babe Ruth. In his quest to shine a brighter light on golf, Corcoran staged some fun promotional events at baseball and football fields. In fact, Corcoran's introduction to Ruth came as a result of a promotion with Snead. The golfer dazzled the crowd at Wrigley Field when he teed off from home plate and bounced golf balls off a new Cubs scoreboard some four hundred plus feet away—something no major league batsman could do. Ruth had tried to get to Wrigley Field to observe the great Snead's performance, but plane connections didn't work out. However, the Babe tracked down Snead and Corcoran postgame in a bar and a lifelong friendship was born.[6] Cobb was another avid post-career golfer who had met Mr. Golf along the way.

In the early forties, Fred convinced Ruth and Cobb to settle their baseball rivalry on the golf course. Both loved the game of golf and fancied themselves as good players. At the time, Cobb was 54 years old and Ruth was 46. Both highly competitive and often combative, Ruth and Cobb deeply respected one another, even though their competitiveness around who was the best baseball player of all time was always in play. Corcoran figured out how to work the players' egos to bring them together on the golf course and raise money for charity in the process. The publicity didn't hurt, either.

It took a lot of massaging Cobb to finally get him to agree to a match. Cobb did not want to lose and wasn't sure this event would be a slam dunk for him. Ruth seemed more self-confident and probably was considered an underdog in this sport, making it a major accomplishment to win and more defensible if he lost. Corcoran worked on Cobb and ultimately convinced him to take the challenge. Judy Corcoran,

Fred's daughter, wrote this about the match in her book, *The Has Beens Cup.*

> "I'll beat him because I care more," Cobb sneered. "But I'd probably have to get him upset. That's how I'd beat him. I'd just get his goat." Cobb believed to beat any opponent was to irritate, embarrass, dare, distract and bully him into losing his composure.
>
> "I bet you would win," Fred said.
>
> The final trick to get Cobb to say yes came about when Corcoran reminded Cobb of a note Fred had received from the Babe. The note said, "I can beat Cobb any day of the week and twice on Sunday at the Scottish game."
>
> Cobb, in finally accepting the match, wrote to Ruth, "I could always lick you on a ball field and I can lick you on a golf course."[7]

The event was named, "The Greatest Championship Golf Match of All Time"—a bit of hyperbole. Ruth called it, "The Left-Handed Has-Beens Golf Championship of Nowhere in Particular."

The first of the three matches between the two was played on June 25, 1941, in Newton, Massachusetts. Cobb won 3 and 2. The second match was played two days later on June 27 at Fresh Meadow in Queens, New York, where Ruth prevailed on the 19th hole 1 up. A final rubber match was played on July 29, 1941, in Detroit at the Grosse Ile Golf Club. Cobb prevailed 3 and 2 to take the series. Cobb said later that the event was one of the highlights of his life and it was later reported that he kept two things on his mantle—his Baseball Hall of Fame plaque and the Has-Beens trophy. Cobb and Corcoran also became life-long friends.

For several years, Scott and Corcoran were the only professional agents dealing with baseball players. While Tom Yawkey and Joe Cronin offered Corcoran the job of traveling secretary for the Boston Red Sox, he turned it down. He was Mr. Golf and baseball was a side business. At first Yawkey and Cronin were very suspicious of Corcoran's relationship with Williams, but once they decided it was not a threat to his baseball activities and maybe even made his baseball commitment stronger, they condoned the arrangement. Later, Corcoran did broaden his base to other special players: St. Louis's Stan Musial and Boston's Tony Conigliaro.

With the end of the Second World War, Corcoran wasted no time in landing off-field deals for Williams

Although he was known as "Mr. Golf," Fred Corcoran served as agent to Ted Williams and other players. For a time, he and Frank Scott were the only agents working with baseball players.

in 1946. His first call was to L.B. Icely at the Wilson Sporting Goods Company, suggested Williams for the company's advisory staff. The result was an immediate contract with a $30,000 guarantee, three percent on all sales, and a ten-year deal. Williams was off and running.

Many of Corcoran's early efforts with Williams tried to make him understand how important it was for him to stop scrapping with the press, and especially with the fans. Image was the lifeblood of his attractiveness to sponsors, and Williams seemed to be doing everything he could to present the wrong one. Corcoran did not always have a great deal of success in modifying Williams's behavior, but he inserted himself often as the buffer between Williams and others. Cobb, who knew and liked Williams, gave Corcoran the following advice:

> Ted is like an outlaw horse that has certain fine ability but tears and pitches in the harness of society and gets many burns and wounds. But that means nothing to him. He retires quickly to those who fawn upon him. Neither you nor I nor anyone else with the interest or desire to help Ted can ever accomplish one thing for him...so it's better to endure him and save one's self.[8]

With Williams and Cobb always in his corner, Corcoran was best friends of two of the orneriest men in baseball. That certainly says something about the man himself. Perhaps Corcoran understood Williams and how his quick temper was a result of a difficult childhood and a distrust that had built up through his formative years. He also knew Williams as one of the most honest and kind people when one got to know him and that he was an extremely loyal friend. It was no accident that the bond developed among the Red Sox core players of that era was anchored by Williams. David Halberstam's book, *The Teammates*, explores this relationship and highlights how Williams fit in among his friends and peers on the team.

Off the field, Williams was an intensely private person, which led to his obsession with fishing, hunting, and the outdoors where he could be peacefully alone and away from the world. Corcoran picked up on how this obsession, when mixed with Williams's baseball fame, could turn into a good commercial opportunity. The actual reward in this area came almost by accident. Corcoran, like a good front man, spent a lot of time where he thought there might be action. In 1950, on a night when he returned from a golf event in the Midwest, he decided to kill some time in New York at Toots Shor's restaurant.

That night, with the Sportsman's Show in New York, he met up with friends from the Bristol Company. They manufactured golf club shafts, but also made fishing rods. Thanks to a chance conversation that night, Corcoran landed a 10-year, $100,000 contract for Williams to endorse Bristol's Horton fishing equipment. It was a perfect fit. Corcoran was making Williams wealthier, and doing it in ways that Williams could shine.

The economic partnership between Williams and Corcoran had its apex during Williams's playing days. As Williams reached retirement, the relationship began to transition into more of a strong personal friendship. The day after Williams officially retired from the Red Sox in 1960, he signed a deal with Sears Roebuck to head up the Sears Sports Advisory Staff. It made him an employee of Sears, and paid $125,000 per year plus a percentage of sales on all "Ted Williams" equipment sold. It also catapulted him into a position of the country's most visible expert on fishing and fishing equipment.

Through Corcoran, Williams had become a close friend of Snead. The golfer and ballplayer had founded a company called Ted Williams Tackle, Inc. that made and sold fishing flies. As part of the Sears deal, that company eventually got swept into Sears's product line.[9]

Prior to Williams settling in with Sears Roebuck, Corcoran got in the middle of another opportunity for Williams to stay in baseball. Dan Topping, the owner of the Yankees, came to Corcoran to see if Williams would be interested in joining the Yankees for the 1961 season just as a pinch hitter. Topping was willing to pay Williams $125,000 for the season. It was certainly a fair offer, but Corcoran told Topping that before he could consider it, the Yankees needed to talk to Yawkey. The Red Sox owner was still paying Williams. Topping refused to get into negotiations with Yawkey, so the offer fizzled. For the long term, Williams having landed with Sears was the right next step.

With Williams happily and safely tucked away under the Sears umbrella and not making on-field headlines any more, the need for Corcoran's services diminished. Williams, however, remained a loyal friend. Still associated with the Red Sox, Williams spent every spring at the Red Sox training camp helping young players. One day following the 1965 season, he called Corcoran and told him about a young player named Tony Conigliaro who, at the age of 20, had just completed his second year in the majors and had hit 32 home runs that season. "I think you should sign him," Williams said as he arranged the meeting.[10] Conigliaro had a similar handshake deal with Corcoran as Williams once had. Corcroan immediately called his old friend Sy Berger at Topps Bubble Gum and signed Conigliaro to his first baseball card contract.

Conigliaro might have been a right-handed Ted Williams for the Red Sox had his career not been derailed in 1967 when he was struck in the face by a pitch from California Angels right-handed pitcher Jack Hamilton. With his eyesight affected, Conigliaro never fully recovered. Batting helmets now have a protective ear-flap, partly due to this incident.

Williams did return to baseball as a manager for the expansion Washington Senators 1969–72, a period that included the team's move to Texas to become the Rangers. Williams was tough on the players and very dogmatic in his theories of the game. His managerial record was below .500. He was much more at home in his post-baseball days hiding out in Florida and spending lots of time with fishing buddies.

The relationship between Corcoran and Williams during the latter's playing career ran deeper than just endorsements and side money. Corcoran honed Williams's image as best he could, given Williams's natural tendency to be quick-tempered and aloof. A classic example of Corcoran's influence came when Williams was recalled into the Marine Corps in 1952, right in the prime of his playing career. Most people today think of Williams's time in the Corps as the epitome of public service selflessly performed by a true patriot. That was not exactly how it started out, but thanks partly to Corcoran, that is how it has come to be viewed.

When Williams first received the call-back to service, he was livid. He was convinced that he was singled out because of his high baseball profile. There were plenty of worthy pilots who could perform those tasks who weren't in the prime of a baseball career and, furthermore, he had been away from flying for long enough to virtually require a re-education on the updated equipment. Because Williams wasn't shy, his natural tendency would have been to make a stink even if it were to be of no avail. Corcoran caught him in time, calmed him down, and convinced him he needed to treat the inevitable as though he was in control. He realized his importance to his country and he would do his duty as any concerned American would. The choice was being a bitter spoiled baseball player or a super-hero patriot. Corcoran knew the right choice and he helped Williams find it.

Corcoran's assistance didn't just come by way of fatherly advice. While Williams was on duty in Korea, he was still being paid by the Red Sox. Corcoran was responsible for watching over those funds. By investing most of them in a company called IBM, Corcoran did quite well for Williams while he was off flying fighter jets.

And Corcoran was instrumental in getting Williams back into baseball after his tour in Korea. By July 1953, Corcoran got word that Williams was coming home, and as soon as he landed in San Francisco, Corcoran got a call from Ford Frick, the Commissioner of Baseball. Frick was calling to see if Williams could fly to Cincinnati to throw out the first pitch at the All-Star Game. Here's an excerpt of the ensuing conversation as reported by Judy Corcoran, Fred's daughter, in *Fred Corcoran: The Man Who Sold the World on Golf.*

> "Everyone wants you at that game," Fred said, "and they want to see you play. You need to get back to Boston."
>
> "Hell, no," Williams said. "I'm out of shape, tired and I'm not feeling well."
>
> "But there's still two months left in the season. Everybody wants you back. I think you ought to try to play this year," Fred pleaded.
>
> "It's the middle of July, already, Fred. The Red Sox aren't going anywhere. I'm not ready to play baseball and Mr. Yawkey says I can do what I feel like doing. I feel like fishing. I'm going fishing."
>
> "But you're not a fisherman," Fred protested. "You're a ballplayer."

> "You've never seen me handle a fly rod. I'm the best there is."
>
> "I'm serious, Ted," Fred said. "You've got to get started. It'll be the best thing in the world for you. Work yourself in gradually, then be ready for a full season next year. Listen to me—baseball is your business."

Fred finally got through to him because Ted agreed to go to Cincinnati where the fans at the All-Star Game gave him one of the warmest receptions he ever got—not a boo in the crowd, and that perked him up some more. And during the second half of 1953, in this shortened season with only 37 games, Ted batted .407.[11]

It was that summer, too, when Williams practiced batting so much to get back in shape that he often got blisters all over his hands. Corcoran happened to be with him on one of these days and gallantly pulled out a golf glove from his bag and suggested Williams wear it while in the batting cage. Williams did and as people around the league saw him wearing it during practice, they started wearing golf gloves. It's sometimes acknowledged that this is how the batting glove was introduced to baseball. There are some, however, who think the batting glove was used earlier. Peter Morris in his book *A Game of Inches* suggests that Hughie Jennings may have used batting gloves as early as 1902, and that Lefty O'Doul and Johnny Frederick used them in 1932, as well as Bobby Thomson in the fifties. Hawk Harrelson, who was also a first-class golfer, is credited by many with being the first ballplayer to wear batting gloves in an actual game.[12] Regardless, it was no doubt Corcoran who told the press and called attention to it.

From the moment Williams left baseball until Corcoran died in 1977, the two men remained best of friends. Corcoran attended Williams's induction into the Baseball Hall of Fame and the two men socialized frequently. Williams was considered a member of the Corcoran family. In the sixties, after Williams was out of baseball, he got to know Corcoran's young daughters through visits to the Corcoran home on the 15th hole of the Winged Foot Golf Club in Mamaroneck, New York. The young girls developed an apt nickname for "Uncle Ted"—calling him "Old Yeller." It was the title of a Disney kids' movie about a dog, but in this case it applied because Williams "was old and a yeller." He had chastised the girls for brushing their hair after breakfast and before lunch while in the dining room. Long after Corcoran died, Williams kept in contact with his widow Nancy, and was highly appreciative of what the family had done for him.

Corcoran may have lived a baseball fan's dream in the fifties and early sixties. Not only did he have the opportunity to spend time with the best hitter in the American League, but he also had the same relationship with the best hitter in the National League, Stan Musial.

While Musial and Williams were both great left-handed hitters, they were polar opposites in temperament. Musial was mild-mannered, controlled, and got along with everyone: sportswriters, fans, opponents. He was a perfect fit for a team that played in St. Louis, the heart of the country whose fans hailed from a number of Midwest states. But Musial was a very different sell for Corcoran. Williams may have had a hot temper and easily alienated people, but he had a big-city personality and charisma. He was also John Wayne handsome. Musial was just quiet competence. As Cobb told Corcoran one day: "You manage both Williams and Musial. Why don't you do more for Musial. Musial is the greatest player in the world, the greatest ballplayer I have ever seen. Ted is a great hitter, but this boy is the greatest all-round player."[13]

Corcoran was sympathetic but he was also a realist. In his own book, *Unplayable Lies*, Corcoran said:

In addition to being a great player, Musial was one of the finest men I ever knew. Yet Musial never moved people like Williams did. Williams had 'color' even when striking out. You could walk down the street with Stan and few people paid any attention or even noticed him, but Williams was a star, like Cobb or Snead or Jack Dempsey in this respect. Walk down the street with any of them and taxi drivers would blow their horns and wave.[14]

In defense of Musial, Corcoran was used to big cities. Were he to walk down the street in St. Louis or Omaha, Nebraska, or Little Rock, Arkansas, Musial would have been "The Man." Williams may have been big on the coasts but Stan was the guy in the middle of the country. Everyone listened to St. Louis radio on KMOX and everyone who could hear that station with Harry Caray and Joe Garagiola announcing Cardinal games was a Musial fan. But national media didn't emanate from St. Louis or Omaha or Little Rock.

Corcoran did a lot for Musial during their relationship. However, Musial was by nature a local guy rather than a national figure. The heavyweight stars of the fifties and sixties were Williams, Jackie Robinson,

Roger Maris, and Mickey Mantle. The Cardinals had their hey-day in the early forties, and by the time Corcoran arrived for Musial, the team had gone past its peak. The Dodgers, the Yankees, the Red Sox, and later the Braves were drawing national attention. The best player in St. Louis was just that, the best player in St. Louis.

In 1949, Musial became a partner in what became a popular St. Louis restaurant called Stan Musial and Biggie's. Musial took the restaurant very seriously, showing strong interest in both the food and the business. In 1948, he had moved his family from their off-season home in Donora, Pennsylvania, to St. Louis. Unlike Williams, who ran off to Florida after each season and lived in a hotel while he was in Boston, Musial and his family became full-time members of the St. Louis community. Musial regularly appeared at the restaurant and became close to his business partner, Biggie Garagnani, who also became his mentor. Musial kept an office in the restaurant and hung out there a lot answering his fan mail and learning about the restaurant business and greeting customers.[15]

Corcoran dealt with Musial's "baseball stuff," such as a major deal with St. Louis-based Rawlings Sporting Goods. He also handled things like signing on with the Hartland Company, which successfully made and marketed small plastic statues of sports figures and Western heroes. Those "Hartlands," as they are called by collectors, are still a big seller on the memorabilia market.

As he did with Williams, Corcoran remained not only an agent but a close friend of Musial. He made sure Musial got his fair share of recognition in sports circles and often accompanied him to events. Musial came out of his shell the night before the All-Star Game in 1960 at Yankee Stadium, and harped to Corcoran on how the managers of All-Star Games should make sure the fans got their fill of the better players (like himself and Ted Williams). He promised he would give the National League fans an idea of what he meant by declaring that if he were put in the game the next day, he would hit a home run. He got in and he did.

When Musial's career came to an end in 1963, unlike Williams, he was still very committed to baseball and his personality made him a good executive and a perfect ambassador for the Cardinals. At one point he was the team's General Manager and remained involved with the Cardinal organization almost his full post-playing-career life. He remained in St. Louis until he died in 2013.

Because Corcoran was such a man-about-town, he pretty much knew everybody. As a result, he had other baseball friendships besides the players he represented. One of the strangest was with Moe Berg, the famous catcher/spy whose life has become a favorite of those who love intrigue. Corcoran and Berg actually roomed together for periods of time. More accurately, Corcoran invited Berg to stay with him when Berg seemed to have nowhere else to go. They got along well, but Berg sometimes became dependent on Corcoran and followed him around, maybe even living vicariously through Corcoran's many friendships and contacts. In 1951, Berg happened to be bunking in with Corcoran when Corcoran proposed to his future wife Nancy. The wedding was a quickly arranged affair with a limited guest list, and Berg was one of those guests. More bizarre, when the Corcorans set off on their honeymoon, which was combined with a golf tournament in Montreal, Berg went along. When Nancy questioned why Berg had been asked to join them, Fred said, "He has nowhere to go and I didn't want to turn him out."[16]

From 1946, when Corcoran first met Williams, until his death in 1977, he remained a name in the world of baseball representation. He was one of the first to show star players how to capitalize on their skills and fan following through off-field endorsements. He not only made those for whom he worked wealthier, but in his worldly wisdom and consummate patience, he helped his clients become better people and understand that their behavior was looked at by others as that of a role model. Admittedly, these are different times today, but many of today's super agents, the Scott Boras types, could take a lesson from Fred Corcoran. It is about the money but it's not always about the money. ∎

Acknowledgment

I'd like to thank Judy Corcoran, daughter of Fred Corcoran, who both helped edit this article and who shared lots of time and stories about her father. Without her help, this story could not have been told with the insight and knowledge that it deserves.

Notes

1. Judy Corcoran, *Fred Corcoran: The Man Who Sold The World On Golf*, New York: Gray Productions, 2010, 101.
2. Michael Seidel, *Ted Williams: A Baseball Life*. Lincoln: University of Nebraska Press, 1991, 118.
3. Corcoran, *Fred Corcoran*, 102.
4. Mark Ahrens, "Christy Walsh—Baseball's First Agent," Books on Baseball, August 4, 2010, accessed January 27, 2021. https://www.booksonbaseball.com/2010/08/christy-walsh-baseballs-first-agent.
5. Deepti Hajela, "Sports Agent Frank Scott Dead At 80," AP News, June 30, 1998, accessed January 27, 2021. https://apnews.com/e80d981756dba5ab5604f8b69802afce.
6. Judy Corcoran, *The Has Been Cup*, New York: Gray Productions, 2016, 21–25.
7. Corcoran, *Fred Corcoran*, 61–68.
8. Corcoran, *Fred Corcoran*, 114.
9. Ben Bradlee, Jr., *The Kid: The Immortal Life Of Ted Williams*, New York: Little, Brown and Company, 2013, 471–4.
10. Corcoran, *Fred Corcoran*, 211.
11. Corcoran, *Fred Corcoran*, 154–5.
12. https://en.wikipedia.org/wiki/Batting_glove.
13. Corcoran, *Fred Corcoran*, 164.
14. Corcoran, *Fred Corcoran*, 164.
15. http://losttables.com/musial/musial.htm.
16. Corcoran, *Fred Corcoran*, 139.

A Slice of Piazza

A Trade Brought the Mets One of the Biggest Superstars in Franchise History

Mike Hoenigmann

On August 9, 2006, the first-place New York Mets were hosting the San Diego Padres at Shea Stadium. The Mets were headed toward their first division title since 1988 and first playoff berth since 2000. It was an ordinary late summer series against an out-of-division team as the Mets held a big 13.5 game lead in the NL East.[1] Yet something strange happened on that otherwise ordinary night: the Padres' 37-year-old catcher hit two home runs off Mets ace Pedro Martinez...and was given a standing ovation both times. In fact, he took a curtain call after the first one, a rare occurrence for an opposing player in any ballpark. The reason this visiting player received such an extraordinary response and so much love from the Mets fans in attendance that night was because he was Mike Piazza, former Met and one of the biggest superstars in the history of the franchise.

Before Piazza came to New York as a superstar, he became a superstar in Los Angeles with the Dodgers. His journey to even become a big league player was nothing short of miraculous. Piazza was drafted in the 62nd round of the 1988 MLB Draft as a favor to Tommy Lasorda, a good friend of Mike's father, Vince who grew up with him. Lasorda's connections had been giving Piazza great opportunities well before he was drafted. Young Mike had actually celebrated with Dodgers players in their locker room after they won the 1977 National League pennant under Lasorda, who was in his first full year as manager.[2] At age 16, he even had the opportunity to have the great Ted Williams watch him take batting practice in a cage in his backyard. Most importantly, his advancement from high school baseball player to professional baseball came through a series of interventions from Lasorda. In his autobiography *Long Shot*, Piazza explains that although he was a great hitter in high school, he was struggling to get recruited onto a college team because he had no position defensively and had ignored his academics. It was only through Lasorda convincing University of Miami coach Ron Fraser that Piazza got an opportunity to join the collegiate team he wanted to play for.[3] When he got barely any playing time as a freshman at Miami, Lasorda again stepped in and helped him transfer to Miami-Dade North, "a busy community college with an excellent baseball program" where he played his sophomore season and batted .364 as their first baseman.[4] As Piazza looked into where he would play ball next (Miami-Dade was a two-year program), Lasorda had him work out as a catcher with one of his big league coaches. When he got a positive report on the workout, he called the scouting director for the Dodgers and told him, "I want you to do me a favor. I want you to draft Michael Piazza."[5] With his foot in the door and the support of Lasorda, Piazza grinded through four and a half years in the minors, including a stint as the first American in the Dodgers' Latin American camp in the Dominican Republic, and became the organization's top prospect before reaching the big leagues in September 1992.

With the Dodgers, Piazza became a perennial All-Star by the mid-90s, and a star both on and off the field. On the diamond, Piazza broke out in 1993 as the NL Rookie of the Year. He put up 35 home runs, a .318 batting average, an impressive 153 OPS+, and 7.0 WAR, all while playing 146 games behind the plate (149 total).[6] Over the next several seasons with the Dodgers, Piazza established himself as one of the best players in baseball as well as one of its most marketable. As a young bachelor and the best player on an iconic baseball team in one of the largest media markets in the world, opportunities began to open up for Piazza that are seldom seen for baseball players today. In his rookie season he was the only baseball player to shoot a commercial with ESPN.[7] He had an endorsement with Pert Plus Shampoo and appeared in a memorable commercial for the company in 1997. But in Los Angeles, Piazza's acting appearances usually came on TV shows. He made cameos on a number of popular shows, including *Married...With Children*, *The Bold and the Beautiful*, and a very humorous appearance on *Baywatch*, all during the 1994 players' strike. In the *Baywatch* episode he played himself, wearing his Dodgers hat and jersey on the beach, "practicing his swing" and eventually helping Pamela

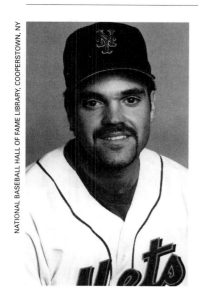

Mike Piazza's big bat and heartthrob good looks made him a Hollywood fixture, until the Dodgers traded him to the Florida Marlins. The Marlins quickly flipped him to the Mets, and his star would continue to rise in the Big Apple.

Anderson's character rescue a woman stuck in a rip tide before walking off with her. According to Piazza, he was dating Anita Hart—the actress in the scene—at that time, which was how he got the cameo.[8] During his time in Los Angeles he also dated another *Baywatch* actress, Debbe Dunning, known for playing the girl from Tim Allen's show-within-a-show *Tool Time* on *Home Improvement*. While on strike, Piazza even presented at the MTV Music Awards, struck up a friendship with Fabio, and golfed with Charles Barkley.[9] Piazza's stardom and popularity really took off during this period, when he had established himself as one of the game's young rising stars and had some time off.

While his play would reach an even higher level in the 1996 and 1997 seasons, his relationship with the Dodgers began to deteriorate. Those two years were probably the best of his Hall of Fame career. In the 1996 All-Star Game, played in Philadelphia near where he grew up, Piazza took home the All-Star Game MVP with a performance that included a double and a massive home run to left field. He also finished in second place in the NL MVP voting in both seasons, batting .336 and .362 in 1996 and 1997 respectively. In 1997 he led the majors in OPS+ (185) and set career highs with 40 homers and 124 RBIs (which he would match with the Mets in 1999). That 1997 season is considered among the best individual seasons of all time, and perhaps the best offensive season ever by a catcher. In fact, Piazza's 9.0 Offensive WAR that season is the highest ever by a catcher in a single season.[10] In total with the Dodgers, Piazza won five Silver Slugger Awards, earned five trips to the All-Star Game, and was clearly their best player as they headed into the 1998 season, which was the last under contract his LA contract.

In his autobiography Piazza suggests that the Dodgers felt he owed them for taking a chance on him by drafting him in the first place, and as a result, always reminded him of it and approached contract negotiations with him as if he were not deserving of the value of an All-Star player.[11] The tension spilled into the media, where Piazza complained about his contract situation to Dodgers beat writer Jason Reid, and later when former Dodger Brett Butler told Bill Plaschke of *The Los Angeles Times* that Piazza was a "moody, self-centered '90s player" and that although he was the greatest hitter he'd been around, a team couldn't build around him since he wasn't a leader.[12] Piazza had also rejected contract offers from the Dodgers in the range of six years and $80 million.[13] It all came to a head in mid-May 1998, when the Dodgers suddenly and shockingly traded him to the defending champion Florida Marlins. The Marlins were no ordinary defending champ, as ownership had already torn the team down, slashing payroll in advance of the sale of the team. In an iconic issue of *Sports Illustrated* with Piazza on the cover and the headline "Trade of the Century," Michael Bamberger shared Piazza's reaction to the trade: "Piazza just laughs. 'I wish I could say it's been a little slice of heaven.'"[14] With the distrust and cloud of uncertainty surrounding Piazza and the Dodgers now gone, the next question on everyone's mind was: where would Piazza, one of the best players in the league in the prime of his career and a pending free agent, be flipped to next?

The answer to that question came just one week later when Piazza was traded to the Mets for three prospects. The date was May 22, 1998, a turning point from which the image and direction of the Mets franchise changed profoundly in the eyes of both the league and the fan base. While with the Marlins, Piazza had heard a number of teams had varying degrees of interest in trading for him, including the Orioles, Rockies, Red Sox, and the team he thought he'd ultimately be traded to, the Cubs. He was shocked when he found out it would actually be the Mets.[15] Before even arriving in New York, his new teammate John Franco (who at the time was the all-time saves leader in NL history) gave up his number 31 so that Piazza could have it. That gesture gave a small insight into the magnitude of Piazza coming to the Mets and what it would mean for the franchise and fan base. At the time Franco remarked, "He's perfect for this city. He's young, single, a billboard kind of guy. Fifth Avenue is going to eat him up. He'll find out that if you're a favorite in New York, the fans will go crazy. It's going to be like when Reggie Jackson came to the

Yankees. He's a marquee guy."[16] Franco foresaw the many marketing opportunities Piazza would have in New York and his manager, Bobby Valentine, echoed many of the same sentiments looking back at the hoopla years later when he said, "I think we got instant credibility with that trade, and we began to build an identity around Mike. The Mets had not had a player of Mike's star quality in many years… From the first day, everything about it was rather bigger than life."[17] It was clear Piazza was a caliber of player and level of star the Mets had not had in years, and that those involved felt that impact at the time and can still feel it with the passage of time. But to turn that groundbreaking move into something more tangible, Piazza would need to perform and the Mets would need to sign him long-term.

Piazza's 1998 season with the Mets featured plenty of ups and downs, but it set the stage for Piazza's re-signing with the team, his unique bond with the fan base, and the continued growth of his stardom. From the start, Piazza could tell New York was different from other places he'd played. Fans were waiting at the airport to greet him and long walk-up lines formed to buy tickets to his first game.[18] He delivered an RBI double in a win in his Mets debut, but he quickly found out that proving himself to New York and its fans was not going to be easy. He started to struggle to drive in runs, and with his not committing to stay with the Mets long-term, fans started to boo him. The booing and constant questions from the media about his future began to weigh on him. It took the Mets announcing that they were postponing contract talks until after the season for him to relax and begin hitting for the last two months, changing the boos to cheers.[19] For a while Piazza thought that there was little chance he would re-sign with the Mets, which would have been a disaster for them, but after receiving a curtain call following a home run against the Cardinals in August, he felt "a page had been turned."[20] He ended that 1998 season having played 109 games with the Mets, posting tremendous numbers including a line of .348/.417/.607 with 23 homers and 76 RBIs.[21] While they had a late lead in the Wild Card race, the Mets ended the season one game back of the Cubs and Giants who were in a tie for the NL Wild Card. Attention quickly turned from the disappointing end to the season to whether or not the Mets and Piazza would agree to continue their relationship.

Although Piazza had felt unsure about re-signing with the Mets during the season, his feelings had begun to change. Management knew the importance of keeping him for the team to be contenders and for the image of the franchise. As Piazza explained, "The more I pondered it, the more I believed that there was a reason I'd been traded to the Mets. I didn't really know what the reason was, but I knew I couldn't walk away from it, just because New York was difficult. I decided that if the Mets wanted me and the contract was acceptable, I'd stay."[22] The negotiations progressed quickly during the World Series, and Piazza and his agent, Dan Lozano, agreed that not dragging it out could send a great message to everyone that he wanted to be in New York and was not interested in going anywhere else.[23] The Mets signed the 30-year-old Piazza to a then-Major League record contract on October 24, 1998. The deal was for 7 years and $91 million, which beat the previous record of 6 years and $75 million the Red Sox had given to Pedro Martinez the previous offseason.[24] The record contract was proof of both the Mets' seriousness in building a winner and of Piazza's status as one of the biggest stars (and best players) in the sport.

With the contract in hand, Piazza spent the next several years establishing himself as one of the most important players in Mets history, while also building on his superstardom that at times transcended the sport. He delivered for the Mets, being the key cog in their lineup as they made the playoffs in consecutive years for the first time in franchise history in 1999 and 2000. Opposing pitchers and managers now had a name they had to circle and plan around in the Mets lineup, one of the few players in the league at any one time who truly strikes fear into the opposition every time they step to the plate. As Piazza felt the pressure of performing under his big new contract early in 1999, he jump-started his season with a walk-off home run against Trevor Hoffman and the Padres. That launched a season that saw him match his career highs in home runs and RBIs (40 and 124) while finishing seventh in the MVP voting. The Mets clinched the NL Wild Card with a 97–66 record to make the playoffs for the first time since 1988.

The 2000 season brought even more success and dramatics centered around the Mets catcher. There was his three-run homer that capped an epic 10-run bottom of the 8th inning to come back and defeat the rival Atlanta Braves, 11–8, on June 30. There was also the season-long drama between Piazza and Yankees pitcher Roger Clemens. For Mets fans, Clemens represented the ultimate villain to their superhero Piazza, who already had great career numbers against Clemens when he hit a grand slam off him in a June game against the Yankees. A month later when they met again, Clemens beaned Piazza, knocking him out with a concussion. The pitch had clear frustration behind it, and the tension grew in the matchup of crosstown rivals. That season Piazza led the Mets to the playoffs again, finishing third in the MVP vote after posting a .324 batting average and 113 RBIs.[25] This time, Piazza and the Mets reached the World Series, the first and only time Piazza reached the Fall Classic in his career. Their opponent was the Yankees, World Series champions the past two seasons, and in three of the last four. Although the Yankees were the favorites, Piazza's presence gave Mets fans hope. He would again clash with Roger Clemens in Game 2 at Yankee Stadium. In the top of the first inning Clemens broke Piazza's bat with an inside fastball. The ball rolled foul and the top half of Piazza's bat landed near the pitcher's mound. Clemens picked it up and chucked it in the direction of Piazza, who had started running up the first base line, not knowing where exactly the ball was. This set off more drama, benches clearing and all. However, Clemens and the Yankees would get the better of Piazza and the Mets that night and in the Series, winning their third straight world championship in five games. Piazza hit two home runs while driving in four.

As great and successful as the 1999 and 2000 seasons were for Piazza and the Mets, a singular moment in 2001 became the most iconic in Piazza's career and an indelible part of Mets and baseball history. Following the terrorist attacks against the United States on September 11, 2001, sports were put on hold as the country, and New Yorkers in particular, turned their attention to the tragedy, rescue missions, and caring for survivors and all of those who were directly affected. The Mets and Yankees both gave their time and presence to help supply efforts and to meet with, talk to, and provide some sort of comfort to those who had either been first responders at the World Trade Center, or families who lost loved ones in the attack. As baseball started up again a week later and through the end of the 2001 season, the two New York baseball teams sort of became "America's Teams," with fans of opposing teams giving them standing ovations and holding up signs of support. The first major sporting event held in New York following the attacks was on September 21 at Shea Stadium, a game between the Mets and their biggest rival and kryptonite, the Atlanta Braves. The night featured lots of extra security, performances by Marc Anthony, Diana Ross, and Liza Minelli, honoring of rescue workers, a 21-gun salute, a pre-game exchange of hugs between the two teams, and an announced crowd of 41,235 fans who came to watch a baseball game that would hopefully be part of the healing process.[26] The biggest moment of the night, however, came in the bottom of the eighth inning with Mets trailing the Braves, 2–1, Desi Relaford on first base, and Piazza stepping up to the plate. In his recap of the game in The New York Times the following day, Tyler Kepner described what transpired next: "With one strike, Piazza got a 96-mile-an-hour fastball and drilled it off the middle tier of a three-tiered camera stand in center field. He took a curtain call from the fans, lifting his helmet with one hand, kissing the fingers of the other and pointing to the crowd."[27] Reflecting back on the moment, Piazza believed they "had" to win this game and remembered how emotional he was before and during the game. He described the homer by saying, "I caught that fastball with the full force of my emotional rush. When it cleared the fence just left of center and caromed off a distant TV camera, I thought the stadium would crumble into rubble."[28] The home run has truly taken on legendary status: it is shown whenever there is a discussion on sports after 9/11 or the biggest moments of Piazza's career. It was evidence of the power of sports to bring some joy and healing to a hurting city, and the power of Piazza to come through in the clutch—to be the team's superstar. The home run, which gave the Mets a 3–2 lead that would be the final score, is so highly thought of that during the final season at Shea Stadium fans voted it the second greatest moment in the history of Shea, behind only the clinching of the 1986 World Series and one spot ahead of the 1969 World Series Game 5 clincher.[29] With one swing of the bat, Piazza cemented his place in Mets and New York history.

New York wasn't just a place where Piazza continued his great play and built on his legacy in baseball. It was also where he continued to grow off the field with commercials and even a cameo in a major movie. In the early 2000s, Piazza had endorsements with MCI (a long distance phone company), Callaway Golf, Nerf, and Claritin. He shot MCI commercials with other stars such as fellow athletes Emmitt Smith, Terry Bradshaw, and Hulk Hogan, country singer Toby Keith, and puppet/sitcom star ALF. Industry experts at the time estimated he pulled in around $3–10 million a year from his endorsements.[30] For reference, in 2019 Bryce Harper made the most money of any MLB player in endorsements with an estimated $6.5 million, and the next highest was Mike Trout at $3 million.[31] So Piazza was potentially pulling in more endorsement money almost 20 years ago than the top baseball player does now, and was definitely pulling in more than any other player in 2019 not named Bryce Harper. That says something about how big of a superstar Piazza was, as

Only two Mets players have had their numbers retired by the team, Tom Seaver ("The Franchise") and Mike Piazza.

well as how baseball is lacking true star power in America today. At the time, a *Los Angeles Daily News* columnist noted, "Show-business people say his blend of good looks, charm and humility make him a natural salesman."[32] Advertising executive Bob Dorfman added, "The fact is he is getting deals…You look at guys who go beyond the shoe deals and the athletic-based deals and Mike has transcended that and I would use that as a yardstick."[33] After a few seasons with the Mets, Piazza had established himself as one of the most marketable players in the game, and in some ways had transcended baseball in a way that very few modern players do.

It wasn't just commercials that Piazza was involved in. The summer he came to New York there was a video game released for Nintendo64 named *Mike Piazza's Strike Zone*. Piazza also appeared as himself in the rom-com movie *Two Weeks Notice* in 2002, which starred Sandra Bullock and Hugh Grant. He graced the cover of *GQ* in 1999 in advance of his first full season with the Mets. He appeared on the cover of *Sports Illustrated* five separate times, twice with the Dodgers, once for the "Trade of the Century," and another two times with the Mets. Bobby Valentine looked at the impact of his celebrity status on the Mets this way: "I think the team needed somebody like Mike. We needed to be able to have that celebrity status because, a) we were in New York, and b) we were competing on a daily basis with a celebrity team across the borough. There was no other chance for us to compete on Page Six [the *New York Post* gossip section] or on talk radio without the celebrity status of Mike."[34] At a time when the Yankees were winning championships seemingly every season and baseball was in a period of national revival following the 1998 home-run-record chase, Piazza was far and away the team's biggest star and with that brought the Mets credibility and attention.

Piazza's play began to decline in the last few years of his contract as age and the wear-and-tear of being a catcher caught up to him, but the mark he had made on the franchise and its fans had been deeply etched. In his last game as a Met at Shea in 2005, the team played a video tribute to him during the game, manager Willie Randolph batted him cleanup for old time's sake, and he was removed in the top of the eighth inning to get one more standing ovation.[35] He played two more seasons after leaving the Mets, one with the Padres and one with the A's. It wasn't long after he retired that he was back involved with the Mets and big moments. When the Mets closed Shea Stadium in 2008 and opened CitiField in 2009, two players took center stage as the last ones off the field and first ones on the new field: Tom Seaver and Piazza. In 2016 Piazza also joined Seaver as the only Mets enshrined in Cooperstown with a Mets cap and the only players to have their numbers retired by the team. Before he had actually been inducted into the Hall, Piazza explained why he wanted to go in as a Met, saying, "Maybe I'm hypersensitive in this respect, but I appreciate appreciation. Over the years, the Mets have shown me theirs. I seldom felt that the Dodgers did."[36]

The bond between Mets fans and Piazza had become as strong as any between an athlete and a fan base in sports. To Piazza, there were two main reasons: "The first was choosing to sign with the ball club after I was relentlessly booed in 1998… The second factor was 9/11. It was a shared and profound experience, the kind that people can only get through together. Everyone suffered, and grew closer for it."[37] The superstar had chosen to stay with the Mets even after the fans and media put him through the wringer in his first season with them. That commitment started the bond and the way he carried himself following the 9/11 attacks combined with his iconic home run in the first game back in New York cemented that bond. Piazza had officially transformed from a star ballplayer to a legendary one in the annals of New York sports.

Piazza's Met career stretched from 1998 through 2005, and during that time he climbed the leaderboard in most Mets career stats. Piazza is fourth on their all-time list in Offensive WAR (30.8); third all-time in batting average (.296), home runs (220), and RBIs (655); second in OPS (.915); and first in slugging percentage (.542). His 124 RBIs in 1999 are tied for the most ever by a Met in a single season with David Wright, who matched him in 2008.[38] He was also a seven-time All-Star with the Mets, making it every year but one with the team, and won five of his Silver Sluggers with them as well. All of these numbers are impressive, but they do not tell the overall impact he had on the team. Piazza's arrival ushered in one of the most successful eras in Mets history, and he was the central factor in that success.

Piazza's success, impact, and superstardom with the Mets puts him in rarefied air in franchise history, a place occupied by Seaver, who is without much doubt the best player in franchise history and a superstar in his own right. He won three Cy Young Awards with the Mets and most importantly, led them to their first World Series Championship in 1969. More recently, David Wright established himself as a lifelong Met, the franchise's career leader in many categories, a fan favorite, and the team captain. He will probably see his number 5 retired next to Piazza's 31 and Seaver's 41, and with it join an exclusive Mets club.

When looking back over the history of the New York Mets, there have only been a few times when the team reached national prominence. Doing so is made more difficult considering that they play in the same city as possibly the most famous sports franchise in America, if not the world, the New York Yankees. At the turn of the century, the franchise made the playoffs in consecutive years for the first time, made the World Series against the Yankees, and gained significant national spotlight. It would be hard to argue that any of that could have happened had it not been for their acquisition of Piazza in May 1998. At no other time in franchise history have they brought in a star in the prime of their career who delivered in as many ways as Piazza did. He was an All-Star on the field and one of the most recognizable and talked about athletes off of it. Piazza was simply one of the biggest superstars in Mets history. ∎

Notes

1. "San Diego Padres at New York Mets Box Score, August 9, 2006," Baseball-Reference.com, accessed February 22, 2021. https://www.baseball-reference.com/boxes/NYN/NYN200608090.shtml.
2. Mike Piazza and Lonnie Wheeler, *Long Shot*, New York: Simon & Schuster, 2013, 3.
3. Piazza and Wheeler, 40.
4. Piazza and Wheeler, 45, 47.
5. Piazza and Wheeler, 49-50.
6. "Mike Piazza," Baseball-Reference.com, accessed February 22, 2021. https://www.baseballreference.com/players/p/piazzmi01.shtml.
7. Piazza and Wheeler, 120.
8. Piazza and Wheeler, 131.
9. Piazza and Wheeler, 132.
10. "Mike Piazza," Baseball-Reference.com.
11. Piazza and Wheeler, 174.
12. Steven Booth, "De-constructing the Piazza trade," *The Hardball Times*, December 16th, 2010, accessed July 2, 2020. https://tht.fangraphs.com/de-constructing-the-piazza-trade.
13. Booth.
14. Michael Bamberger, "Playin' the Dodger Blues." *Sports Illustrated*, May 25th, 1998, accessed July 6, 2020. https://vault.si.com/vault/1998/05/25/playin-the-dodger-blues-in-the-course-of-a-few-traumaticdays-mike-piazzas-world-turned-upside-down and-si-was-there-when-he-heard-the-news-that-his-la-dayswere-over.
15. Piazza and Wheeler, 185.
16. George Vecsey, "Sports of The Times; Will the Numbers Work Out for Piazza as He Shifts to New York?" *The New York Times*, May 24th, 1998, accessed July 3, 2020. https://www.nytimes.com/1998/05/24/sports/sports-times-will-numbers-work-for-piazza-he-shifts-new-york.html?searchResultPosition=12.
17. Piazza and Wheeler, 187.
18. Piazza and Wheeler, 186.
19. Jason Diamos, "BASEBALL: The Mets Agree to Make Piazza Baseball's Richest Player; Leiter Says He Is Close to a $32 Million Deal," *The New York Times*, October 25th, 1998, accessed July 2, 2020. https://www.nytimes.com/1998/10/25/sports/baseball-mets-agree-make-piazza-baseball-s-richestplayer-leiter-says-he-close.html?auth=login-google1tap&login=google1tap.
20. Piazza and Wheeler, 194.
21. "Mike Piazza," Baseball-Reference.com.
22. Piazza and Wheeler, 195.
23. Piazza and Wheeler, 197.
24. Diamos.
25. "Mike Piazza," Baseball-Reference.com.
26. Tyler Kepner, "BASEBALL; Mets' Magic Heralds Homecoming," *The New York Times*, September 22nd, 2001, accessed July 30, 2020. https://www.nytimes.com/2001/09/22/sports/baseball-mets-magicheralds-homecoming.html?searchResultPosition=4.
27. Kepner.
28. Piazza and Wheeler, 247.
29. Piazza and Wheeler, 342.
30. Liz Mullen, "Piazza catching on as pitchman and as actor," *Sports Business Journal*, October 7, 2002, accessed July 5, 2020. https://www.sportsbusinessdaily.com/Journal/Issues/2002/10/07/Special-Report/Piazza-Catching-On-As-Pitchman-And-As-Actor.aspx.
31. Kurt Badenhausen, "Baseball's Highest-Paid Players 2019: Mike Trout Leads With $39 Million," *Forbes*, April 1, 2019, accessed July 16, 2020. https://www.forbes.com/sites/kurtbadenhausen/2019/04/01/baseballs-highest-paid-players-2019-mike-trout-leads-with-39-million/#287db8fd6cc7.
32. Matt McHale, "Piazza makes splash in commercials," *Los Angeles Daily News*, August 17th, 2001, accessed July 3, 2020. https://www.chron.com/sports/astros/article/Piazza-makes-splash-incommercials-2052297.php.
33. Mullen.
34. Piazza and Wheeler, 201.
35. Piazza and Wheeler, 313.
36. Piazza and Wheeler, 343.
37. Piazza and Wheeler, 344.
38. "New York Mets Top 10 Career Batting Leaders," Baseball-Reference.com, accessed February 22, 2021. https://www.baseball-reference.com/teams/NYM/leaders_bat.shtml.

Dave Nicholson, Revisited

Mike Kaszuba

He was forever young on his baseball card—6-foot-2, with a square jaw, and a passing resemblance to Mickey Mantle. He was 24, and I was in the third grade. It was the summer of 1963.

I never minded that he set a record for strikeouts in a single season that year, which is how many people—if they recall him at all—remember him. He was my guy, No. 11 in the black-and-white pinstripes. I grew up on the Southside of Chicago as a White Sox fan—a team with pitching, speed, and fielding, but little power—and Dave Nicholson was my home run hitter.

And now he was old, reeling from lung surgery. He sounded hoarse and tired. "I'm trying to recover," he said on a Friday in January 2016, a half-century after he led the White Sox in home runs in his best season. But he was not very convincing. He had a chunk of his lung removed during a six-day hospital stay that ended on Christmas Eve; it was as big as his fist, he reported by phone.[1]

He was 76 at the time, and had once smoked a pack-and-a-half of cigarettes a day. I was retired, after 40 years as a newspaper reporter, and interested in finding out what happens to heroes. I had never met him in person, though my journey in the end would bring me to his doorstep.

I had gotten out of the hero worship business long before. Though I spent much of my time covering government for the *Minneapolis Star Tribune*, I had ended my career in journalism reporting on the money of sports—the endless appetite for new stadiums, the sweeping corporate takeover of sports, and the scandals both big and small. The athletes, instead of inspiring a small boy, were too often doing things that hardly made them heroes.

It had always been there, I suppose, but everything now seemed to be on steroids.

I was worried meanwhile that Nicholson was fading, and quickly. And, as I began an odd relationship with him, calling him every six weeks or so to check in, I hung on his every word.

It would go on for nearly two years—me calling, hoping to catch him in a talkative mood, and trying to get myself invited for a visit and a sit-down interview. Most times he talked, recalling in detail a long-ago home run or the latest inconclusive trip to the doctor. Occasionally, he was terse and nearly hung up, depressed because his energy was sapped, forcing him to sit in a chair most of the day.

"I am not feeling too good," he told me during our fifth conversation, this one in February 2016. "I got about another nine weeks before I'm out of the woods. [I] haven't been in a very good mood. I didn't expect the kind of operation I had. I've been kind of in the dumps."[2]

He rebounded but, nearly a year later, relapsed. I learned from Jeannie, his wife, that he was again in the hospital in late 2016. "I don't like being alone," she said, missing her husband. She had taken him golfing, hoping to get him more active, and feared she may have caused more problems.[3]

I first cold-called Nicholson on a gray Tuesday in October 2015—the first night of the World Series between the Kansas City Royals and New York Mets. He said he did not watch baseball very much anymore; didn't like the way the game was now played. He was of course puzzled—skeptical, even—about what I wanted.

I told him I was interested in something more than an autograph. He laughed when he heard he was my childhood hero. I wasn't very smart, he said.[4]

Dave Nicholson would never be confused with the era's greats—Willie Mays, Mickey Mantle, Hank Aaron, or Roberto Clemente. When he hit 22 home runs in 1963, he batted just .229. A year later, he was relegated to a part-time role. There would be no Ted Williams-type home run in his final at bat. In his last game, he went 0-for-3.[5]

When I talked to Gary Peters, the White Sox pitching ace during the early 1960s, he told me that he had occasionally pinch-hit for Nicholson when the slugger was scheduled to face a pitcher who was particularly tough on him. It was highly unusual—but, of course, classically White Sox—for a pitcher to bat in place of the team's supposed power hitter. "I pinch hit for Dave a few times," Peters said. "He didn't like that very good. He had a lot of trouble with certain guys who had good sliders." Peters, in fact, claimed he once hit a home run pinch-hitting for Nicholson.[6]

"He swung hard," said Peters, who won 19 games for the White Sox in 1963, and was a 20-game winner for the team the following year. But Nicholson "couldn't adjust for the breaking ball very good."[7]

Rooting for Nicholson meant forgetting those kinds of things. But for one brief moment, it all came together—for me, and for him. It was the first summer that I lived and died with each White Sox game, often listening to them on a transistor radio on my front step in Calumet City with my best friend, Jerry Gorak. It was a Polish neighborhood, surrounded by steel mills and an oil refinery. The twin steeples of a Catholic Church, three doors away, loomed over our duplex; the Czechanski Funeral Home was across the street. On Sunday afternoons, my dad listened to live polka music on the radio from Club 505 in the nearby Hegewisch neighborhood of Chicago .

Against that background, I spent the summer worshipping a hitter who couldn't hit.

One could always dream, though, and I kind of did. In the early 1960s, any real fan played Strat-O-Matic Baseball, a card and dice game that matched real players from real teams with surprisingly real results. It was addictive. My parents bought me the 1963 starter set: five teams—the New York Yankees, San Francisco Giants, St. Louis Cardinals, Los Angeles Dodgers and White Sox. A couple of years later I added three more, including the Chicago Cubs.

I purposely added the 1966 Cubs—being a White Sox fan, I hated the Cubs—knowing that in reality they had lost 103 games that year and would likely suck at Strat-O-Matic Baseball. They did not disappoint.

Nicholson did not disappoint either. In my league, Big Nick was a monster. He hit 53 home runs, including four grand slams, in 1966.

In 1967, the White Sox won the pennant by one game over the Giants in my league and Nicholson finished fifth with 37 home runs, two of them grand slams. My pretend White Sox, led by Nicholson, were way more satisfying than the real thing.

Not bad production, considering it was fictional. On his Strat-O-Matic card, there were 33 possible outcomes every time the dice were rolled. Of the 33, there were only five ways Nicholson could get a hit, and just a total of 10 ways he could get on base. On his card, meanwhile, there was more than a one in three chance he would strike out. But the dice, for some reason, were kind to him.[8]

As I got married, moved to Minnesota, had a kid, got divorced, got married and had more kids, Nicholson faded from my consciousness but never completely disappeared. In the basement, my copy of Operation White Sox, the team's 50-cent year book from 1964, had survived nearly six decades. Nicholson was pictured on page 123, rounding the bases. The write-up was glowing: "Dave, the $100,000 bonus baby sought by all in 1958, was part of the gigantic Baltimore-Chicago deal of the winter of 1962. He responded spectacularly 449 times at bat slamming 22 homers and driving in 70 runs."[9]

My White Sox memories, though fogged slightly by time, remained vivid. There were the bus rides to Comiskey Park, sponsored by my dad's American Legion post, which featured beer and pop on ice in a tub in the aisle. As we swept through the dingy Southside neighborhoods, and inched closer to the stadium, we ducked as kids threw rocks at our bus.

The old ballpark was cavernous, and smelled of beer and cigars. On humid nights, the players warmed up in a haze of cigarette smoke that hung over the field—this was, after all, the 1960s. Andy the Clown, who was always kind of creepy, roamed the stands as the team's unofficial mascot. The exploding scoreboard was in straight-away center field.

Meanwhile, I sucked at baseball. In Little League, I was chubby, slow, and short—a bad combination. For some reason, I batted leadoff and often got on base by purposely getting hit by the ball. Our manager seemed to encourage me to lean into the pitch. Our team was sponsored by an A&W Root Beer stand, and we lost nearly all of our games.

I was the son of a Catholic fork-lift operator, and was taught to keep my head down and brace for disappointment. In that sense, Nicholson was the perfect hero—the guy who might win the game, but more than likely would not.

As I neared retirement, I found myself strangely circling back to Nicholson and a once-upon-a-time world.

And for any Nicholson fan, that meant heading to May 6, 1964. That was the night Nicholson hit a ball over the left field roof, and out of Comiskey Park. Only Jimmie Foxx, Eddie Robinson, and Mantle had ever done it before, or so the story went. The team estimated it traveled 573 feet—and into the hands of 10-year-old Mike Murillo Jr. who, according to the *Chicago Tribune*, was standing outside the stadium and listening to the game on the radio.[10]

The newspaper called it "one of the most prodigious homers in major league history," claiming that

Nicholson's home run was the second longest ever hit in the major leagues, behind only a 600-foot home run by Babe Ruth.[11]

Murillo gave the ball to Nicholson in exchange for one of Nicholson's bats, an autographed baseball, and a picture with the slugger. The *Tribune* documented it all on the front page of the next day's sports section.[12] For a fleeting moment, Nicholson was the toast of the town.

But the controversy over Nicholson's biggest moment started almost immediately. Fans in the left field upper deck claimed they heard a bang as the ball went over the roof, suggesting maybe it had bounced on the roof and did not go over on a fly. Still, the *Tribune* quoted John Cook, an electrician working on the roof that night, as saying the ball cleared the roof.[13]

I found Paul Junkroski, who was a high school sophomore sitting in the left field upper deck when the ball was hit.

"He hit the ball, and immediately you could see that there was no doubt, this was going to be a home run," said Junkroski, by then a retired school teacher living in the Chicago area. "And then, suddenly, it dawns to all of us in the stands there that this ball's going to come into the upper deck. It's just coming up and up and up.[14]

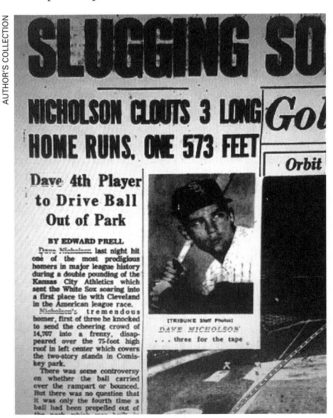

The Chicago Tribune *trumpeted Nicholson's feat.*

"Then...we realized it's not even coming into the upper deck, it's going over."[15]

Five decades after the event, he recalled it vividly. "As it disappeared above us, over the roof [that's] when we heard a noise. Everybody sitting there heard something—something fell."[16]

Junkroski worked as an usher at the ballpark that year. "That was an old wooden roof in that stadium. A lot of people didn't realize that," he told me. "There were always people up there—electricians or somebody who worked there." The roof was 75-feet high. The ballpark, built in 1910, was torn down in 1991.[17]

Nearly two years after first calling him, I found both Nicholson and the ball outside Benton, Illinois.

He recalled that night. "When I hit the ball really good, I never watched them," he said. But "I knew I really hit it good. There was always speculation it hit on the roof, over the roof, whatever—it got over the roof someway because the kid picked it up in the park across the street." After he hit his famous home run that night, he told a reporter he was unsure whether it was the furthest one he had ever hit—there were a couple that he had hit in spring training, Nicholson explained, that might have gone even further.[18,19]

Nicholson hit three home runs that night during a doubleheader sweep of the then-Kansas City Athletics, which vaulted the White Sox temporarily into a first-place tie with the Cleveland Indians. His two home runs in the first game—including his moon shot—were off Moe Drabowsky, whom the newspaper the next morning noted "was once a Cub."[20]

Entering the game, Nicholson had been scuffling, batting just .209, and up until that day had only two extra-base hits in 43 at-bats. He would be traded after the 1965 season.[21]

"I just didn't hit enough," he said, looking back. His best year—1963—was the "only decent year I had."[22]

"We had a pretty good year, we finished second," said Nicholson. "The only bad thing is, I struck out so much."[23]

After not talking to Nicholson for several months—he was sick and not interested in talking anymore, he said—I wrote him a get-well card during the summer of 2017.

Out of the blue, he called. Still puzzled over what I wanted, he invited me down. The White Sox, perhaps sensing my sudden optimism, completed a sweep that day of the Houston Astros, who would go on to win the World Series. As I headed off to Illinois, my wife sent me a text: "There is still a 10 year old boy inside my guy, and a 24 year old baseball star inside that boy's 'guy'. Go find them both and introduce them to each other."

It took me 23 hours to get there, and we had a four-hour visit.

It was the first day of September, and the White Sox were firmly in last place. Three days before, Nicholson had turned 78. I was 63. The red mailbox in front of his home read N-I-C-H-O-L-S-O-N.[24]

He was 182 pounds—frail, but feeling better. He nodded to the small lake outside his living room window, describing how winded he got walking up the hill from the boat dock. "This getting older is not the 'Golden Years,'" he lamented.[25]

But just that day, Nicholson said, he had autographed some baseball cards a collector had sent. Oddly, the requests for autographs still come, and he sometimes grows tired of driving to the post office after signing them to mail them back. The autograph requests, he said, "come from everywhere. I signed a bunch [a] couple months ago from Europe, from—what the heck was it—the Ukraine, or something like that."[26]

The interest is hard to explain. Yet people do remember.

In March 2016, with Nicholson fighting an assortment of health problems and cursing his doctors, a young White Sox slugger with unfulfilled potential launched a mammoth home run in a spring training game. "Wow! That was some shot by Avi [Garcia]!" wrote one fan on a White Sox website. "It was Dave Nicholsonish."[27]

In Benton, Nicholson lives in relative obscurity.

At a museum in the old jail near the city's downtown, Bill Owens recited the names of the famous and near-famous who were born near Benton: John Malkovich, the actor, was a Benton-area native, as was Gene Rayburn, the TV gameshow host. And George Harrison, the quiet Beatle, visited his sister in Benton before the band's first appearance on the *Ed Sullivan Show*.

And Dave Nicholson?

"Does he live here in Benton?" Owens asked, pausing to consider the name. "Dave Nicholson—I've never heard of him, and I'm a baseball historian."[28]

A week after my visit with Nicholson, the reference librarian at the National Baseball Hall of Fame in Cooperstown, New York, put an even bigger dent into my favorite player.

I had asked her about Nicholson's mammoth home run in 1964. "As for the home run," Cassidy Lent emailed back. She pointed me to a *Baseball Almanac* article that listed the home run "among the other great exaggerations in the history of tape measure home runs" and said the alleged 573-foot blast had been calculated by "White Sox mathematicians." The article concluded:

"These unidentified individuals based their calculations on the assumption that the ball traveled completely over the left-center field roof. [However], subsequent investigation indicated that the ball landed on the back of the roof before bouncing into the night."[29]

Ouch.

The ball Nicholson hit that night—now yellowed and ancient-looking—sat in a small case in a bedroom at his home. On the ball, there are these words: "May 6 1964 over the roof White Sox Park 500+." One of his favorite old gloves is on a nearby shelf. And so is the ball that the Minnesota Twins' star, Harmon Killebrew, gave to the White Sox slugger when Nicholson broke Killebrew's single-season record of 142 strikeouts. Killebrew had just himself set the record the year before, in 1962. "From one champ to another—Congratulations," Killebrew wrote on it.[30]

There was one other baseball, and a story I had never heard before. Holding a ball with a partially torn off cover, Nicholson said this one had bounced off a car bumper in a parking lot after he hit the ball more than 500 feet. I asked him if he had ever seen *The Natural*, the 1980s movie where the fictitious Roy Hobbs in one scene literally hits the cover off the ball. "Phony as phony can get," Nicholson said, laughing at the movie moment he, too, had seen. "But I liked it."[31]

Five decades later, it was obvious that striking out 175 times in one season still stung Nicholson. Never mind that a lot of players had since broken his record. Mark Reynolds holds the current record—he struck out 223 times in 2009. Nicholson is now tied at No. 85 on the single-season strikeout list. "He's got me by 50," strikeouts, Nicholson said of Reynolds.[32,33]

Jeannie Nicholson, who was mostly quiet that day in Benton, suddenly began talking of how the sports reporters covering the White Sox seemed to rub in Nicholson's strikeout problems. "That [was] kind of aggravating that they really harped on that—not that much attention to all the home runs he hit."[34]

The Over-The-Roof ball that Nicholson keeps at his home.

"They beat it to death," Nicholson added. "Every damn article that was written about me, mentioned that."[35]

In a hallway near the front door later that day, Nicholson moved on to happier memories. He paused by a picture of him in his White Sox pinstripes. He was young, with muscled biceps. His arms were extended, and he was swinging away. He even went into detail about his bat, a Louisville Slugger, Model N26.

"People said I looked a little like Mickey Mantle."[36]

Right after my visit with Nicholson, Jim Landis died. He was 83, and had played mostly center field for the White Sox while Nicholson, for a couple of years at least, was next to him in left field. But Landis, who played on the White Sox World Series team in 1959, was much better known. Landis's death was another sign that, one-by-one, his teammates were disappearing.[37]

The point of it all, of course, was mortality. Nicholson had emerged from a rough couple of years.

The worst stretch may have been March and April 2016. When I called in late March, it was Jeannie who answered, and she spoke to me for the longest she had ever talked. Her husband had been in the hospital three times in the past two months, she reported. The next day, she said, she planned to bring him home from his most recent stay.[38]

Nicholson, right, and the author in September 2017.

The worry tumbled out of her. She was 15 when she met Nicholson, and married him at 19. Now she herself was 75.[39]

He was better, she said, but "he's bored to death."[40]

Opening Day for the White Sox that year was on April 4—a Monday—and I found myself briefly talking to a slightly upbeat Nicholson. The White Sox beat the A's, 4–3, behind their then-ace Chris Sale, who struck out eight.[41]

"I haven't even paid any attention," he said when I asked him about Opening Day.[42]

Charlie Philpott, Nicholson's grandson, has in many respects been the keeper of his grandfather's flame. A longtime baseball fan himself, Philpott said his grandfather made him appreciate what may have been baseball's golden age. Today's athletes seem like celebrities who are "almost removed from society," he said. In Nicholson's time, the players "were regular everyday people and also somehow super human at the same time."[43]

Though Nicholson had more recently opened up about his career, Philpott added, he did not seem too eager before that. "I've gotten the impression [the strikeout record] was maybe part of his reticence," Philpott said. "[Maybe he] felt he didn't have as good a career as he thought he should have."[44]

During my sophomore year in high school, Nicholson's career sputtered to a close with the Omaha Royals, a minor league team. His last year in the majors was 1967; he played in just 10 games for the Atlanta Braves. He struck out nine times in 25 at-bats. He had found a glimmer of hope in 1968, hitting 34 home runs for the minor league Richmond Braves. But he struck out 199 times.[45]

After his playing days ended, Nicholson owned a sporting goods store in suburban Chicago.[46]

With college and career in front of me, I lost track of him.

In the ensuing years I found new baseball heroes—White Sox sluggers like Dick Allen, Carlos May, Ron Kittle, and Frank Thomas. But it was never the same; the moment had come and gone. Even when the White Sox won the World Series in 2005, ending nearly a century of disappointment, I was happy but detached.

Fifty years after Nicholson played, I lived in a world where cynicism came easy. I covered the Minnesota Twins' quest to use a boatload of taxpayer money to build a new ballpark—even though the team's owners were incredibly affluent. On the night the public subsidy package passed the state legislature, I watched as a sports columnist from my own newspaper sat with team officials and cheered on the vote. What I was writing about then, I remember telling myself, had nothing to do with the actual game.

Nicholson believed he played at a special time. He hit his last home run, he claimed, off Sandy Koufax, the Hall of Fame pitcher and baseball legend.[47] He faced, among many others, Bob Gibson, the St. Louis Cardinals' intimidating right-hander and two-time Cy Young Award winner who is now also a Hall of Famer. He saw Ted Williams take the last swing of his major league career.[48]

I had not lived in Chicago since the early 1970s, but I did go to a White Sox game while visiting a couple of years ago.

The White Sox' old stadium had been gone for a quarter century. But the spot that marks the stadium's old home plate is in a nearby parking lot. Standing there, looking north toward a hazy Chicago skyline, I could still picture how far the ball traveled on that Tuesday night in 1964 before it reached Murillo.

The White Sox lost that day, 10–2—but that was not the worst of it. At about the time of my Chicago visit, the website Sportsbreak came out with a list of the 15 longest home runs in American and National League history. I had never heard of the website, but sports fans—me included—love lists. So, I bit, and clicked on it. Nicholson's name was nowhere to be found.[49,50]

When I found John Nicholson, Dave's younger brother by nearly three years, he still lived in St. Louis where the family grew up on the city's west side. Yogi Berra, the famed Yankees catcher, had grown up nearby. Dave had the baseball talent, he said. "I was no good," said John. Even as a teenager, Dave was hitting long home runs, and drawing major league scouts. "He was like my dad, [and] my dad was a very strong [guy]" said John.[51]

John retired after more than 40 years in the machine trades. Though he lived for a while in Chicago, and attended White Sox games, he couldn't recall ever seeing his brother hit a major league home run in person.[52]

Now it hurt to see his brother in pain. "He looks [like] a shadow of what he used to be."[53]

So "I say a little prayer every night."[54]

As my visit with Nicholson came to an end, Jeannie took a picture of the two of us in front of the fireplace. Though I did not notice at first, Nicholson was smiling.

I thought of asking Nicholson for his autograph. As a kid, I never had it. But I never did ask, thinking it would cheapen the moment. I had found a long-ago hero who was now an old man, but who still tugged at something inside of me. We had, for now, both survived a strange journey from the past to the present. For me, that was enough. ∎

Notes

1. Dave Nicholson, telephone interview, January 8, 2016.
2. Dave Nicholson, telephone interview, February 10, 2016.
3. Jeannie Nicholson, telephone interview, November 29, 2016.
4. Dave Nicholson, telephone interview, October 27, 2015.
5. Baseball-Reference.com, baseball box scores, October 1, 1967.
6. It should be noted that there's no evidence of this home run. Gary Peters, telephone interview, September 21, 2016.
7. Gary Peters, telephone interview, September 21, 2016.
8. Strat-O-Matic Baseball, Dave Nicholson, 1963 card.
9. Operation White Sox, team yearbook, 1964, 123.
10. Edward Prell, "Slugging Sox Win 2; Cubs Beat Giants," Chicago Tribune, May 7, 1964, 3–1.
11. Edward Prell, "Slugging Sox Win 2; Cubs Beat Giants," Chicago Tribune, May 7, 1964, 3–1.
12. Edward Prell, "Slugging Sox Win 2; Cubs Beat Giants," Chicago Tribune, May 7, 1964, 3–1.
13. Edward Prell, "Slugging Sox Win 2; Cubs Beat Giants," Chicago Tribune, May 7, 1964, 3–1.
14. Paul Junkroski, telephone interview, January 27, 2016.
15. Paul Junkroski, telephone interview, January 27, 2016.
16. Paul Junkroski, telephone interview, January 27, 2016.
17. Paul Junkroski, telephone interview, January 27, 2016.
18. Dave Nicholson, telephone interview, November 5, 2015.
19. Edward Prell, "Slugging Sox Win 2; Cubs Beat Giants, Chicago Tribune, May 7, 1964, 3–1.
20. Edward Prell, "Slugging Sox Win 2; Cubs Beat Giants, Chicago Tribune, May 7, 1964, 3–1.
21. Edward Prell, "Slugging Sox Win 2; Cubs Beat Giants, Chicago Tribune, May 7, 1964, 3–1.
22. Dave Nicholson, telephone interview, November 5, 2015.
23. Dave Nicholson, telephone interview, November 5, 2015.
24. Baseball-Reference.com, baseball standings, September 1, 2017.
25. Dave Nicholson, in-person interview, September 1, 2017.
26. Dave Nicholson, in-person interview, September 1, 2017.
27. SBNation.com SBNation.com/users/grinnellsteve/search/2?q=avi+garcia+and+march-9,+2016&type=comment.
28. Bill Owens, in-person interview, September 1, 2017.
29. Cassidy Lent, reference librarian, Baseball Hall of Fame, September 7, 2017.
30. Dave Nicholson, in-person interview, September 1, 2017.
31. Dave Nicholson, in-person interview, September 1, 2017.
32. Baseball-Reference.com, Single-Season Strikeout Leaders.
33. Dave Nicholson, in-person interview, September 1, 2017.
34. Jeannie Nicholson, in-person interview, September 1, 2017.
35. Dave Nicholson, in-person interview, September 1, 2017.
36. Dave Nicholson, in-person interview, September 1, 2017.
37. Baseball-Reference.com, Jim Landis biography, October 7, 2017.
38. Jeannie Nicholson, telephone interview, March 25, 2016.
39. Jeannie Nicholson, telephone interview, February 13, 2017.
40. Jeannie Nicholson, telephone interview, March 25, 2016.
41. Baseball-Reference.com, baseball box scores, April 4, 2016.
42. Dave Nicholson, telephone interview, April 4, 2016.
43. Charlie Philpoa, telephone interview, October 6, 2017.
44. Charlie Philpoa, telephone interview, October 6, 2017.
45. Baseball-Reference.com, Dave Nicholson, biography.
46. Dave Nicholson, in-person interview, September 1, 2017.
47. His last home run was off of Larry Jackson.
48. Dave Nicholson, in-person interview, September 1, 2017.
49. Baseball-Reference.com, baseball box scores, August 7, 2016.
50. Sportsbreak.com Sportsbreak.com/mlb/the-15-longest-home-runs-ever-hit.
51. John Nicholson, telephone interview, September 6, 2017.
52. John Nicholson, telephone interview, September 6, 2017.
53. John Nicholson, telephone interview, September 6, 2017.
54. John Nicholson, telephone interview, September 6, 2017.

Black Swans in Baseball

The Case of the Unexpected MVP Season

Douglas Jordan, PhD

> First, it is an outlier, as it lies outside the realm of regular expectations, because nothing in the past can convincingly point to its possibility. Second, it carries an extreme impact (unlike the bird). Third, in spite of its outlier status, human nature makes us concoct explanations for its occurrence after the fact, making it explainable and predictable.
>
> — Nassim Nicholas Taleb,
> *The Black Swan: The Impact of the Highly Improbable*

INTRODUCTION

The epigraph from Taleb's book was written about very low-probability events in financial markets. Taleb compares Australian black swans (that were unknown in Europe for centuries) to rare, violent market movements that are impossible to predict in advance. He argues that these events occur without warning and that investors must be prepared for them in spite of their rarity. But black swan events are not confined to the world of finance. Although the term black swan is not usually associated with baseball, unpredictable and rare events certainly occur on the diamond. The 23 perfect games (27 batters up, 27 batters out) thrown in MLB history are a good example.[1]

But black swans in baseball are not confined to a single game; an entire season can be considered to be one. For an individual player, a noteworthy season is often referred to as a career year. This kind of season could be called a black swan depending on how far above the norm it is for that player. If the career year is especially noteworthy, it's possible that the player may merit MVP consideration. Therefore, the purpose of this article is to determine if there have been any black swan MVP seasons. Have there been any players whose performance in previous years gave no indication that they would win an MVP award?

The question then, is how to define that the player gave no such indication. The definition used in this paper is that the player wins an MVP award without having been recognized in a previous season for any aspect of his performance. The player never won, nor even got a vote for, any seasonal award such as Rookie of the Year, Gold Glove, or Silver Slugger, and was never on an All-Star team. Pitchers cannot have a previous Cy Young Award to their credit. For purposes of this paper, these definitions are taken to mean that the

awards column in the Baseball-Reference.com statistics for the player is empty every year prior to the year that the player wins an MVP. Analysis begins in 1931 when the Baseball Writers' Association of America started voting for the MVP. All of the data in this article are taken from Baseball-Reference.com.

RESPONSE TO AN OBJECTION

One possible objection to the results of this study is to argue that the player in question should not have won the award at all. This appears to be an easy argument to make if modern metrics such as Wins Above Replacement (WAR) are retroactively accounted for. For example, in 2006, Justin Morneau won the AL MVP with a WAR of 4.3. Derek Jeter came in second in the MVP voting that year with a WAR of 5.6 and Johan Santana came in seventh with a WAR of 7.6. An argument could be made that Morneau should not have won, and therefore claiming his season as a black swan is misleading.

This objection is disingenuous. Morneau actually won the award. To say that someone else should have won the award is simply hindsight bias. Bill James argues, "...the fact is that the MVP voting system is awfully well designed, and the right man does win the award the great majority of the time."[2] James goes on to say that the MVP voting represents the best judgment of baseball writers at that time regarding who was the most valuable player. That judgment should not be swept away by asserting that we know better now because we have more advanced statistics. The "we know better now" argument is discussed at length by Anthony Kronman, who writes about the issue in academia, but the core idea is the same. He says, "...we, even with our more enlightened ideals, are human beings, with the same imperfections as our predecessors, bedeviled by the same tendency to overestimate ourselves and confronting the same gap between ideals and reality."[3] We need to be very careful about thinking that we can better judge a player's abilities because we augment the eye test with complex formulas. The Appendix on page 54 contains the letter sent to MVP voters with their ballots.[4] The subjective nature of the process is made clear in the first line of the letter where it says, "There is no clear-cut definition of what Most Valuable means."

BLACK SWAN MVP NON-PITCHERS

An MVP-winning season is very special. Not only does the player have to have a historically excellent season, but it has to be a better season than any other great player of his era. Intuition suggests that such an outstanding campaign is highly unlikely to come without warning. It seems almost impossible that a previously mediocre player would be able to improve his performance significantly enough from one year to the next to win an MVP award. And in fact, the vast majority of MVP award-winning seasons have been preceded by being a previous MVP or an All-Star or a Rookie of the Year, getting some votes for MVP or Rookie of the Year,

winning a Gold Glove or Silver Slugger, or some combination of the above.

It should be noted that although the previous sentence is correct, the standard of a completely empty awards column in a player's Baseball-Reference.com statistics prior to winning the MVP award is a high bar. There have been a number of players who have only one of the above listed accomplishments in one season (and even more in just two seasons) prior to winning the MVP. For example, Keith Hernandez won the MVP in 1979 (along with Willie Stargell) in his sixth season. His only award prior to that season was a 1978 Gold Glove. Roger Maris won the MVP in 1960 in his fourth season after being an All-Star in 1959. It's reasonable to argue that these players' MVP seasons were unexpected, and hence should be included in this analysis. But lines have to be drawn somewhere, and in this paper, it is a completely empty awards column.

That's why there have been only three non-pitchers who have won an MVP award without receiving any previous awards. Those players are Justin Morneau in 2006, and Steve Garvey and Jeff Burroughs in 1974. Selected data for these players' MVP seasons and the seasons that preceded them are shown in Table 1.

Table 1. Select Data for Black Swan MVP Position Players

Justin Morneau select data

Year	Age	Tm	G	AB	R	H	2B	HR	RBI	BB	SO	BA	OBP	SLG	OPS	Awards
2003	22	MIN	40	106	14	24	4	4	16	9	30	0.226	0.287	0.377	0.664	
2004	23	MIN	74	280	39	76	17	19	58	28	54	0.217	0.34	0.536	0.875	
2005	24	MIN	141	490	62	117	23	22	79	44	94	0.239	0.304	0.437	0.741	
2006	25	MIN	157	592	97	190	37	34	130	53	93	0.321	0.375	0.559	0.934	MVP-1, SS

Steve Garvey select data

Year	Age	Tm	G	AB	R	H	2B	HR	RBI	BB	SO	BA	OBP	SLG	OPS	Awards
1969	20	LAD	3	3	0	1	0	0	0	0	1	0.333	0.333	0.333	0.667	
1970	21	LAD	34	93	8	25	5	1	6	6	17	0.269	0.31	0.355	0.665	
1971	22	LAD	81	225	27	51	12	7	26	21	33	0.227	0.29	0.382	0.673	
1972	23	LAD	96	294	36	79	14	9	30	19	36	0.269	0.312	0.422	0.734	
1973	24	LAD	114	349	37	106	17	8	50	11	42	0.304	0.328	0.438	0.766	
1974	25	LAD	156	642	95	200	32	21	111	31	66	0.312	0.342	0.469	0.811	AS, MVP-1, GG

Jeff Burroughs select data

Year	Age	Tm	G	AB	R	H	2B	HR	RBI	BB	SO	BA	OBP	SLG	OPS	Awards
1970	19	WSA	6	12	1	2	0	0	1	2	5	0.167	0.286	0.167	0.452	
1971	20	WSA	59	181	20	42	9	5	25	22	55	0.232	0.319	0.365	0.683	
1972	21	TEX	22	65	4	12	1	1	3	5	22	0.185	0.243	0.246	0.489	
1973	22	TEX	151	526	71	147	17	30	85	67	88	0.279	0.355	0.487	0.842	
1974	23	TEX	152	554	84	167	33	25	**118**	91	104	0.301	0.397	0.504	0.901	AS, MVP-1

Fred Lynn select data

Year	Age	Tm	G	AB	R	H	2B	HR	RBI	BB	SO	BA	OBP	SLG	OPS	Awards
1974	22	BOS	15	43	5	18	2	2	10	6	6	0.419	0.49	0.698	1.188	
1975	23	BOS	145	528	**103**	175	**47**	21	105	62	90	0.331	0.401	**0.566**	**0.967**	AS, MVP-1, RoY-1, GG

Ichiro Suzuki select data

Year	Age	Tm	G	AB	R	H	2B	HR	RBI	BB	SO	BA	OBP	SLG	OPS	Awards
2001	27	SEA	157	**692**	127	**242**	34	8	69	30	53	**0.35**	0.381	0.457	0.838	AS, MVP-1, RoY-1, GG, SS

Bold means led the league

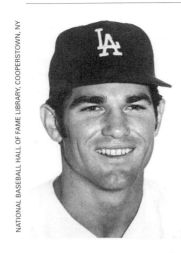

Steve Garvey had his breakout MVP season in 1974 at the age of 25.

Justin Morneau won the MVP at 25 years old in his fourth season. There was little to suggest he would have such an excellent season in his previous three seasons. He batted only .226 in 106 at bats during his rookie year. He improved his batting average to .271 with 19 home runs and 58 RBIs in 74 games the next year but the totals are low because he didn't become a full-time player until mid-July. His first full season as a starter was 2005. He played in 141 games, got 117 hits, blasted 22 home runs, and drove in 79 runs. His batting average declined to .239 and his slugging average was .437. With the exception of his batting average, these are good numbers for a season but they certainly aren't MVP caliber. That said, his performance that year was hindered by a concussion he suffered in the third game of the season when he was hit in the head by a pitch from Seattle's Ron Villone.[5]

He didn't win any awards during those first three seasons. But he had a breakout year his fourth season in 2006. He played in 157 games, had 190 hits, and put 34 balls over the fence. He also drove in 130 runs, batted .321, and slugged .559. His reward for these efforts was 15 out of 28 first-place votes for MVP and a total of 320 MVP points to Derek Jeter's second place 306 points. Morneau's play helped the Twins win 96 games and the AL Central division title before getting swept by the A's in the ALDS. It is also interesting to note that Morneau did not make the All-Star team the year of his MVP campaign. This suggests that the quality of his season was not even apparent during the early portion of that season. Morneau's MVP season appeared to have come out of nowhere.

Steve Garvey's inclusion on this list of unexpected MVP seasons is surprising given all he accomplished during his 19-year career. But most of what we remember him for came in the wake of his MVP performance, not before it. After just three at bats as a 20-year-old in September 1969, Garvey played four seasons before his MVP award-winning year in 1974 when he was 25. He played in only 34 games in 1970 and batted .269 in 93 at bats. During 1971 he appeared in 81 games with 225 at bats, seven home runs, and a .227 batting average. He got more playing time in 1972, 96 games, but his home run total only went up to nine even though his batting average increased to .269. His slow increase in playing time continued during 1973 when he appeared in 114 games. During that season he had 349 at bats, 106 hits, 50 RBIs, and eight home runs with a .304 batting average. His performance during 1973 and earlier does not suggest that an MVP season is imminent. He did not win any awards nor was voted to any All-Star teams in any of those five years.

But 1974 was a different story. Garvey played in almost every Dodger game that year (156) and had 642 at bats. He got 200 hits, slammed 21 balls out of the park, and drove in 111 runs. He batted .312 and slugged .469 that year. His reward for these outstanding numbers was the 1974 NL MVP award. In the MVP voting, Garvey got 13 out of 22 first-place votes and a total MVP vote count of 270 points. Lou Brock (who stole a modern-day second-best 118 bases that year) was second with 233 points. Garvey's efforts contributed to the Dodgers' 102-win season and their run to the World Series, where they lost in five games to the Oakland A's (who won the third of three consecutive titles in 1974). Justin like Morneau (I couldn't resist the pun), Garvey's MVP season appeared to have come out of nowhere.

The third position player to win an unexpected MVP award, also in 1974, was Jeff Burroughs. Burroughs won the award at age 23 during his fifth season in the majors. In spite of the fact that Burroughs was a promising power hitter, there's very little to note about his first three seasons, 1970–72.[6] He appeared in a total of 87 games those three years, his best effort being five home runs and a .232 batting average in 1971. Lower back problems limited his playing time in 1972. But unlike Morneau and Garvey, Burroughs had a better than average season the year before winning the MVP award even though he didn't win any awards for it. In 1973 Burroughs played in 151 games, batted .279 and slugged .487. He collected 147 hits and drove in 85 runs. And he finally exhibited the power he was expected to display when he hit 30 home runs to challenge Reggie Jackson (who hit 32) for the AL home run title. Given this output in 1973, it's not too surprising that he won the MVP the next year. It's more surprising that he wasn't named on any MVP ballots in 1973 in spite of such good numbers.

Burroughs had an outstanding season in 1974. He

improved his batting numbers in every category except home runs. He appeared in 152 games, got 167 hits and 33 doubles, while driving in a league-leading 118 RBIs and batting .301. His home run total declined to 25 but that was still fourth best in the league. His slash line of .301/.397/.504 was almost exactly the classic great season of .300/.400/.500. In the MVP voting, Burroughs got 10 of 23 first place votes and a total vote count of 248. Joe Rudi came in second with 161 points. Burroughs's efforts helped the Rangers to a second-place finish in the AL West, five games behind the A's.

BLACK SWAN MVP PITCHERS

Despite a school of thought that says pitchers shouldn't win the MVP because they don't play every day, there are pitchers who have won the MVP award. But just like other players, the same question can be asked: are there any pitchers who have won an MVP award without ever having won any other award? And just like position players, the answer is yes. There are four pitchers who meet this criterion: Willie Hernandez (1984), Vida Blue (1971), Jim Konstanty (1950), and

Carl Hubbell (1933). Selected data for these players are shown in Table 2.

Outside of Detroit, Willie Hernandez is not very well remembered three and a half decades after the heroics that won him both the Cy Young and MVP in 1984. There's a good reason for that. Beside that year, he had a relatively undistinguished 13-year career, primarily with the Cubs and the Tigers, plus one year with the Phillies. Most of his national exposure came from the six games he pitched in during the 1983 and 1984 World Series.

Hernandez got to the big leagues with the Cubs in 1977 at age 22. His rookie season was his best year prior to 1984. Being utilized mostly in relief, he went 8–7 with a 3.03 ERA in 67 games and 110 innings pitched. His ERA+ that year was 145 which means that the league's average ERA was 45 percent higher than his (ballpark adjusted). This was a fine rookie season, but Hernandez was not able to repeat the performance. Using ERA+ as a guideline, his performance was slightly better or worse than average between 1978 and 1983 with the exception of 1982, when he had an

Table 2. Select Data for Black Swan MVP Pitchers

Willie Hernanadez select data

Year	Age	Tm	W	L	ERA	G	GS	SV	IP	ER	HR	BB	SO	ERA+	WHIP	Awards
1977	22	CHC	8	7	3.03	67	1	4	110	37	11	28	78	145	1.109	
1978	23	CHC	8	2	3.77	54	0	3	59.2	25	6	35	38	107	1.542	
1979	24	CHC	4	4	5.01	51	2	0	79	44	8	39	53	83	1.57	
1980	25	CHC	1	9	4.4	53	7	0	108.1	53	8	45	75	90	1.477	
1981	26	CHC	0	0	3.95	12	0	2	13.2	6	0	8	13	97	1.61	
1982	27	CHC	4	6	3	75	0	10	75	25	3	24	54	125	1.307	
1983	28	TOT	9	4	3.28	74	1	8	115.1	42	9	32	93	112	1.223	
1983	28	CHC	1	0	3.2	11	1	1	19.2	7	0	6	18	121	1.119	
1983	28	PHI	8	4	3.29	63	0	7	95.2	35	9	26	75	110	1.244	
1984	29	DET	9	3	1.92	**80**	0	32	140.1	30	6	36	112	204	0.941	AS, CYA-1, MVP-1

Vida Blue select data

Year	Age	Tm	W	L	ERA	G	GS	SV	IP	ER	HR	BB	SO	ERA+	WHIP	Awards
1969	19	OAK	1	1	6.64	12	4	1	42	31	13	18	24	52	1.595	
1970	20	OAK	2	0	2.09	6	6	0	38.2	9	0	12	35	171	0.828	
1971	21	OAK	24	8	**1.82**	39	39	0	312	63	19	88	301	183	**0.952**	AS, CYA-1, MVP-1

Jim Konstanty select data

Year	Age	Tm	W	L	ERA	G	GS	SV	IP	ER	HR	BB	SO	ERA+	WHIP	Awards
1944	27	CIN	6	4	2.8	20	12	0	112.2	35	11	33	19	126	1.296	
1946	29	BSN	0	1	5.28	10	1	0	15.1	9	2	7	9	67	1.565	
1948	31	PHI	1	0	0.93	6	0	2	9.2	1	0	2	7	438	0.931	
1949	32	PHI	9	5	3.25	53	0	7	97	35	9	29	43	121	1.309	
1950	33	PHI	16	7	2.66	**74**	0	22	152	45	11	50	56	151	1.039	AS, MVP-1

Carl Hubbell select data

Year	Age	Tm	W	L	ERA	G	GS	SV	IP	ER	HR	BB	SO	ERA+	WHIP	Awards
1928	25	NYG	10	6	2.83	20	14	1	124	39	7	21	37	137	1.113	
1929	26	NYG	18	11	3.69	39	35	1	268	110	17	67	106	124	1.269	
1930	27	NYG	17	12	3.87	37	32	2	241.1	104	11	58	117	122	1.328	
1931	28	NYG	14	12	2.65	36	30	3	248	73	14	67	155	139	1.121	
1932	29	NYG	18	11	2.5	40	32	2	284	79	20	40	137	149	1.056	
1933	30	NYG	**23**	12	**1.66**	45	33	5	**308.2**	57	6	47	156	193	**0.982**	AS, MVP-1

NATIONAL BASEBALL HALL OF FAME LIBRARY, COOPERSTOWN, NY

Jim Konstanty receiving his 1950 MVP award from Ford Frick, then president of the National League.

ERA+ of 125. Seven years into his career, Hernandez had done little to suggest that he was anything more than an average pitcher. He hadn't won any awards during those seven years.

But the story changed when the Phillies traded him to Detroit in 1984. Hernandez became a key contributor to an excellent Tigers team that started the year 35–5 and won the World Series. He had seven saves during that initial 40-game run. His excellent performance continued the rest of that season. Hernandez appeared in almost half the team's games (a league-leading 80), compiling a 9–3 record with a 1.92 ERA and a season total of 32 saves with only one blown save. His ERA+ of 204 means that his ERA that year was about half of the league average. He lowered his WHIP to 0.94 from 1.22 the year before. This perfect example of a black swan year earned Hernandez 16 out of 28 first place votes in the MVP voting and a total of 306 points. Kent Hrbek was second in the voting with 247 points. Hernandez never again appeared in the Cy Young or MVP voting although he was an All-Star in both 1985 and 1986.

Vida Blue's relatively short path to the Cy Young and MVP awards he won in 1971 at age 21 was very different from the long route taken by Hernandez. Blue had started a grand total of ten games, with a combined record of 3–1, over his initial two big-league seasons before winning the awards in his first full season. But Blue's award-winning season was foreshadowed by the no-hitter he threw as a September call-up in 1970.[7] This performance, combined with a one-hitter in another start that month, led to great expectations for 1971. It's hard to believe that he exceeded those expectations.

Blue's accomplishments over the first half of 1971 were truly remarkable. After giving up four runs (only one of them earned) in 1⅔ innings, and taking the loss in his first start of the year, he didn't get a decision in just two of his next 21 starts. He won 17 of those 21 games and had a 17–3 record at the All-Star break. Most astoundingly by today's standards, he pitched nine innings in 16 of his first 22 starts and 11 shutout innings in another. Ironically, the 11-inning shutout was one of his two non-decisions. The A's eventually won that game (July 9 versus the Angels) 1–0 in the bottom of the 20th inning.

Blue's numbers for the whole season are very impressive too. He started 39 games, compiling a 24–8 record with 24 complete games and 8 shutouts in 312 innings. He struck out 301 batters. He led the league in ERA (1.82), shutouts (8), WHIP (0.952), hits per nine innings (6.0), and strikeouts per nine innings (8.7). These efforts earned him 14 out of 24 first-place votes in the MVP voting and a total of 268 points. His teammate, Sal Bando, was second in the voting with 182 points.

The year 1950 was a long time ago. So you may not be familiar with the name Jim Konstanty. As with Hernandez, there are good reasons for that. Konstanty had an almost completely undistinguished 11-year pitching career between 1944 and 1956. But the word "almost" is needed because Konstanty managed to put a classic black swan season together in 1950 when he became the first relief pitcher to win an MVP award. He's the only man on this list who has a clear awards column both before *and* after his MVP season.

Konstanty was a relief pitcher for the Philadelphia "Whiz Kids" Phillies who won the NL pennant in 1950 before getting swept by the Yankees (who were in the midst of winning a record five consecutive titles) in the World Series. Usually pitching in long relief, Konstanty went 16–7 with a 2.66 ERA. He led both leagues in games (74), games finished (62), and saves (22). Konstanty was an ironman in relief that year, throwing 152 innings while giving up 108 hits and just 45 earned runs.[8] This body of work earned him 18 out of 24 first-place votes in the MVP voting and a total of 286 points. Stan Musial was second with 158 points. But Konstanty was unable to repeat this excellent performance. The next year his ERA jumped to 4.05 and he won only four games against 11 losses.

Hall of Famer Carl Hubbell won the MVP award in 1933 as a 30-year-old in his sixth season. He started 45 games, completed 22 of them, and compiled a 23–12 record with a 1.66 ERA. He led the league in wins (23), ERA (1.66), shutouts (10), innings pitched (308.2),

ERA+ (193), and WHIP (0.982). With these impressive numbers he won the MVP vote with 77 vote points to Chuck Klein's 48 vote points. His Baseball-Reference.com awards column is empty for the first five years of his career.

Therefore, according to the definition in this paper, this is a black swan season. But like Ichiro Suzuki (discussed in the next section) it's arguable that this season does not really qualify as a black swan. In 1932 Hubbell went 18–11 with a 2.50 ERA and he led MLB in WHIP at 1.056. These numbers are better than Bob Brown put up that year (14–7, 3.30 ERA) and got ten MVP award vote points and better than Dizzy Dean's numbers (18–15, 3.30 ERA) and got four MVP award vote points. Hubbell should have gotten some votes for MVP in 1932; leading baseball in WHIP the previous year means that his excellent campaign in 1933 was not completely unexpected. In addition, Hubbell was more likely to have a clear Awards column prior to 1933 because there were no All-Star games before that year, and the Cy Young and Gold Glove awards didn't start until 1956 and 1957 respectively.

THE SPECIAL CASE OF ROY AND MVP

Almost by definition, rookies are not expected to win an MVP award. That's why only two men have managed to win the MVP in their rookie year. Select data for those two players are shown in Table 1. The first man to do it was Fred Lynn in 1975. Although Lynn played in 15 games in 1974, he still was officially a 23-year-old rookie in 1975 when he had one of the best rookie seasons of all time, and paced the Red Sox to a 95-win season and an appearance in a thrilling seven-game World Series. He played in 145 games, batted .331, hit 21 home runs, and drove in 105 runs. He led the league in runs scored (103), doubles (47), slugging average (.566), and OPS (.967). In the MVP voting, he got 22 out of 24 first place votes and a total of 326 points. John Mayberry of the Royals was second with 157 points. Although Lynn showed some promise in AAA in 1974 (he batted .282 and hit 21 homers in 124 games[9]) that's not enough to expect an MVP type season the next year. Lynn's MVP season in 1975 is clearly a black swan event.

The second man to win ROY and MVP in the same season was 27-year-old Ichiro Suzuki in 2001. But even though Ichiro (he is usually referred to by his first name) was technically an MLB rookie that year, he was far from a typical first-year player. Before coming to Seattle in 2001, he had already played for nine years in the Japan Pacific League, where he appeared in 951 games and compiled a Japanese lifetime batting average of .353. Ichiro was a superstar in Japan but he wanted to compete in the US.[10]

When he got that chance in 2001, he excelled. He appeared in 157 games, scored 127 runs, and hit 34 doubles. He led the American League in plate appearances (738), at bats (692), stolen bases (56), and batting average (.350). And, in addition to all of that, he got an amazing 242 hits (ninth best all-time at the time). The MVP vote was very close. Ichiro got 11 first-place votes and 289 MVP vote points total. Jason Giambi got eight first-place votes and 281 points. But even though Ichiro technically meets the definition in this paper, it's hard to argue that his 2001 season actually belongs in the black swan season camp. Given his Japanese performance, it's not surprising he had a noteworthy inaugural campaign.

CONCLUSION

Of the nine players discussed in this article who had black swan MVP seasons, only Konstanty didn't win at least one award in the years that followed their MVP season. Therefore, in the context of a complete career, Jim Konstanty's MVP campaign in 1950 is the best example of a black swan MVP season. ■

Acknowledgments

My thanks to two anonymous reviewers for taking the time to carefully review the paper and provide feedback. Their comments improved the final product.

Notes

1. https://www.baseball-reference.com/bullpen/Perfect_game.
2. Bill James, *The Politics of Glory: How Baseball's Hall of Fame Really Works*, New York: Macmillan, 1994, 74.
3. Anthony Kronman, *The Assault on American Excellence*, New York: The Free Press, 2019, 176.
4. Brian Cohn, "Defining MVP—and why it matters for voting," SB Nation: The Crawfish Boxes, September 13, 2019, accessed January 25, 2021. https://www.crawfishboxes.com/2019/9/13/20862347/defining-most-valuable-player-lemahieu-bregman-trout-mlb-mvp-houstonastros-yankees-angels-voting.
5. Eun Jung Decker, "Justin Morneau Biography," JockBio.com, 2013, accessed January 25, 2021. https://www.jockbio.com/Bios/Morneau/Morneau_bio.html.
6. David E. Skelton, "Jeff Burroughs," SABR, 2019, accessed January 25, 2021. https://sabr.org/bioproj/person/2df1caea.
7. Rich Puerzer, "Vida Blue," SABR, accessed January 25, 2021. https://sabr.org/bioproj/person/397acf10.
8. C. Paul Rogers III, "Jim Konstanty," SABR, 2018, accessed January 25, 2021. https://sabr.org/bioproj/person/ad95bdcc.
9. Tom Nahigian, "Fred Lynn," SABR, 2005, rev. 2014, accessed January 25, 2021. https://sabr.org/bioproj/person/7fb674d5.
10. https://en.wikipedia.org/wiki/Ichiro_Suzuki#Career_in_Japan.

Appendix
The letter sent to MVP voters

Dear Voter:

There is no clear-cut definition of what Most Valuable means. It is up to the individual voter to decide who was the Most Valuable Player in each league to his team. The MVP need not come from a division winner or other playoff qualifier.

The rules of the voting remain the same as they were written on the first ballot in 1931:

1. Actual value of a player to his team, that is, strength of offense and defense.

2. Number of games played.

3. General character, disposition, loyalty and effort.

4. Former winners are eligible.

5. Members of the committee may vote for more than one member of a team.

You are also urged to give serious consideration to all your selections, from 1 to 10.
A 10th-place vote can influence the outcome of an election. You must fill in all 10 places on your ballot. Only regular-season performances are to be taken into consideration.

Keep in mind that all players are eligible for MVP, including pitchers and designated hitters.

Did Batters of Long Ago Learn During a Game?

Jay Wigley

Modern baseball analysis has established without a doubt that the longer a pitcher stays in the game, the better the batters will perform against him. Beginning in 1996, analysts evaluated the starting lineup's plate appearances and later coined an acronym for the rule: TTOP, for the "Times Through (the) Order Penalty." That is, "As the game goes on, the hitter has a progressively greater advantage over the starting pitcher."[1] Has this TTOP always been there? This article examines whether Deadball Era batters improved their performance against the starting pitcher in the same way as their modern counterparts. Using Retrosheet data for the seasons 1916–2019, we will see that while Deadball batters also learned their opposing pitcher during a game, the pattern of their learning was different.

The differences between the Deadball Era game and that of today are many, but two of them stand out when it comes to batters and pitchers.

First, Deadball Era baseballs were kept in play as long as reasonably possible, primarily to minimize team expenses. Whereas modern batters see a new ball at least at the beginning of every inning (and often several new ones are put in play during a single plate appearance), Deadball Era batters were trying to make quality contact with a ball that had been darkened by dirt and by the pitcher using a variety of foreign substances.

Second, Deadball Era batters aimed their hits between fielders, producing line drives into the outfield, not driving the ball out of the park, which was a futile approach in most ballparks of the time. Babe Ruth's powerful uppercut swing, which helped transform the game in the 1920s, was a lesson not yet learned by hitters in the Deadball years.

Considering these two substantial differences in how the game was played, we might expect there to be a difference in how the battle at the plate progressed as batter and pitcher became more and more familiar with each other.

WHAT HAS ALREADY BEEN DONE

David Smith discovered the TTOP in 1996, writing about it in his article "Do Batters Learn During a Game?" He examined the outcomes of sequential plate appearances between starting pitchers and hitters in every game from 1984 to 1995. Smith's study showed that batters learn faster than the pitchers can adjust during their first three times at the plate. He found the phenomenon consistent across both the American and National leagues and for both home and away batters. Thanks to the work of a host of folks at Retrosheet, our dataset has grown to allow us to examine the TTOP for every season since 1916.[2] While Smith's original study used the standard metrics of 1996 (batting average, on-base average, and slugging average), here we will rely on wOBA, an "all-in-one offensive rate statistic" on the scale of traditional on-base average.[3] The wOBA measure uses season-specific values to weight hitters' outcomes across all plate appearances.[4] If you're familiar with linear weights, you understand wOBA. But even without looking at a single formula, anyone familiar with standard on-base average (OBA) can think of wOBA as OBA's smarter cousin.

DID DEADBALL BATTERS LEARN?

Figure 1 (following page) shows the wOBA of all batters (excluding pitchers at the plate) during their first three plate appearances against the starting pitcher, organized into five-year clusters from 1916 through 2019. We see that for all half-decades after 1920, batters improved their wOBA every time they faced the same pitcher in a game: The second time up is better than the first, and the third time up is even better than the second. The notable exception is the half-decade 1916–20.

There are some limitations with the data. For example, play-by-play for the seasons of 1916–27 is incomplete as I write in the summer of 2020; approximately 75 percent of games are available, a quantity that assures statistical significance. However, for seasons 1928 and beyond, all games are available from Retrosheet. Also, I have excluded the fourth time at the plate from Figure 1, as its wOBA is uniformly greater than the third time for all clusters through 1985 (including 1916–20). Therefore, the fourth time up is not different in 1916–20 and is not considered here.[5]

Focusing on the Deadball years of 1916–20, the outcomes from first to third plate appearances expressed as wOBA form a "U," with a dip in batter performance the second time around. For shorthand, we will name that Deadball dip the "STUD" (Second Time Up Dip). We also note that the batters improved their third-time outcomes to a level only equal to their first time up, but not improving on it. As mentioned above, the fourth time up is greater still for Deadball batters (not presented in Figure 1). In short, while these batters of long ago *did* learn, improving their performance during the course of a game, the pitchers maintained a remarkable advantage (illustrated by the STUD) until the batter came to the plate a fourth time.

A NOTE ABOUT 1920

Many baseball historians and analysts consider the 1920 season at best wedged between two eras, and many place it fully with the 1920s for statistical analysis, and that makes sense when looking at traditional rate statistics like runs per game or slugging average, which suggest that the 1920 season had more in common with the 1920s than the 1910s. But when evaluating play-by-play data from 1920 compared to the season immediately afterward (Figure 2), the patterned performance of batters in 1920 games has more in common with the Deadball STUD we saw in Figure 1 than with seasons afterward.

WHAT CREATED THE STUD?

Looking back at Figure 1, we can eliminate some potential causes of the STUD, such as the overall weak offensive statistics in the Deadball Era. We see the TTOP present consistently even during the reduced of-

Figure 1. wOBA, first through third plate appearances, starting batters against starting pitchers (pitcher batting removed).

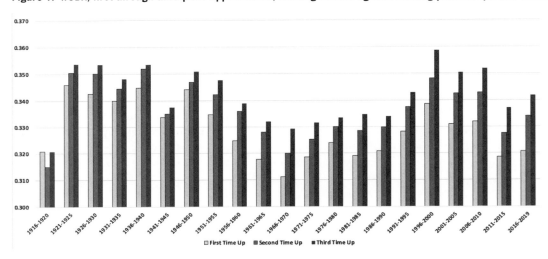

Figure 2. The wOBA pattern across the first three plate appearances in 1920 argues that the batters' experience that season was still Deadball. The STUD departed in 1921.

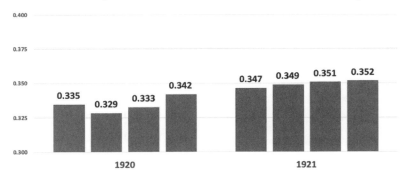

fense of the 1960s, and it remains steady even as offense rises significantly in the late 1990s, so the STUD isn't a product of the run environment. The STUD was also not the product of differences in the rules. At times of other significant changes, such as changing the height of the pitching mound in the late 1960s or the addition of the designated hitter in the American League in the early 1970s, we see no disruption in the TTOP at all. The TTOP was stable through integration (1947) and expansion (1961 and five times since). Even the introduction of significant numbers of replacement players during World War II did not disrupt the TTOP, which Figure 1 shows to be a remarkably stable characteristic of post-1920 baseball.

The STUD must have been a result of the ball itself. The timing of the STUD's disappearance is the tell. When the "no trick pitches" rule was issued early in 1920, umpires began replacing balls during games more frequently, even as the press complained.[6] Prior to 1920, teams used a single baseball as long as possible. Every incident of contact loosened the ball's cover, and that loose cover, darkened by dirt and tobacco juice, marred with cuts and scrapes, allowed pitchers to fling the ball with an erratic flight, reducing the chance of good contact by the batter. Changing the rules alone did not eliminate the STUD—*implementing* the change did, as umpires removed balls from play more often to enforce the new rule, which gave batters a cleaner, tighter ball to hit on a more regular basis. And when the power-hitting revolution took hold in 1921, following Ruth's example, not only umpires but batters were replacing the ball more often by knocking more and more pitches out of the park.

How sure can we be that the condition of the ball is to blame for the STUD? And why did the STUD persist in 1920 (see Figure 2) when the ban on trick pitches was already in effect?

To explore those questions, we divide the 1920 data into two leagues. If the ball was to blame, we should find a STUD in common between the American and National Leagues during the Deadball Era, since league balls were nearly identical and manufactured on the same equipment. Figure 3 shows that while both leagues did demonstrate the STUD, National League batters had a smaller dip, only two points of wOBA, while American League batters dropped 21 points of wOBA their second time up.

The difference in the league STUDs seems puzzling at first glance. League balls had only slight, primarily cosmetic differences: the color of some of the stitches.[7] If the magnitude of the STUD was driven by how much each league played with a battered ball, the difference between the leagues' STUDs should be related to the rate at which the ball was replaced. Thanks to a National League press release in December 1920, we can determine that NL teams used about 43 percent more balls per game in 1920 than they had in 1919.[8] Focusing on only the National League for just those two seasons, I found that the NL STUD is typical for the Deadball Era in 1919 (about 6 points of wOBA) but nearly gone—less than two points—in 1920. The 1919 and 1920 American League STUD is fully present in both seasons, with a substantial gap of over 12 points (data not presented). The difference in the leagues for these two seasons supports the theory that the condition of the ball was responsible for the STUD. While examining data for only two seasons league by league is slicing very thin, the result is suggestive.[9]

Why might the AL umpires have been replacing the baseball less often than their NL counterparts? Imagine the situation in 1920: Ban Johnson, his authority waning as American League president, strives to keep the waters calm.[10] All these new baseballs cost owners money. At some point in the season, he directs the umpires to cut down on ball replacement, tilting the balance toward the pitchers in the AL and deepening the STUD (as the data show). But after the death of Ray Chapman in August, a tragedy blamed as much on a ball that was difficult to see as on pitcher Carl Mays, the danger of Johnson's directive becomes obvious. Soon, Kenesaw Mountain Landis is on his way in as commissioner, and there's nothing to stop more frequent ball replacement in 1921—helping to boost the offense and drive everyone even more baseball crazy.[11]

Figure 3. wOBA, 1916–20, first through third times at the plate, NL and AL

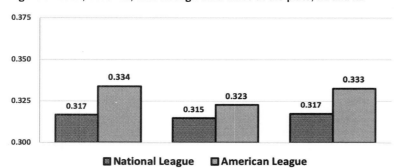

National League   American League

WAS THE DEADBALL STUD CONSISTENT FOR VISITING AND HOME BATTERS?

While AL and NL hitters swung at balls damaged to different extents, we can be sure that both the visiting and home teams swung at the same ball during a game. Yet Figure 4 shows that the difference between visiting and home batter performance was much greater than the difference between the leagues. From first to fourth times up, the visitors underperformed compared to the home team, but both teams' batters improved after climbing out of the STUD. Both teams peak the fourth time up relative to their first three appearances. But while the better performance of any era's home team batters is not unusual, we notice that the Deadball home team batters also enjoy another advantage: they seem to barely suffer the STUD effect at all.[12] Their second-time-up performance is practically as good as their first! Why would the visiting batters' STUD be so much larger, when both teams must have used the same battered, dirty ball?

It's the first inning. When the visiting batters took the field against the home pitcher in the top of the first, they swung at a clean ball with a tight cover. But in the bottom half, home team batters began with a ball that had almost certainly been in play for at least three batters. So the home batters faced a handicap in the first inning that the visitors did not. The visitors were sure of an advantage the home team could never have: beginning the game with a fresh ball. The home batters performed more poorly their first time up, rather than better-than-expected their second time up. Therefore, the visitors' STUD is exaggerated while the home team's STUD is minimized due to never batting with a clean ball in the first inning.

WHAT ABOUT THE PITCHERS?

While wOBA is a fine metric to evaluate batter performance, we can learn more about the Deadball Era's difference by examining the pitchers' perspective. We will use the strikeout-to-walk ratio (K/BB), which measures how well pitchers control the ball as they attempt to make strikes look like balls and balls look like strikes. K/BB isolates two outcomes over which the pitcher has great influence. If the ball was becoming invisible and disfigured more and more until it was replaced, we would expect strikeouts to increase as walks decrease, as batters could not see the ball well enough to make contact or judge well a pitch's path relative to the strike zone.

Figure 5 shows that in these late Deadball years, first-time-up batters struck out with the same frequency as they drew walks. But the pitchers gained an advantage of eight strikeouts per 100 walks the second time around, and only by the fourth time up did the batters' walks exceed their strikeouts. Inducing the swing and miss became more and more difficult as the ball was replaced. Therefore, the decreasing advantage to the pitchers, especially the fourth time around, is expected. By then, batters had seen all the starter's pitches and could see all of them *well*, thanks in part to a cleaner ball.

Figure 4. wOBA, first through fourth times up, visitor and home batters evaluated separately.

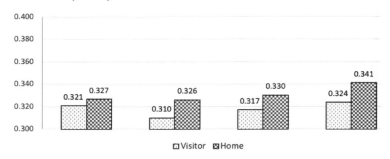

Figure 5. K/BB, 1916–20, first through fourth times at the plate.

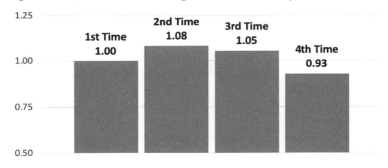

Figure 6. K/BB, 1921–29, first through fourth times at the plate.

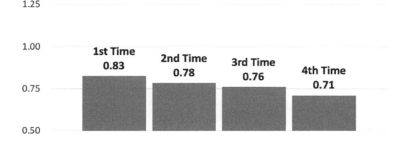

What about the pitchers of the 1920s?

Consistent with other measures of offense like runs per game or wOBA, Figure 6 shows that the pitchers lost a lot of their advantage when the leagues eliminated trick pitches. Pitchers in the 1920s never again enjoyed any in-game improvement in K/BB as they had in the Deadball years (when facing batters their second time up). Each time through the order, we see a decreasing ability to fool the batter into swinging at a ball or letting a strike go by. Strikeouts never exceeded walks, not even close, not even for batters in their first time at the plate. And by the fourth time around, batters had seen the pitcher's offerings enough to eliminate 12 strikeouts per 100 walks, on average, compared to the first time up.

CONCLUSIONS

We can draw the following conclusions from our study of the TTOP for late Deadball Era batters and pitchers:

Batters in 1916–20 saw their performance (defined by wOBA) dip their second time at the plate compared to the first time up, an experience distinctly different from that of batters in seasons since 1920.

The second-time-up-dip (STUD) ended because umpires beginning in 1920 replaced the ball more often to enforce the rules change against trick pitches, a practice accelerated after the death of Ray Chapman in August of that year. Prior to 1921, the ball was not replaced often enough to eliminate the STUD phenomenon.

The 1916–20 STUD is consistent in both American and National Leagues, and for both home and visiting batters. However, the magnitude of the dip was greater for the visiting batters because they always began the game with a fresh baseball, while home batters almost never did. Thus the home batters in the first inning played with a disadvantage that disproportionally depressed their performance for that inning, compared to the first inning for the visiting batters.

The pitchers' command of the strike zone (as evaluated by the ratio of strikeouts to walks) was better in the 1916–20 period, with strikeouts exceeding walks during batters' second time at the plate. After 1920 through at least 1929, walks always exceeded strikeouts across all times up, with the batters' advantage growing during the course of the game. ∎

Sources

Steve Steinberg, "The Spitball and the End of the Deadball Era," *The National Pastime* 23 (2003): 7–17.

David J. Gordon, "The Rise and Fall of the Deadball Era," *Baseball Research Journal* 47 (Fall 2018).

Notes

1. Tom Tango, Mitchel Lichtman, and Andrew Dolphin, *The Book: Playing the Percentages in Baseball* (CreateSpace Independent Publishing Platform, 2014), 191.

2. Smith's original study was most recently published in *SABR 50 at 50: The Society for American Baseball Research's Fifty Most Essential Contributions to the Game*, edited by Bill Nowlin, et al., (Lincoln: University of Nebraska Press, 2020), and was last revised in 2005, using all the Retrosheet data available then. Both Smith's and this study, therefore, used information obtained free of charge from and copyrighted by Retrosheet. Interested parties may contact Retrosheet at 20 Sunset Rd., Newark, DE 19711.

3. Michael Lichtman, "Everything You Always Wanted to Know About the Times Through the Order Penalty," Baseball Prospectus, November 5, 2013. https://www.baseballprospectus.com/news/article/22156/baseball-proguestus-everything-you-alwayswanted-to-know-about-the-times-through-the-order-penalty. wOBA multiplies the run values of various offensive events, divides by a batter's plate appearances, and produces a metric on the scale of on-base average.

4. To calculate each wOBA in this study I used the weights provided by Fangraphs at https://www.fangraphs.com/guts.aspx.

5. Batters since the late 1980s have shown a consistent decline in their fourth-time-up performance, as noted by Smith and others. The decline has been evaluated in some detail elsewhere. For example, see Smith's study, as well as Lichtman, "Everything You Always Wanted to Know."

6. "A Waste That Should Be Checked," *The Sporting News*, August 5, 1920. This view was likely a channeling of the owners' frustration with the increasing expense of all those new baseballs.

7. "The only difference [in the baseball itself] is the label and the red and blue stitches used in the American League ball as opposed to the red and black stitches used in the National League ball." Russell Wright, *A Tale of Two Leagues* (Jefferson, N.C.: McFarland and Company, 1999), 11.

8. "Most Successful Season," *The Brooklyn Daily Eagle*, December 15, 1920. The story explains that 27,924 balls were used in the NL for the 1920 season, and provides comparable data for 1919. The total number of baseballs used would include spring training games, exhibition games, and batting practice balls, so a simple "balls per game" metric is not possible. However, we can compare the two seasons to derive the 43 percent estimate with confidence.

9. There are other indications that NL umpires were stricter in enforcing the ban on trick pitches. For example, see the ejection of Slim Sallee for using a foreign substance on the ball, as described in "Giants Win Final Clash from Reds," *The New York Times*, June 12, 1920.

10. For more on Johnson's struggle to maintain authority over the AL owners, see Michael Lynch's *Harry Frazee, Ban Johnson and the Feud That Nearly Destroyed the American League* (Jefferson, N.C.: McFarland and Company, 2008).

11. "Umpires Criticize Mays," *The New York Times*, August 19, 1920. The story, published three days after Chapman's beaning, makes it clear that Johnson had directed umpires to leave nondangerous balls in play "as long as possible" at some point earlier that season.

12. David W. Smith, "Do Batters Learn During a Game?" Retrosheet, June 7, 1996. https://www.retrosheet.org/Research/SmithD/batlearn.pdf. Smith explained in his study that the visiting pitchers must adjust to an unfamiliar mound, and the home batters are more familiar with the hitting background and idiosyncrasies of the home park. Such factors combine to visiting batters) throughout the game.

Who Threw the Greatest Regular-Season No-Hitter since 1901?

Gary Belleville

A pitcher usually needs good command and quality stuff to toss a no-hitter.[1] Stellar fielding and a dollop of good luck doesn't hurt, either. A bad-hop single or a flare off the end of the bat that falls for a hit is all it takes to break one up. Between 1901 and 2020, a no-hitter was thrown in the American, National, or Federal League 263 times.[2] It has been done just once in every 769 regular-season games.[3]

Although joining this exclusive club is a significant accomplishment, some no-hitters are more impressive than others. The two no-hitters thrown under postseason pressure, Don Larsen's perfect game in the 1956 World Series and Roy Halladay's no-no in the 2010 NLDS, are truly remarkable. At the other end of the scale are the no-hitters thrown in the dying days of the season against a weak-hitting, second-division club. In extreme cases, a pitcher may have the dubious honor of tossing a no-hitter in a losing cause, which is exactly what happened to Baltimore's Steve Barber when he walked 10 batters in his combined no-hitter with Stu Miller in 1967.

Setting aside the two postseason no-hitters, an interesting question comes to mind: Who threw the greatest regular-season no-hitter since 1901?[4] Some might suggest Max Scherzer's 17-strikeout, zero-walk performance against the New York Mets on October 3, 2015, was the best of them all. I'd argue it may be the most dominant no-hitter of all time, but it's not the greatest. It's probably not even the most commendable no-hitter that Scherzer threw in 2015. Less than four months before his no-no at Citi Field, he no-hit a much stronger Pittsburgh lineup, striking out 10 without walking a single batter.

Rather than focusing on who threw the most dominant no-hitter, this paper will identify a short list of the greatest no-hitters thrown since 1901 based on their difficulty. An objective, quantitative method will be used. The results are not intended to be a definitive list, because different methodologies may lead to different results.

This article will also highlight the particularly noteworthy no-hitters identified and list some of the more interesting bits of trivia uncovered during the data analysis.

METHODOLOGY

The key factor when assessing the difficulty of each no-hitter is the batting average of the hitters in the opposing lineup. Statistics that measure speed, on-base ability, and power are important in generating runs, yet they are less relevant when it comes to breaking up a no-hitter.

The end-of-season batting average will be used for each player instead of the batting average at the time of the no-hitter. This will provide a better measurement of a hitter's ability, since batting averages in early-season no-hitters can be misleading. For example, all Chicago White Sox batters had a .000 batting average immediately after Bob Feller's Opening Day gem in 1940.

Neutralized batting averages (BA_n) will be used instead of regular batting averages to eliminate the impact of a player's home ballpark. This will allow, for instance, the batting averages of the 1996 Colorado Rockies to be compared fairly to those of the 1905 Chicago White Sox.[5]

A weighted neutralized batting average (BA_{wn}) will be calculated for each no-hit lineup. This figure will be weighted based on the number of official at-bats in the game by each batter. For example, the BA_n of a

Ernie Shore had one of the most improbable no-hit pitching performances in 1917, relieving Babe Ruth after Ruth had faced a single batter (a walk), and proceeding to set down the next 26 men in a row.

NATIONAL BASEBALL HALL OF FAME LIBRARY, COOPERSTOWN, NY

pinch-hitter who had one at-bat in the game will have one-third of the impact on BA_{wn} as the BA_n of a player who had three at-bats. One of the benefits of weighting by at-bats instead of plate appearances is that a pitcher will not get credit for walking a dangerous hitter, which may be done to help preserve the no-hitter.

A composite batting average (BA_c) of the no-hit lineup will be calculated by adjusting the weighted neutralized batting average by the one-year park factor for hits (divided by 100) of the ballpark in which the no-hitter occurred. This composite batting average will approximate the combined season batting average of the opposing lineup had they played all their regular-season games in that ballpark, with each player having the same proportion of at-bats during the season as in the no-hitter.

The park factor for hits is not to be confused with the much more common park factor for runs, which is less relevant to no-hitters. The one-year park factor is used instead of the three-year version, since many ballparks, such as Braves Field in Boston, have undergone frequent modifications.[6]

DATA

A list of no-hitters was downloaded from Retrosheet. All 263 no-hitters thrown between 1901 and 2020 in the National, American, and Federal Leagues were included in the analysis.

Batting data for each of the 263 no-hitters were downloaded from the Regular Season Box Score Event Files, Regular Season Event Files, and Post-Season Event Files on the Retrosheet web site. The neutralized season batting averages for the players in the no-hit lineups were obtained from the Baseball-Reference.com web site, as were the yearly league-wide batting averages. The one-year park factors for hits were gleaned from the Ballparks Database on the Seamheads.com web site.[7] The Retrosheet and Baseball-Reference.com player and team identifiers were cross-referenced using the Teams and People tables in the Lahman Baseball Database, which is available at SeanLahman.com.

No-hitters thrown in the Negro Leagues and the All-American Girls Professional Baseball League were not included because the required (structured) data are not currently available.

All data were loaded into an Oracle 18c database. SQL queries were used to generate the results.

DISCUSSION
Historical Trends

As the chart in Figure 1 shows, there is a strong negative correlation between the major-league batting average and the frequency of no-hitters in a decade. It's no surprise the 2010s saw the highest frequency of no-hitters since the 1960s given that the batting average in the big leagues plummeted from .269 in 2006 to just .252 in 2019. If batting averages continue to decline, no-hitters may soon be as frequent as they were in the Deadball Era and the 1960s.

Summary Data by No-Hitter Type

Of the 263 no-hitters thrown between 1901 and 2020, there were 238 nine-inning no-hitters with baserunner(s), four 10-inning no-hitters with baserunner(s),

Figure 1. Regular-Season No-Hitters in the National, American and Federal Leagues (1901–2019)

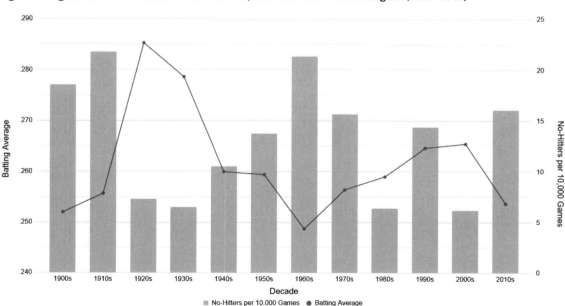

and 21 (nine-inning) perfect games.[9] Because of their varying degrees of difficulty, this article will treat each category of no-hitter separately. Refer to Table 1 for summary statistics on each type of no-hitter.

Table 1. Summary Data by No-Hitter Type

No-Hitter Type	Games	Average BA_wn	Average Park Factor	Average BA_C
Nine Innings, Baserunner(s)	238	.253	98	.248
Perfect Games	21	.250	97.5	.245
Ten Innings, Baserunner(s)	4	.260	103	.268
All No-Hitters	263	.253	98	.248

As one would expect, most no-hitters are thrown in pitchers' parks. That is, those with a one-year park factor for hits below 100. Only 25.5 percent of no-hitters (67 of 263) have been thrown in hitters' parks.[10]

The data also show that the weighted neutralized batting average of the opposing lineup in perfect games is on average 2.8 points lower than in nine-inning no-hitters with baserunner(s). Likewise, the composite batting average is 3.5 points lower.

The summary data for ten-inning no-hitters suffer from a small sample size and are skewed by one particularly difficult 10-inning no-hitter, which will be highlighted later in the paper.

Top 20 Nine-Inning No-Hitters with Baserunner(s)

The Top 20 nine-inning no-hitters with baserunner(s) ranked by composite batting average can be found in Table 2. At the top of the list is the unlikely no-hitter thrown by Hideo Nomo at Coors Field on September 17, 1996.

This notoriously extreme hitters' park hosted 2,047 regular-season games between 1995 and 2020. Nomo's no-hitter was the only one thrown at "Coors Canaveral" during that time. Amazingly, he turned the trick against the Rockies in 1996, the year in which the Denver ballpark was at its most severe for hits.[11] Its one-year park factor for hits was a stunning 129 that season. Nomo's extraordinary accomplishment was as much a conquest of Coors Field as it was the Rockies, since the Colorado club hit .343 at home and a paltry .228 on the road in 1996.

The lineup Nomo faced included five hitters who finished in the National League Top 20 in batting average: Ellis Burks, Eric Young Sr., Dante Bichette, Vinny Castilla, and Andrés Galarraga. Future Hall of Famer Larry Walker, a key member of the Blake Street Bombers, was out of action that evening because of lingering pain from a broken collarbone suffered three months earlier.[12]

Nomo used his fastball and a devastating split-fingered pitch to shut down the Rockies, who hit just

Table 2. Top 20 Nine-Inning No-Hitters by Composite Batting Average

	Pitcher (IP)	Pitcher Tm	Date (DH Game)	Score	Ballpark (Park Factor)	BA_C
1.	Hideo Nomo	Los Angeles	9/17/1996	Dodgers 9, Rockies 0	Coors Field (129)	.302
2.	Ken Holtzman	Chicago	8/19/1969	Cubs 3, Braves 0	Wrigley Field (106)	.289
3.	Clay Buchholz	Boston	9/1/2007	Red Sox 10, Orioles 0	Fenway Park (112)	.288
4.	Babe Ruth (0), Ernie Shore (9)	Boston	6/23/1917 (1)	Red Sox 4, Nationals 0	Fenway Park (105)	.284
5.	Nolan Ryan	California	5/15/1973	Angels 3, Royals 0	Royals Stadium (107)	.284
6.	Jim Colborn	Kansas City	5/14/1977	Royals 6, Rangers 0	Royals Stadium (105)	.282
7.	Miles Main	Kansas City	8/16/1915	Packers 5, Blues 0	International Fair Assoc. Grounds (104)	.282
8.	Kent Mercker (6) Mark Wohlers (2) Alejandro Peña (1)	Atlanta	9/11/1991	Braves 1, Padres 0	Atlanta-Fulton County Stadium (111)	.282
9.	Ray Caldwell	Cleveland	9/10/1919 (1)	Indians 3, Yankees 0	Polo Grounds V (100)	.281
10.	Vern Kennedy	Chicago	8/31/1935	White Sox 5, Indians 0	Comiskey Park I (104)	.280
11.	Nick Maddox	Pittsburgh	9/20/1907	Pirates 2, Superbas 1	Exposition Park III (108)	.280
12.	Ed Lafitte	Brooklyn	9/19/1914 (1)	Tip-Tops 6, Packers 2	Washington Park IV (100)	.279
13.	Dwight Gooden	New York	5/14/1996	Yankees 2, Mariners 0	Yankee Stadium I (104)	.278
14.	Jordan Zimmermann	Washington	9/28/2014	Nationals 1, Marlins 0	Nationals Park (106)	.278
15.	Phil Niekro	Atlanta	8/5/1973	Braves 9, Padres 0	Atlanta Stadium (113)	.277
16.	Bob Gibson	St. Louis	8/14/1971	Cardinals 11, Pirates 0	Three Rivers Stadium (100)	.275
17.	Sal Maglie	Brooklyn	9/25/1956	Dodgers 5, Phillies 0	Ebbets Field (101)	.274
18.	Ernie Koob	St. Louis	5/5/1917	Browns 1, White Sox 0	Sportsman's Park III (98)	.274
19.	Bob Forsch	St. Louis	4/16/1978	Cardinals 5, Phillies 0	Busch Stadium II (100)	.274
20.	Milt Pappas	Chicago	9/2/1972	Cubs 8, Padres 0	Wrigley Field (109)	.273

Ken Holtzman of the Cubs shut down a powerful Braves lineup at Wrigley Field on August 19, 1969.

three balls sharply all game.[13] Not a single spectacular play was required in the field.[14] Because of the wet conditions, Nomo abandoned his deceptive, whirling delivery in the later innings to stabilize his footing.[15] The Rockies still struggled against him. Nomo ended the night by striking out Burks, a .344 hitter, on a filthy split-fingered fastball. He struck out eight and walked four Colorado batters.

One notable aspect of the Top 20 nine-inning no-hitters is that six of them occurred in the Deadball Era. This shouldn't be too much of a surprise, since the first two decades of the twentieth century still featured a fair number of teams with solid batting averages. For example, Ernie Koob of the St. Louis Browns no-hit the 1917 White Sox, a 100-win team that went on to defeat the New York Giants in the World Series. Koob faced a Chicago lineup containing four players with a neutralized batting average greater than .300: Happy Felsch (.325), Shoeless Joe Jackson (.318), Eddie Collins (.306), and Buck Weaver (.301). In a bizarre twist, the game ended with Koob having been credited with a one-hitter. Following the game, the official scorer changed a first-inning hit by Buck Weaver to an error. The next day's headline in the *Chicago Tribune* erroneously read "Koob Tames Sox in One Hit Game, 1–0."[16]

The entry in Table 2 for the combined no-hitter by Babe Ruth and Ernie Shore does *not* contain a misprint;

Ruth did in fact pitch zero innings in that 1917 game. After he walked the Nationals leadoff hitter, Ray Morgan, a heated argument ensued over two alleged missed strike calls by home plate umpire Brick Owens. Ruth punched Owens during the altercation and was ejected from the game, forcing Ernie Shore to come on in relief. After Morgan was caught stealing, Shore retired the next 26 batters in order.[17]

The first of Nolan Ryan's record seven no-hitters ranks fifth. The 26-year-old fireballer completely shut down Kansas City at Royals Stadium on May 15, 1973, which was no easy feat. The Royals finished second in runs scored in the American League that year, fueled by a .277 team batting average in their new, spacious ballpark.

In the introduction, Max Scherzer's two no-hitters in 2015 were used as an example of a common pitfall in evaluating no-nos. Scherzer's 17-strikeout performance at Citi Field ranks 196th out of the 238 nine-inning no-hitters with baserunner(s) using the methodology outlined in this article. The Mets lineup had a composite batting average of only .232, roughly 16 points less than an average no-hitter of that type. However, his no-hitter against the Pirates at Nationals Park less than four months earlier ranked 37th all-time with a solid .269 composite batting average.

Ten-Inning No-Hitters

A list of the four 10-inning no-hitters tossed between 1901 and 2020 can be found in Table 3. George "Hooks" Wiltse of the New York Giants threw the most difficult of the four by an exceedingly wide margin. His 1908 masterpiece came against a Phillies lineup that had a robust composite batting average of .293. Even more impressively, Wiltse would have thrown a 10-inning perfect game were it not for circumstances reminiscent of Armando Galarraga's lost perfect game more than a century later.[18]

Wiltse had overtaken a fading "Iron Man" Joe McGinnity as the Giants' number two starter that season, forming a dominant lefty-righty combination with Christy Mathewson. Together, the duo combined to pitch 720⅔ innings and record the win in 60 of the Giants' 98 victories.[19]

Table 3. Ten-Inning No-Hitters Sorted by Composite Batting Average

	Pitcher (IP)	Pitcher Tm	Date (DH Game)	Score	Ballpark (Park Factor)	BA_c
1.	Hooks Wiltse	New York	7/04/1908 (1)	Giants 1, Phillies 0	Polo Grounds IV (107)	0.293
2.	Francisco Córdova (9), Ricardo Rincón (1)	Pittsburgh	7/12/1997	Pirates 3, Astros 0	Three Rivers Stdm (100)	0.263
3.	Fred Toney	Cincinnati	5/02/1917	Reds 1, Cubs 0	Weeghman Park (103)	0.261
4.	Jim Maloney	Cincinnati	8/19/1965 (1)	Reds 1, Cubs 0	Wrigley Field (102)	0.253

The heart of the Philadelphia lineup facing Wiltse consisted of John Titus, Sherry Magee, and Kitty Bransfield, all of whom finished in the Top 10 in the NL batting race in 1908. Bransfield was one of just five .300 hitters in the entire National League that season.

Wiltse twirled his gem on Independence Day morning at the Polo Grounds, the wooden ballpark that opened in 1890 for the New York team that played in the Players' League.[20] With its distinctive horseshoe shape, the Polo Grounds was the most extreme hitters' park (for hits) in the National League in 1908.[21] In theory, the Phillies hitters were far more dangerous there than they were in their home park, the Baker Bowl, which played as a pitchers' park in 1908.[22] However, the ballpark in Coogan's Hollow proved to be of no help to the Phillies that game.[23]

Wiltse breezed through the Philadelphia lineup, retiring the first 26 men in order. The fielders behind him weren't required to make any outstanding plays, although right fielder "Turkey" Mike Donlin made a nice running catch in the fourth inning.[24] Wiltse, one of the best-fielding pitchers of his era, took care of two other difficult chances himself.[25]

With two outs in the top of the ninth inning and the game still scoreless, Wiltse faced his mound opponent, George McQuillan. On a 1-and-2 count, the Giants hurler threw a curveball that started outside and broke sharply to "cut the heart out of the plate."[26] Home plate umpire Cy Rigler, normally an excellent judge of balls and strikes, called it a ball.[27] Even the *Philadelphia Inquirer* admitted Wiltse had "fanned" McQuillan.[28] The plate appearance continued. The very next pitch from Wiltse hit McQuillan in the shoulder, and the perfect game was no more. The next batter, Eddie Grant, grounded out to end the inning.

After the Giants failed to score in the bottom of the ninth, Wiltse returned to the mound and retired Otto Knabe, Titus, and Magee in order. New York finally scored a run in the bottom of the 10th inning, giving Wiltse the first extra-inning no-hitter in the National or American League.[29] The 28-year-old moundsman retired 30 of 31 batters, with the only runner reaching base on a hit-by-pitch immediately following a missed strikeout call by Rigler. The respected umpire later acknowledged he made the wrong call. "Every time I saw Charlie Rigler after that he gave me a cigar," Wiltse recalled in 1953. "He admits (the disputed ball) was one of the pitches he missed."[30]

Top 10 Perfect Games

A list of the Top 10 perfect games by composite batting average can be found in Table 4. Charlie Robertson's immaculate outing against the 1922 Detroit Tigers leads the way with a .291 composite batting average, almost 19 percentage points better than the second-ranked perfect game, which was thrown by Catfish Hunter in 1968.

One day after being shut out by future Hall of Famer Red Faber and his grandfathered spitball, the mighty Tigers expected to maul Robertson, an unheralded 26-year-old righthander making his fifth big league appearance. The Detroit lineup featured three sluggers who finished in the Top 10 in the American League batting race: Ty Cobb (.401), Harry Heilmann (.356), and Bobby Veach (.327).

Navin Field had a neutral park factor of 100 in 1922, although it was potentially more hitter-friendly during Robertson's outing considering there was a large overflow crowd standing in the outfield. As it turned out, the fans in the outfield didn't have a significant impact on the game. When Veach led off the second inning by sharply hitting a ball towards the roped-off area in left field, the Detroit crowd graciously gave way to allow Johnny Mostil to make an easy grab.[31] The only standout defensive play of the game came two batters later when Harry Hooper made a "splendid running catch" on a ball hit by Bob Jones.[32]

Table 4. Top 10 Perfect Games by Composite Batting Average

	Pitcher	Pitcher Tm	Date (DH Game)	Score	Ballpark (Park Factor)	BA_C
1.	Charlie Robertson	Chicago	4/30/1922	White Sox 2, Tigers 0	Navin Field (100)	0.291
2.	Catfish Hunter	Oakland	5/08/1968	Athletics 4, Twins 0	Oakland-Alameda County Coliseum (101)	0.272
3.	Tom Browning	Cincinnati	9/16/1988	Reds 1, Dodgers 0	Riverfront Stadium (104)	0.270
4.	Jim Bunning	Philadelphia	6/21/1964 (1)	Phillies 6, Mets 0	Shea Stadium (101)	0.269
5.	Mike Witt	California	9/30/1984	Angels 1, Rangers 0	Arlington Stadium (103)	0.268
6.	Addie Joss	Cleveland	10/02/1908	Naps 1, White Sox 0	League Park III (104)	0.268
7.	Dennis Martínez	Montreal	7/28/1991	Expos 2, Dodgers 0	Dodger Stadium (100)	0.259
8.	Kenny Rogers	Texas	7/28/1994	Rangers 4, Angels 0	The Ballpark in Arlington (99)	0.253
9.	Mark Buehrle	Chicago	7/23/2009	White Sox 5, Rays 0	U.S. Cellular Field (97)	0.251
10.	Randy Johnson	Arizona	5/18/2004	Diamondbacks 2, Braves 0	Turner Field (98)	0.250

Hideo Nomo's 1996 no-hitter against the Colorado Rockies at hitter-haven Coors Field is exceedingly impressive not only because of the immense park factor (129) but the hitting prowess of the lineup he faced.

The frustrated Tigers began to lose their cool once Robertson's perfect game lasted into the middle innings. During his fifth-inning at-bat, Heilmann complained to home plate umpire Frank Nallin that the White Sox hurler was discoloring the ball. He continued to carp about it for the remainder of the game, as did Cobb, the Detroit player-manager.[33] Cobb had first baseman Earl Sheely's glove checked for evidence in the eighth inning, and in the ninth he had Robertson's clothing inspected.[34] Nothing untoward was uncovered. The unfazed Robertson retired the side in the final frame, including two left-handed-hitting pinch-hitters, to seal the perfect game.

"Had any student of baseball even dared to suggest that any pitcher could qualify to keep the Tigers away from first base and retire 27 men in order he would have been carted away to some state institution for the mentally unbalanced," opined the *Detroit Free Press*.[35] The writer's hyperbole could be forgiven, because almost a century later those Tigers still possessed the highest weighted neutralized batting average (.291) of any lineup victimized by a perfect game—or any no-hitter for that matter.[36]

Hunter's perfect game in 1968 is also noteworthy, considering the weighted neutralized batting average

of the Twins lineup he faced was almost 40 points higher than the league-wide batting average (.230) in the "Year of the Pitcher." Not only is it the largest such differential for any of the 21 perfect games, but it's also the largest in all 263 no-hitters.

Bottom 10 No-Hitters

Although throwing a no-hitter is never easy, let's turn our attention to those that were the least difficult to achieve according to the methodology outlined in this paper. A list of the 10 no-hitters with the lowest composite batting average can be found in Table 5. Two no-hitters stand apart from the others: Sandy Koufax's perfect game against the Cubs in 1965 and Jimmy "Nixey" Callahan's no-hitter against the 1902 Tigers.

The September 9, 1965, game between the Dodgers and Cubs was one of the most memorable regular-season games in baseball history. Koufax struck out 14 Chicago batters en route to becoming the first pitcher to record four no-hitters in the American, National, or Federal League.[37] His mound opponent, Bob Hendley, limited the Dodgers to just one unearned run on one hit and one walk. As of the end of the 2020 season, this thrilling contest still held the big-league record for the fewest combined hits (1) and baserunners (2).

The Cubs lineup, sporting a composite batting average of .166, was incredibly weak. Five of their starters were rookies, including 19-year-old Don Young and 22-year-old Byron Browne, who were both playing in their first major league game.[38] Browne had spent most of the season playing single-A ball, and to make his debut even more challenging, he had only arrived in Los Angeles earlier that afternoon.[39]

The Chicago batting order had three easy outs, as Young and Browne combined to go 2-for-41 with the Cubs in 1965, and Hendley came into the game with a career .093 batting average. Only three batters in the starting lineup finished the season with a batting

Table 5. The 10 No-Hitters with the Lowest Composite Batting Average

	Pitcher	Pitcher Tm	Date (DH Game)	Score	Ballpark (Park Factor)	BA$_C$
263.	Sandy Koufax (Perfect Game)	Los Angeles	9/9/1965	Dodgers 1, Cubs 0	Dodger Stadium (92)	.166
262.	Jimmy Callahan	Chicago	9/20/1902 (1)	White Sox 3, Tigers 0	South Side Park III (83)	.167
261.	Addie Joss	Cleveland	4/20/1910	Naps 1, White Sox 0	South Side Park III (91)	.193
260.	Lucas Giolito	Chicago	8/25/2020	White Sox 4, Pirates 0	Guaranteed Rate Field (98)	.195
259.	Larry Dierker	Houston	7/9/1976	Astros 6, Expos 0	Astrodome (88)	.198
258.	A.J. Burnett	Florida	5/12/2001	Marlins 3, Padres 0	Qualcomm Stadium (89)	.200
257.	Frank Smith	Chicago	9/20/1908	White Sox 1, Athletics 0	South Side Park III (92)	.200
256.	Juan Marichal	San Francisco	6/15/1963	Giants 1, Colt .45s 0	Candlestick Park (92)	.203
255.	Bill Singer	Los Angeles	7/20/1970	Dodgers 5, Phillies 0	Dodger Stadium (89)	.203
254.	Edinson Vólquez	Miami	6/3/2017	Marlins 3, Diamondbacks 0	Marlins Park (94)	.205

average over .239. To Koufax's credit, he was dominant enough that day to throw a perfect game against any team. The heart of the Chicago lineup—Billy Williams, Ron Santo, and Ernie Banks—combined to go 0-for-9 with six strikeouts.

Callahan threw his no-hitter for the White Sox at South Side Park III, the most extreme pitchers' park in American League history.[40] Although the ballpark hosted only 721 White Sox games between 1901 and 1910, four of those games featured a no-hitter.[41]

Callahan easily handled a feeble Detroit lineup that had only three hitters with a neutralized batting average above .227. Tigers manager Frank Dwyer even let his weak-hitting starting pitcher, Wish Egan, bat for himself with the team trailing by three runs in the eighth inning, a move that was not uncommon in the early twentieth century.[42] Egan struck out to end the inning.

Miscellaneous Observations on No-Hit Lineups

During the data analysis for this research paper, several interesting observations were made while inspecting the batting data of no-hit lineups.

Even casual baseball fans know that Nolan Ryan holds the record for tossing the most no-hitters (seven). But which batter has been the victim of the most no-hitters? That distinction is shared by three individuals, two of whom were teammates on the Philadelphia Phillies. Between 1960 and 1969, Johnny Callison and Tony Taylor played together in the same six no-hit lineups.[43] Callison, a fine-hitting outfielder, went 0-for-18 with two walks and four strikeouts in the six no-hitters, while Taylor went 0-for-16 with three walks and five strikeouts. Their record was tied in 1977 when Bert Campaneris was no-hit for the sixth time.[44] Campy went 0-for-19 with three walks and four strikeouts in the six no-hitters.

As of January 2021, the Internet was teeming with web pages that listed the record for the most walks in a no-hitter as 10. Yes, Jim Maloney did walk 10 batters in his 10-inning no-no against the Cubs in 1965, as did Steve Barber in his nine-inning combined no-hitter with Stu Miller in 1967. However, the record for walks in a no-hitter is 11, set in 1976 by Chicago's Blue Moon Odom and Francisco Barrios in their combined no-hitter against the Oakland Athletics. Odom walked eight batters in the first five innings. When he issued his ninth free pass to open the bottom of the sixth, White Sox manager Paul Richards summoned Barrios from the bullpen. He walked two more over the final four innings. Odom earned the win and Barrios picked up the save in a 2–1 White Sox victory. Although the

no-hitter may have been messy, the Oakland lineup had a respectable composite batting average of .256, which ranks 87th out of the 238 nine-inning no-hitters with baserunner(s).

The single-game record for walks by a batter in a no-hit lineup is three, held by seven players. The hitters (and pitchers) are: Earl Torgeson (Cliff Chambers) in 1951, Dale Long (Sam Jones) in 1955, Mickey Stanley (Steve Barber) in 1967, Reggie Jackson (Jim Palmer) in 1969, Steve Huntz (Dock Ellis) in 1970, Bill Hall (Justin Verlander) in 2007, and Juan Pierre (Francisco Liriano) in 2011.

The single-game record for strikeouts by a batter in a no-hit lineup is four, held by Tony Graffanino of the Milwaukee Brewers. He donned the Golden Sombrero in Justin Verlander's 2007 no-hitter. Verlander struck out 12 and walked four in the game.

No batter in a no-hit lineup has ever reached base on a hit-by-pitch (HBP) more than once in a game. The only batter with two career HBP in a no-hit lineup is Bill Freehan, who was plunked on April 30, 1967, by Barber and again just over four months later in Joel Horlen's no-no. The two hit-by-pitches weren't out of the ordinary for Freehan, as the Tigers catcher led the major leagues with 20 HBPs that season.

For additional information on no-hitters, the reader is invited to visit NoNoHitters.com, an excellent website created by journalist and SABR member Dirk Lammers.

CONCLUSIONS

This paper introduced a methodology for objectively comparing the difficulty of each no-hitter thrown in the American, National, or Federal League between 1901 and 2020. This mathematical model produced a short list of the most impressive no-hitters in that period.

Hideo Nomo's nine-inning no-hitter at Coors Field in 1996 was one of the greatest pitching accomplishments in baseball history. The Rockies lineup that he no-hit had a composite batting average of .302. No other pitcher was able to throw a no-hitter in the 2,047 regular-season games played at Coors Field between 1995 and 2020.

Charlie Robertson threw the greatest regular-season perfect game in 1922 when he waltzed through a powerful Detroit lineup that included Ty Cobb, Harry Heilmann, and Bobby Veach. As of the end of the 2020 season, those Tigers still had the highest weighted neutralized batting average (.291) of any lineup victimized by a perfect game—or any no-hitter for that matter.

But who threw the greatest regular-season no-hitter since 1901? The author believes that distinction belongs to Hooks Wiltse for his incomparable 10-inning no-hitter and near-perfect game against a tough Phillies lineup at the Polo Grounds in 1908. In 31 Philadelphia plate appearances, the sole batter to reach base did so on a hit-by-pitch immediately following a missed strike-three call, an error later acknowledged by the home-plate umpire, Cy Rigler. Many believe that Armando Galarraga, the victim of another unfortunate umpiring error over a century later, deserves to be recognized for throwing a perfect game. So, too, does George "Hooks" Wiltse. ∎

Author's note

Shortly after beginning the data analysis for this article, I noticed that Retrosheet and Baseball-Reference.com listed one more no-hitter than I was expecting—the 1901 Pete Dowling no-hitter. As luck would have it, this was mere days after Retrosheet posted the box score for it. This started me on my quest to solve the case of the lost Dowling no-hitter, and it culminated with the publication of the SABR Games Project article titled "June 30, 1901: Cleveland's Pete Dowling tosses the American League's first no-hitter — or does he?"

Acknowledgments

Thanks to fellow SABR member Kevin Johnson for generating park factors for 1901–05 and for answering my questions about the Ballparks Database at Seamheads.com.

Notes

1. The pitching term "stuff" is not easily defined. However, the following definition is as good as any: "Stuff is a pitcher's pitches, judged by how inherently hard those pitches are to hit." Tom Scocca, "Here Is What "Stuff" Means in Baseball," Deadspin, October 7, 2015, http://deadspin.com/here-is-what-stuff-means-inbaseball-1734592813, accessed January 29, 2021.

2. As of December 2020, Retrosheet and Baseball-Reference.com recognized 263 major-league no-hitters thrown between 1901 and 2020. However, Major League Baseball only recognized 262. The one discrepancy is the June 30, 1901, outing by Pete Dowling of Cleveland against the Milwaukee Brewers. This paper will include all 263 no-hitters. Gary Belleville, "June 30, 1901: Cleveland's Pete Dowling tosses the American League's first no-hitter—or does he?," SABR Games Project, 2020, http://sabr.org/gamesproj/game/june-30-1901-clevelands-petedowling-tosses-the-american-leagues-first-no-hitter-or-does-he, accessed January 26, 2021.

3. There were 261 no-hitters thrown in the 401,330 regular-season team-games in the National, American, and Federal Leagues between 1901 and 2020. Two no-hitters were thrown in the postseason (a perfect game in 1956 and a no-hitter in 2010).

4. This paper will only consider no-hitters thrown since 1901, the year the American League was first designated as a major league. As of December 2020, the Retrosheet.org web site didn't provide box scores or event data files for the 1900 season.

5. The neutralized batting averages of the 1996 Colorado Rockies can be found at http://baseballreference.com/teams/COL/1996-batting.shtml#all_players_neutral_batting, accessed January 26, 2021.

6. It is not possible to generate meaningful one-year park factors for ballparks hosting a small number of games in a season. The San Diego Padres played three home games in Estadio Monterrey in 2018; an estimated park factor of 100 was used. The Houston Astros played two home games in Miller Park in 2008 because of Hurricane Ike;

the Brewers' 2008 park factor for Miller Park (98) was used for those games. The Braves played 29 home games in Fenway Park in 1914; the Red Sox's 1914 park factor for Fenway Park (94) was used for those games. The White Sox played 28 home games at South Side Park III in 1910 before moving to Comiskey Park I; the 1909 park factor for South Side Park III (91) was used for the games played there in 1910.

7. Unlike some other web sites, the park factors at Seamheads.com are not automatically divided by two to account for the fact that half of all regular-season games are played at home. For instance, a park factor for hits of 108 on Seamheads is equivalent to a Fangraphs park factor of 104. In this example, eight percent more hits were recorded at that ballpark than a league-average park. Likewise, a Seamheads one-year park factor for hits of 94 is equivalent to a Fangraphs park factor of 97.

8. The data used to generate the chart in Figure 1 (batting average by decade and number of no-hitters per decade) have a correlation of -0.73.

9. An extra-innings perfect game has never been thrown. Pittsburgh's Harvey Haddix threw 12 perfect innings against the Milwaukee Braves on May 26, 1959, before the perfect game, no-hitter, and shutout were broken up in the 13th inning. He lost the game 1–0. Although he was initially credited with throwing a no-hitter, that decision was reversed in 1991 by Major League Baseball's Committee for Statistical Accuracy. Their revised definition of a no-hitter ("a game in which a pitcher or pitchers complete a game of nine innings or more without allowing a hit") resulted in the elimination of 50 no-hitters from the record books, dating back to the 1890 season.

10. No-hitters were thrown in pitchers' parks 67.7 percent of the time (178 of 263) and in neutral parks 6.8 percent of the time (18 of 263).

11. There were three seasons (1995, 1999, and 2000) in which Coors Field was more extreme for home runs than 1996. However, 1996 was peak Coors Field in terms of the one-year park factor for hits.

12. Quinton McCracken substituted for Larry Walker in the lineup Hideo Nomo faced. Walker had broken his collarbone on June 9, 1996, crashing into the fence at Coors Field. He returned to action on August 15. Walker left a September 7 game against the Astros because of pain in his left clavicle, and he made his final plate appearance of the year on September 12. He was limited to use as a pinch-runner and defensive replacement for the remainder of the year. A healthy Walker won the NL MVP award the following season.

13. Bill Staples Jr., "September 17, 1996: Hideo Nomo No-Hits Colorado Rockies at Hitter-Friendly Coors Field," SABR Games Project, 2017, http://sabr.org/gamesproj/game/september-17-1996-hideo-nomo-no-hitscolorado-rockies-at-hitter-friendly-coors-field, accessed January 26, 2021.

14. Bob Nightengale, "NooooooooooMo," *Los Angeles Times*, September 18, 1996, p35.

15. Associated Press, "Nomo Gets No-No," *The Daily Sentinel* (Grand Junction, Colorado), September 18, 1996, 23.

16 Gregory H. Wolf, "May 5, 1917: On Second Thought, It's a No-Hitter for Ernie Koob," SABR Games Project, 2017, http://sabr.org/gamesproj/game/may-5-1917-on-second-thought-its-a-no-hitter-for-ernie-koob, accessed January 26, 2021.

17. Michael Clair, "Ernie Shore Once Threw a Quasi-Perfect Game…after Babe Ruth Punched an Umpire," CUT4, June 23, 2015, http://mlb.com/cut4/ernie-shore-threw-quasi-perfect-game-after-babe-ruth-ejection/c-132245176, accessed January 26, 2021.

18. On June 2, 2010, Armando Galarraga of the Detroit Tigers retired the first 26 Cleveland batters he faced. The 27th batter of the game, Jason Donald, hit a groundball in the hole to first baseman Miguel Cabrera, who threw to Galarraga covering first. Video replays showed that Donald was clearly out, but first base umpire Jim Joyce called him safe. It was ruled an infield single, breaking up the perfect game and no-hitter. The next batter, Trevor Crowe, grounded out to end the game.

19. Hooks Wiltse went 23–14 with a 2.24 ERA in 330 innings pitched in 1908, while Christy Mathewson went 37–11 with a 1.43 ERA in 390⅔ innings on the hill.

20. This facility, known precisely as "Polo Grounds IV," was originally named Brotherhood Park. It burnt down in April 1911 and was replaced later in the season by the steel-and-concrete version of the Polo Grounds ("Polo Grounds V") that served as the Giants' home until they moved to San Francisco following the 1957 season.

21. The Polo Grounds had a one-year park factor for hits of 107 in 1908. Its dimensions were 258 feet to right field, 277 feet to left, and 500 feet to straightaway center field. South End Grounds III, home of the Boston Braves, was the most extreme hitters park in the National League for runs in 1908.

22. Over its history, the Baker Bowl was generally considered a hitters' park, especially for left-handed batters. While it greatly inflated home run numbers beginning in 1911, the Baker Bowl had a one-year park factor for hits of 96 in 1908. The Phillies hit .243 at home and .245 on the road that season. Not a single Phillies batter hit a home run at the Baker Bowl in 1908.

23. The Polo Grounds were built on farmland known as Coogan's Hollow.

24. Joe Cox, *Almost Perfect: The Heartbreaking Pursuit of Pitching's Holy Grail* (Guilford, CT: Lyons Press, 2017).

25. "Wiltse's No-Hit Game," *Sporting Life*, July 11, 1908, 6.

26. "Giants Win Two Games," *Brooklyn Citizen*, July 5, 1908, 6.

27. David Cicotello, "Cy Rigler," SABR Bio Project, 2004, http://sabr.org/bioproj/person/cy-rigler, accessed January 26, 2021.

28. "Wiltse Too Much for the Phillies,"*Philadelphia Inquirer*, July 5, 1908, 24.

29. As of December 2020, the only previous extra-inning no-hitter in the big leagues (recognized by Retrosheet and Baseball Reference) was thrown in the American Association by Sam Kimber of Brooklyn against Toledo on October 4, 1884. The game ended in a scoreless tie when it was called on account of darkness.

30. Cox.

31. David Fleitz, "April 30, 1922: Charlie Robertson's Perfect Game," SABR Games Project, 2016, http://sabr.org/gamesproj/game/april-30-1922-charlie-robertsons-perfect-game/, accessed January 26, 2021.

32. Jacob Pomrenke, "Charlie Robertson," SABR Bio Project, http://sabr.org/bioproj/person/charlierobertson, accessed January 26, 2021.

33. Irving Vaughan, "Kid Robertson Flings Perfect Game for Sox," *Chicago Tribune*, May 1, 1922, 23.

34. "Tigers Helpless before Robertson Who Pitches Perfect Game and Wins 2–0," *Detroit Free Press*, May 1, 1922, 12.

35. "Tigers Helpless before Robertson Who Pitches Perfect Game and Wins 2–0."

36. The second-highest weighted neutralized batting average (.287) of a no-hit lineup was in 36-year-old Hoyt Wilhelm's nine-inning no-hitter of the 1958 Yankees at Baltimore's Memorial Stadium. However, that ballpark's one-year park factor for hits was a mere 94, so Wilhelm's no-no ranks 35th in composite batting average (.270) out of 238 nine-inning no-hitters with baserunner(s). Memorial Stadium had a massive amount of foul territory. According to the Ballparks Database at Seamheads.com, its dimensions in 1958 were 309 feet down the lines, 405 feet to each power alley, and 410 feet to straightaway center field. Center field was even deeper during Memorial Stadium's first four years (1954–57).

37. Koufax's three other no-hitters ranked 48th (May 11, 1963, versus the San Francisco Giants), 118th (June 4, 1964, versus the Philadelphia Phillies), and 218th (June 30, 1962, versus the New York Mets) out of the 238 nineinning no-hitters with baserunner(s).

38. The three other rookies in the Chicago lineup were 25-year-old Chris Krug (playing in his 50th majorleague game), 23-year-old Don Kessinger (92nd major-league game), and 24-year-old Glenn Beckert (134th majorleague game).

39. Jane Leavy, *Sandy Koufax: A Lefty's Legacy* (New York: HarperCollins, 2002), 22.

40. Eric Enders, "Exploring Extreme Ballparks Past," *The Hardball Times*, November 16, 2018, http://tht.fangraphs.com/exploring-extreme-ballparks, accessed January 26, 2021.

41. The White Sox played 718 regular-season games and three World Series contests at South Side Park III. It was the home of the Chicago White Sox from 1900 until June 27, 1910, when the team moved into Comiskey Park I. The other three no-hitters thrown at South Side Park III between 1901 and 1910 were by Jesse Tannehill of the Boston Americans (August 17, 1904 versus the White Sox), Chicago's Frank Smith (September 20, 1908 versus the Athletics), and Cleveland's Addie Joss (April 20, 1910 versus the White Sox). The ballpark was renamed Schorling's Park in 1911 and it served as the home of the Chicago American Giants until 1940. Several no-hitters were thrown there during that period, including a near-perfect game by Frank Wickware of the Chicago American Giants against the Indianapolis ABCs on August 26, 1914. Both teams were part of the Western Independent Clubs circuit in 1914.

42. James Elfers, "September 20, 1902: Chicago's Nixey Callahan throws American League's first no-hitter," SABR Games Project, 2017, http://sabr.org/gamesproj/game/september-20-1902-chicagos-nixey-callahan-throwsamerican-leagues-first-no-hitter, accessed January 26, 2021.

43. The six no-hitters against lineups that included Johnny Callison and Tony Taylor were pitched by Lew Burdette of the Milwaukee Braves (August 18, 1960), Warren Spahn of the Milwaukee Braves (September 16, 1960), Don Nottebart of the Houston Colt .45s (May 17, 1963), Sandy Koufax of the Los Angeles Dodgers (June 4, 1964), George Culver of the Cincinnati Reds (July 29, 1968 - Game 2), and Bill Stoneman of the Montreal Expos (April 17, 1969).

44. Bert Campaneris was victimized by no-hitters thrown by Jim Palmer of the Baltimore Orioles (August 13, 1969), Clyde Wright of the California Angels (July 3, 1970), Jim Bibby of the Texas Rangers (July 30, 1973), Dick Bosman of the Cleveland Indians (July 19, 1974), Blue Moon Odom and Francisco Barrios of the Chicago White Sox (July 28, 1976), and Jim Colborn of the Kansas City Royals (May 14, 1977).

Actual Pennant Winners Versus Pythagorean Pennant Winners, 1901–2020

What Might Have Been

Campbell Gibson, PhD

This paper will provide a general comparison of actual pennant winners and Pythagorean pennant winners for the National and American Leagues from 1901 to 2020. In part, this is a presentation of data, but it is also an exercise in what might have been. With Pythagorean pennant winners, many teams that did not reach the World Series would have done so. And some Hall of Famers who never played in a World Series would have had the opportunity to do so. Additionally, this paper will include a discussion of luck versus skill in the comparison of actual and Pythagorean pennant winners. All of the data presented herein derive from data on Baseball-Reference.com.

Various terms, such as the Pythagorean Theorem of Baseball (used by Baseball-Reference.com) or the Pythagorean Expectation (used in the Wikipedia article), have been used to describe the formula developed by Bill James in his *Baseball Abstract* annual volumes to predict the number of games a team "should" have won in a season based on the numbers of runs scored and runs allowed. The formula used currently by Baseball Reference may be expressed as:

$$WP = 1/\{1 + (OR/R)^{1.83}\}$$

where WP is the predicted winning proportion (i.e., wins divided by the sum of wins and losses), OR is opponents' runs, and R is runs.

While Pythagorean predictions are shown widely, including on the Baseball Reference website and in the sabermetric literature, I have never come across an illustration showing how OR/R and WP are related, including quantifying the relationship of a change in R/OR with a change in predicted WP. In this regard, successive increases of 0.1 in R/OR starting from 1.0 are associated with declining increases in WP. For example, as R/OR increases from 1.0 to 1.1, predicted WP increases from .500 to .543, or by .043; and as R/OR increases from 1.7 to 1.8, predicted WP increases from .725 to .746, or by .021. The relationship between R/OR and actual and predicted WP is shown in Table 1, comparing modeled values of R/OR ranging from 1.0 to 1.8 and actual values of R/OR for pennant-winning teams ranging from about 1.0 to about 1.8. An R/OR value of 0.6 is included also to provide an example of how the formula applies to a very weak team.

In most cases shown in Table 1, the Pythagorean prediction of WP is very close to the actual winning proportion, and by extension, the Pythagorean prediction of team wins is usually very close (perhaps within three) to actual team wins. There are occasional outliers, illustrated here by Cincinnati in 1961, which won 10 more games than its Pythagorean prediction. Even though the Pythagorean predictions are usually highly

Table 1. EXAMPLES OF PYTHAGOREAN PREDICTIONS COMPARED TO ACTUAL PERFORMANCE

Pythagorean model		Actual performance								Pythagorean prediction		Actual wins less Pyth. wins
R/OR	WP	Year	League	Team	R/OR	W-L	Pct.	R	OR	WP	W-L	
1.0	.500	1973	NL	NY	1.03	82-79	.509	608	588	.515	83-78	-1
1.1	.543	1961	NL	CIN	1.09	93-61	.604	710	653	.538	83-71	+10
1.2	.583	1996	NL	ATL	1.19	96-66	.593	773	648	.580	94-68	+2
1.3	.618	1904	AL	BOS	1.30	95-59	.617	608	466	.619	95-59	0
1.4	.649	1943	NL	STL	1.43	105-49	.682	679	475	.658	101-53	+4
1.5	.677	1969	AL	BAL	1.51	109-53	.673	779	517	.679	110-52	-1
1.6	.703	1927	AL	NY	1.63	110-44	.714	975	599	.709	109-45	+1
1.7	.725	1939	AL	NY	1.74	106-45	.702	967	556	.734	111-40	-5
1.8	.746	1906	NL	CHI	1.85	116-36	.763	704	381	.755	115-37	+1
0.6	.282	1915	AL	PHI	0.61	43-109	.283	545	889	.290	44-108	-1

accurate, the closeness of many pennant races, with the winning margin often being no more than three games, means that there have been many pennant races in which the actual winner and the Pythagorean winner have been different. In addition, outliers like that Cincinnati team add to the number of cases where the actual and Pythagorean winners have differed. And lastly, the introduction of division play in 1969, with postseason playoffs to determine pennant winners, has decreased greatly the probability of the Pythagorean pennant winner being the actual pennant winner.

OVERVIEW OF ACTUAL AND PYTHAGOREAN PENNANT WINNERS

The actual and Pythagorean pennant winners for each season in the National and American Leagues from 1901 to 2020 are shown in Table 2. Calculations of Pythagorean won-lost records were rounded to whole numbers of wins and losses (reflecting the fact that actual won-lost records do not have fractions), and thus there are a few cases with ties for the Pythagorean pennant winner. From 1901 to 1968, before the introduction of division play, the actual pennant winner was also the Pythagorean pennant winner in the large majority of seasons.

A few notable differences in the history of actual and Pythagorean pennant winners are noted here. The Chicago Cubs won four pennants in five years from 1906 to 1910, and won the Pythagorean pennant in 1909, even though the great Pittsburgh Pirates team (110–42) won that actual pennant. The Brooklyn Dodgers, who won six pennants in the 10 years from 1947 to 1956, won six Pythagorean pennants in that decade, including five consecutive ones from 1949 to 1953. The Milwaukee Braves, who won pennants in 1957 and 1958, won four consecutive Pythagorean pennants from 1956 to 1959. And the Cincinnati Reds, who won one actual pennant in the 1960s (1961) won two subsequent Pythagorean pennants (1964 and 1965).

In the American League, the Cleveland Indians, who did not win an actual pennant until 1920, won three Pythagorean pennants in five years: 1904, 1906, and 1908. Three of their great players during those years, Hall of Famers Nap Lajoie, Addie Joss, and Elmer Flick, never played in a World Series. The Detroit Tigers, who won three consecutive pennants from 1907 to 1909, won the Pythagorean pennant in only the first of these three years. The Boston Red Sox won the pennant in 1915 and 1916, but the Chicago White Sox won the Pythagorean pennant in both seasons. Thus Boston won only two Pythagorean pennants from 1912 to 1918 (compared with four actual pennants), and Chicago won four Pythagorean pennants from 1915 to

1919 (compared with only two actual pennants). The St. Louis Browns, who won their only actual pennant in 1944, won the 1922 Pythagorean pennant with the best team in their history, led by Hall of Famer George Sisler, who also never got to play in a World Series.

The New York Yankees and Philadelphia Athletics, loaded with Hall of Fame players, dominated the American League from 1926 to 1931, with three pennants for the Yankees followed by three pennants for the Athletics. The Pythagorean pennant winners for those six years present a different picture: Cleveland (1926), New York (1927), Philadelphia (1928 and 1929), Washington (1930), and New York again (1931). The Yankees dominated the American League with 14 pennants in the 16 years from 1949 to 1964, but won "only" 11 Pythagorean pennants during those 16 years, with Boston (1949) and Chicago (1960 and 1964) also winning Pythagorean pennants.

From 1901 to 1968, there were 136 total seasons of National and American League play. These included 104 seasons in which the actual pennant winner was also the Pythagorean pennant winner, two seasons with a tie for the Pythagorean pennant, and 30 seasons (22 percent) in which the Pythagorean winner differed from the actual winner.

As noted earlier, the introduction of division play and postseason playoffs starting in 1969 changed things dramatically. From 1969 to 1993, with two divisions per league (East and West), there was one tier of playoffs to determine pennant winners. Since 1995, with three divisions per league (East, Central, and West), there have been two tiers of playoffs. (There was no postseason in 1994.) And since 2012, there has been a wild-card game before the two tiers of playoffs to determine pennant winners. In contrast to the 1901 to 1968 period, when the Pythagorean winner was also the actual winner a large majority of the time, since 1969 the Pythagorean winner has had to survive an increasing number of short postseason series to be the actual winner as well.

As a result, there are fewer cases of repeat winners since 1969, with only three cases of a team winning three consecutive actual pennants and Pythagorean pennants, all in the American League: Baltimore, 1969 to 1971; New York, 1976 to 1978; and Oakland, 1988 to 1990. Among the many cases of teams winning the Pythagorean pennant, but not the actual pennant, are the Chicago Cubs (1969 and 1970) and the Seattle Mariners (2001 and 2003). As a result Hall of Famers Ernie Banks and Edgar Martinez, and likely future Hall of Famer Ichiro Suzuki never had the opportunity to play in a World Series.

Table 2. ACTUAL AND PYTHAGOREAN PENNANT WINNERS BY LEAGUE AND YEAR: 1901 TO 2020

National League			American League		
Year	Actual	Pyth.	Year	Actual	Pyth.
1901		PIT	1901		CHI
1902		PIT	1902		PHI
1903		PIT	1903		BOS
1904		NY	1904	BOS	CLE - 4
1905		NY	1905	PHI	CHI - 2
1906		CHI	1906	CHI	CLE - 3
1907		CHI	1907		DET
1908	CHI	NY - 2	1908	DET	CLE - 2
1909	PIT	CHI - 2	1909	DET	PHI - 2
1910		CHI	1910		PHI
1911		NY	1911		PHI
1912		NY	1912		BOS
1913		NY	1913		PHI
1914		BOS	1914		PHI
1915		PHI	1915	BOS	CHI - 3
1916		BRO	1916	BOS	CHI - 2
1917		NY	1917		CHI
1918		CHI	1918		BOS
1919		CIN	1919		CHI
1920	BRO	*below	1920	CLE	*below
1921		NY	1921		NY
1922		NY	1922	NY	STL - 2
1923		NY	1923		NY
1924		NY	1924		WAS
1925		PIT	1925		WAS
1926		STL	1926	NY	CLE - 2
1927		PIT	1927		NY
1928		STL	1928	NY	PHI - 2
1929		CHI	1929		PHI
1930		STL	1930	PHI	WAS- 2
1931		STL	1931	PHI	NY - 2
1932		CHI	1932		NY
1933		NY	1933		WAS
1934	STL	NY - 2	1934		DET
1935		CHI	1935		DET
1936	NY	CH - 2	1936		NY
1937		NY	1937		NY
1938		CHI	1938		NY
1939		CIN	1939		NY
1940		CIN	1940		DET
1941		BRO	1941		NY
1942		STL	1942		NY
1943		STL	1943		NY
1944		STL	1944		STL
1945		CHI	1945	DET	NY - 4
1946		STL	1946		BOS
1947	BRO	STL - 2	1947		NY
1948		BOS	1948		CLE
1949		BRO	1949	NY	BOS - 2
1950	PHI	BRO - 2	1950		NY
1951	NY	BRO - 2	1951		NY
1952		BRO	1952		NY
1953		BRO	1953		NY
1954		NY	1954		CLE
1955		BRO	1955		NY
1956	BRO	MIL - 2	1956		NY
1957		MIL	1957		NY
1958		MIL	1958		NY
1959	LA	MIL - 2	1959	CHI	CLE - 2
1960		PIT	1960	NY	CHI - 3
1961	CIN	SF - 3	1961		NY
1962		SF	1962		NY
1963	LA	STL - 2	1963		NY
1964	STL	CIN - 2	1964	NY	CHI - 2
1965	LA	CIN - 4	1965		MIN
1966		LA	1966		BAL
1967		STL	1967		BOS
1968		STL	1968		DET
*1920: BRO-1/NY-2			*1920: CLE-1/NY-3		

National League			American League		
Year	Actual	Pyth.	Year	Actual	Pyth.
1969	NY-1E	CHI-2E	1969		BAL-1E
1970	CIN-1W	CHI-2E	1970		BAL-1E
1971		PIT-1E	1971		BAL-1E
1972	CIN-1W	PIT-1E	1972		OAK-1W
1973	NY-1E	CIN-1W	1973	OAK-1W	BAL-1E
1974		LA-1W	1974		OAK-1W
1975		CIN-1W	1975	BOS-1E	OAK-1W
1976	CIN-1W	PHI-1E	1976		NY-1E
1977		LA-1W	1977		NY-1E
1978		LA-1W	1978		NY-1E
1979		PIT-1E	1979		BAL-1E
1980		PHI-1E	1980	KC-1W	BAL-2E
1981		LA-2W	1981*		NY-3E
1982	STL-1E	*below	1982		MIL-1E
1983	PHI-1E	ATL-2W	1983	BAL-1E	BAL-1E/CHI-1W
1984	SD-1W	CHI-1W	1984		DET-1E
1985		STL-1E	1985	KC-1W	TOR-1E
1986		NY-1E	1986	BOS-1E	CAL-1W
1987	STL-1E	NY-2E/SF-1W	1987	MIN-1W	TOR-2E
1988	LA-1W	NY-1E	1988		OAK-1W
1989		SF-1W	1989		OAK-1W
1990	CIN-1W	NY-2E	1990		OAK-1W
1991	ATL-1W	PIT-1E	1991		MIN-1W
1992		ATL-1W	1992	TOR-1E	MIL-2E
1993	PHI-1E	ATL-1W	1993	TOR-1E	CHI-1W
1994	(none)	MON-1E	1994	(none)	CHI-1C
1995	ATL -1E	ATL-1E/CIN-1C	1995		CLE-1C
1996		ATL -1E	1996	NY-1E	CLE-1C
1997	FLA-2E	ATL-1E	1997	CLE-1C	NY-2E
1998	SD-1W	ATL-1E/HOU-1C	1998		NY-1E
1999	ATL-1E	ARI-1W	1999		NY-1E
2000	NY-2E	SF-1W	2000	NY-1E	OAK-1W
2001		ARI-1W	2001	NY-1E	SEA-1W
2002		SF-2W	2002		ANA-2W
2003	FLA-2E	ATL-1E	2003	NY-1E	SEA-2W
2004		STL-1C	2004		BOS-2E
2005	HOU-2C	STL-1C	2005	CHI-1C	CLE-2C
2006	STL-1C	NY-1E	2006	DET-2C	DET-2C/NY-1E
2007		COL-2W	2007		BOS-1E
2008	PHI-1E	CHI-1C	2008	TB-1E	BOS-2E
2009	PHI-1E	LA-1W	2009		NY-1E
2010	SF-1W	PHI-1E	2010	TEX-1W	NY-2E
2011	STL-2C	PHI-1E	2011	TEX-1W	NY-1E
2012	SF-1W	WAS-1E	2012	DET-1C	NY-1E/TB-3E
2013		STL-1C	2013		BOS-1E
2014	SF-2W	WAS-1E	2014	KC-2C	LA-1W
2015	NY-1E	STL-1C	2015	KC-1C	TOR-1E
2016		CHI-1C	2016	CLE-1C	BOS-1E
2017		LA-1W	2017	HOU-1W	CLE-1C
2018		LA-1W	2018	BOS-1E	HOU-1W
2019	WAS-2E	LA-1W	2019		HOU-1W
2020		LA-1W	2020	TB-1E	*below

*1982: STL-1E/LA-2W/MON-3E

*1981: Because of the extra level of playoffs in 1981 (due to a split season), the pennant winner did not have to be a division winner.

*2020: TB-1E/MIN-1C/CHI-2C(t)

NOTES: For years in which one team is shown, that team was both the actual and the Pythagorean pennant winner. For years in which the actual and Pythagorean pennant winners differed, the actual pennant winner is shown on the left, and the Pythagorean winner is shown on the right with its place in the actual standings. For years with two divisions per league (1969–93), and for years with three divisions per league (1994–2020), when actual pennant winners were not necessarily division winners, both actual place in the standings and the team's division are shown.

During the 1969 to 1993 period, there were 50 total seasons of National and American League play. These included 28 seasons in which the actual pennant winner was also the Pythagorean pennant winner, three seasons with a tie for the Pythagorean pennant, and 19 seasons (38 percent) in which the Pythagorean winner differed from the actual winner. From 1995 to 2020, there were 52 total seasons of play. These included 19 seasons in which the actual winner was also the Pythagorean winner, five seasons with a tie for the Pythagorean pennant, and 28 seasons (54 percent) in which the Pythagorean winner differed from the actual winner. Thus seasons in which the Pythagorean winner differed from the actual winner increased from 22 percent before divisional play to 38 percent when there were two divisions and to 54 percent in the current three-division-plus-wild-card period.

LARGEST DIFFERENCES BETWEEN ACTUAL AND PYTHAGOREAN PENNANT WINNERS

The most interesting seasons in my opinion are those in which there was the greatest total change in the won-loss records of the actual and the Pythagorean pennant winners, the leading case being the 1970 National League. Chicago won the Pythagorean pennant by three games over Cincinnati (94–68 versus 91–71). Cincinnati, which won the postseason playoff to win the pennant, had a 102–60 record compared with 84–78 for Chicago. Thus there is a 21-game difference in the actual and Pythagorean won-loss records of these two teams.

The second largest change involves the great Philadelphia Athletics team of 1931, with a 107–45 won-lost record (and a winning average of .704), which won the pennant by 13.5 games. They outperformed their Pythagorean prediction by 10 games while the New York Yankees, the Pythagorean pennant winner, underperformed by six games.

Data for the 12 seasons with a total change of 10 or more games in going from the Pythagorean pennant winner to the actual pennant winner are shown in Table 3. Seasons with a tie for the Pythagorean pennant are excluded. As in Table 2, the actual pennant winner is listed first; however, the data shown in Table 3 start with the R/OR ratio and the corresponding Pythagorean won-lost record, then show the actual won-lost record to show how the season evolved compared with the Pythagorean prediction. Data are shown also on the team's actual record in one-run games and extra-inning games, which may shed light on the change from predicted to actual performance.

It should be noted that with postseason playoffs starting in 1969, the actual pennant winner may have been outclassed in both its actual and Pythagorean won-lost records. One example of this is the 1987 American League season, when Minnesota, a very average team during the season (R/OR = 0.98) won the American League pennant in postseason play. Toronto had a much better Pythagorean won-lost record than Minnesota (100–62 versus 79–83), and both Detroit (98–64) and Toronto (96–66) had much better actual won-lost records than did Minnesota (85–77).

What accounts for the large changes shown in Table 3? Not surprisingly, teams that had a better actual won-lost record tended to do well in one-run games, and teams that had a better Pythagorean record tended not to do as well in such contests. (Data shown on extra-inning games are not discussed here because such records are subject to more random variation due to being fewer in number.) In the first season in the table, 1970 in the National League, the differences were pronounced. Cincinnati had a 27–15 record in one-run games (12 games over .500), while Chicago had a 17–21 record (four games below .500). Among the 12 seasons shown in Table 3, the differences ranged from pronounced to no appreciable difference. An example of the latter is provided by the 1987 American League season discussed above. The won-lost records in one-run games were nearly identical for Minnesota (24–22) and Toronto (27–24).

It would be expected that differences in performance in games decided by more than one run also could account for some of the differences noted between actual and Pythagorean records. In this regard, data on games by margin of victory are shown below for Cincinnati and Chicago in 1970. Not only did Cincinnati do better in one-run games than Chicago (27–15 versus 17–21), but also in two-run games (22–9 versus 9–19), three-run games (17–10 versus 15–12), four-run games (14–5 versus 10–9), and five-run games (8–1 versus 7–8). Chicago did better only in games decided by six or more runs (26–9 versus 14–20). Among games decided by five or fewer runs (the large majority of games), the won-lost records were 88–40 for Cincinnati and 58–69 for Chicago. Cincinnati's nickname—the Big Red Machine—gained prominence in 1970 when the team won 70 of its first 100 games. Perhaps "winner of close games" would have been more accurate, since Chicago scored more runs during the season than Cincinnati (806 versus 775).

LUCK AND SKILL

There has been a lot of research in recent decades on the role of luck in how well a team performs over the

Table 3. LARGEST CHANGES IN WON-LOST RECORDS FOR PYTHAGOREAN AND ACTUAL PENNANT WINNERS: 1901 TO 2020

Yr. & League Total change in wins (in bold)	Team	R/OR	Pyth. W-L	GB	Actual W-L	GB	One-run games W-L	Net	Ext.-inn. games, W-L	Yr. & League Total change in wins (in bold)	Team	R/OR	Pyth. W-L	GB	Actual W-L	GB	One-run games W-L	Net	Ext.-inn. games, W-L
1970, NL	CIN	1.14	91-71	3	102-60	-	27-15	+12	7-3	**1960, AL**	NY	1.19	89-65	1	97-57	-	30-18	+12	10-7
11- (-10) = 21	CHI	1.19	94-68	-	84-68	18	17-21	-4	4-6	**8 - (-3) = 11**	CHI	1.20	90-64	-	87-67	10	22-23	-1	10-5
1931, AL	PHI	1.37	97-55	2.5	107-45	-	19-14	+5	7-4	**2005, AL**	CHI	1.15	91-71	5	99-63	-	35-19	+16	11-8
10 - (-6) = 16	NY	1.40	100-53	-	94-59	13.5	19-20	-1	5-11	**8 - (-3) = 11**	CLE	1.23	96-66	-	93-69	6	22-36	-14	6-8
1961, NL	CIN	1.09	83-71	6	93-61	-	34-14	+20	6-3	**2018, AL**	BOS	1.35	103-59	6	108-54	-	25-14	+11	8-5
10- (-4) = 14	SF	1.18	89-65	-	85-69	8	29-27	+2	7-6	**5 - (-6) = 11**	HOU	1.49	109-53	-	103-59	5	24-24	0	5-6
2015, AL	KC	1.13	90-72	12	95-67	-	23-17	+6	10-6	**1909, NL**	PIT	1.56	105-47	3.5	110-42	-	33-13	+20	13-4
5 - (-9) = 14	TOR	1.33	102-60	-	93-69	2	15-28	-13	8-6	**5 - (-5) = 10**	CHI	1.62	109-44	-	104-49	6.5	25-15	+10	8-4
1915, AL	BOS	1.34	95-56	3.5	101-50	-	29-21	+8	7-4	**1930, AL**	PHI	1.27	93-61	2	102-52	-	25-14	+11	6-1
6 - (-7) = 13	CHI	1.41	100-54	-	93-61	9.5	23-26	-3	6-4	**9 - (-1) = 10**	WAS	1.30	95-59	-	94-60	8	23-21	+2	6-5
1906, AL	CHI	1.23	90-61	7	93-58	-	29-19	+10	11-1	**1987, AL**	MIN	0.98	79-83	21	85-77	11	24-22	+2	9-2
3 - (-9) = 12	CLE	1.38	98-55	-	89-64	5	21-25	-4	6-9	**6 - (-4) = 10**	TOR	1.29	100-62	-	96-66	-	27-24	+3	10-7

NOTES

1. Total change in wins (in bold) is the change in wins for the actual pennant winner (going from Pythagorean to actual) minus the change in wins for the Pythagorean pennant winner (going from Pythagorean to actual). For example, in the first case shown (1970, NL), Cincinnati's wins increased by 11, and Chicago's wins decreased by 10. Thus, 11- (-10) = 21. This number (21) is by definition, the same as the change in games behind (GB). In the Pythagorean pennant race, Cincinnati finished 3 games behind Chicago, while in the actual pennant race, Chicago finished 18 games behind Cincinnati. Thus the total change in games behind is: 3 + 18 = 21.

2. One-run games and extra-inning games are not mutually exclusive.

3. In addition to a team's W-L record in one-run games, wins minus losses is shown as net.

course of a season. The Baseball Reference website, in its tables showing detailed standings by season, includes each team's actual and Pythagorean records and labels the difference between them as "luck," and quantifies it as actual games won minus Pythagorean games won. Bill James, in his 2004 article "Underestimating the Fog" (*BRJ*, Vol. 33, pages 29–33) said that with regard to the assertion that winning or losing close games is luck: "it would be my opinion that it is probably not *all* luck," suggesting that it was mostly luck. Examples of research focused on the role of luck over the course of a season include Phil Birnbaum in his 2005 article, "Which Great Teams Were Just Lucky?" and Pete Palmer in his 2017 article, "Calculating Skill and Luck in Major League Baseball."[1]

Both Birnbaum and Palmer stress the fact that, for an average team with an 81–81 record, one standard deviation corresponds to 6.36 wins, calculated as the square root of (162 x .5 x .5). Rounding one standard deviation to the nearest whole number (six) means that an average team's record would range from about 75–87 to about 87–75 about 68 percent of the time (reflecting the proportion of the area under a bell-shaped curve within one standard deviation of the mean). Two standard deviations correspond to 12.72 wins. Rounding two standard deviations to the nearest whole number (13) means that an average team's record would range from about 68–94 to about 94–68 about 95 percent of the time (reflecting the proportion of the area under a bell-shaped curve within two standard deviations of the mean). Thus about five percent of the time, an average team's record for a season would be 94–68 or even better, or 68–94 or even worse! (These results are identical to those for the results of flipping a fair coin 162 times, expressed as the numbers of heads and tails.)

While a team with an 87–75 record might have been viewed traditionally as slightly above average and a team with a 94–68 record might have been viewed traditionally as a good team, the reality is not so simple because random variation plays a major role in a team's performance for a season. For example, a comparison of two teams, one with a 100–62 won-lost record and the other with a 90–72 record yields the following. Their standard deviations in wins are 6.19 and 6.32, respectively. The standard error of the difference between these two values, calculated as the square root of (6.19 squared + 6.32 squared) is 8.85. The difference in wins between the two teams (10) divided by the standard error of the difference (8.85) is about 1.13, frequently referred to as the z-score. A z-score of 1.0 or more means that there is a 68 percent chance that the 100-win team is actually better than the 90-win team. A z-score of 1.13 corresponds to a 74 percent chance. A z-score of 2.0 would correspond to a 95 percent chance that the 100-win team is better. It is a matter of judgment what z-score value is used and depends how much the researcher wants to avoid concluding that the 100-win team is truly superior when this is not the case. However, it is most prudent (as in the case of most medical research) to use the more rigorous standard: a z-score of 2.0 or more corresponding to a 95-percent-plus confidence level before concluding that the difference in records was not due entirely to luck.

It has seldom been the case that the actual and Pythagorean pennant winners differed in wins by nine or more (corresponding generally to one standard deviation or more) and never by as much as 18 or more (two standard deviations or more). The largest difference was in the 1987 American League when, as discussed earlier, the difference between Minnesota's actual pennant-winning record and Toronto's Pythagorean pennant-winning record was 15 wins. It may be noted that it is also extremely rare that the "best team" (not necessarily the actual or Pythagorean pennant winner) in a season can be determined. This is because a season (with "only" 162 games) does not provide a large enough sample size to conclude that a team is the best team in its league unless it wins 18 or more games than any of its opponents.

It should be stressed, however, that the Pythagorean pennant winners are the result of a statistical model. A team's record is determined by the aggregate performance of its players (batting, base running, fielding, and pitching). But this is a two-stage process. Player performance determines, subject to some variation, the numbers of runs scored and runs allowed by the team, which in turn determines the team's won-lost record. In each of these two phases, a team can under-perform, perform as predicted, or over-perform. All the calculations above, starting with the 6.36 standard error for an average team's won-lost record, reflect these two phases. The Pythagorean pennant winners are predicted with a model that starts with the team's numbers of runs scored and runs allowed, thus excluding the variation inherent in an actual baseball season. Thus it may be the case that standard errors calculated for Pythagorean pennant winners should be different (and somewhat lower) than for actual pennant winners. It is my guess that it

would still be the case that only a small proportion of the seasons with different actual and Pythagorean pennant winners would differ by one standard deviation or more in their records and that seasons with differences of two standard deviations or more would be extremely rare (perhaps just the 1987 American League).

SUMMARY

The purpose of this paper has been to provide a general comparison of actual pennant winners and Pythagorean pennant winners for the National and American Leagues from 1901 to 2020. From 1901 to 1968, before the introduction of postseason play to determine pennant winners, the actual and Pythagorean pennant winners differed only 22 percent of the time in 136 seasons of play. The corresponding figure for the 50 seasons of play in the 1969 to 1993 period, with one round of playoffs to determine pennant winners, was 38 percent. For the 1995 to 2020 period, with two or more rounds of playoffs to determine pennant winners, the corresponding figure for the 52 seasons of play was 54 percent. There have been 12 seasons with different actual and Pythagorean pennant winners in which the total change in actual and Pythagorean won-lost records was 10 or more games. The most extreme case was in the National League in 1970 when Chicago won the Pythagorean pennant by 3 games over Cincinnati, but Cincinnati actually won 18 more games than Chicago did, a net change of 21 games. Finally, it appears that for all or virtually all seasons in which the actual and Pythagorean pennant winners differed, the differences between the two teams' won-lost records fell within the range of sampling error on their won-lost records (using a 95-percent confidence level) and thus could be attributed to luck. ∎

Acknowledgment

The author would like to acknowledge the comments and suggestions of two anonymous reviewers.

Notes

1. Phil Birnbaum, "Which Great Teams Were Just Lucky?" *Baseball Research Journal*, Volume 34 (2005): 60–68; Pete Palmer, "Calculating Skill and Luck in Major League Baseball," *Baseball Research Journal*, Volume 46, No. 1 (2017): 56–60).

Friends of SABR

You can become a Friend of SABR by giving as little as $10 per month or by making a one-time gift of $1,000 or more. When you do so, you will be inducted into a community of passionate baseball fans dedicated to supporting SABR's work.

Friends of SABR receive the following benefits:
- ✓ Recognition in This Week in SABR, SABR.org, and the SABR Annual Report
- ✓ Access to the SABR Annual Convention VIP donor event
- ✓ Invitations to exclusive Friends of SABR events

SABR On-Deck Circle - $10/month, $30/month, $50/month

Get in the SABR On-Deck Circle, and help SABR become the essential community for the world of baseball. Your support will build capacity around all things SABR, including publications, website content, podcast development, and community growth.

A monthly gift is deducted from your bank account or charged to a credit card until you tell us to stop. No more email, mail, or phone reminders.

Josh Gibson

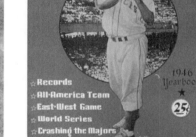
Jackie Robinson

Cool Papa Bell

Join the SABR On-Deck Circle

Payment Info: __Visa __Mastercard __ Discover

Name on Card: _____

Card #: _____

Exp. Date: _____ Security Code: _____

Signature: _____

- ○ $10/month
- ○ $30/month
- ○ $50/month
- ○ Other amount _____

Go to sabr.org/donate to make your gift online

Third Things First

Carl Zamloch and the Brief History of Reversible Baseball

Dan Schoenholz

On February 15, 1928, the University of California baseball squad took on a local semi-pro team by the name of the Ambrose Tailors in an early-season exhibition game. Such a contest normally would have generated little interest from the baseball-viewing public, who tended to wait for intercollegiate play before turning out to support the Bears. But on this day, "a crowd of 500 fans, two motion picture cameras, and four newspaper photographers" made the trek to West Field on the Berkeley campus to watch the action.[1] Spectators were treated not only to a seesaw affair that saw California pull out an 11–10 victory in the bottom of the ninth; they also witnessed what they had come for in the first place, a field trial of Coach Carl Zamloch's proposed revision to the rule books, what he called "reversible" baseball.

What exactly was reversible (also sometimes referred to as "left-handed" or "ambidextrous") baseball? Simply put, batters were given the option of running to either first or third base after putting the ball in play. Fielders were forced to take note of where the batter was going, and to adjust accordingly. If a batter chose to run to third base and reached safely, all offense in that half inning was reversed: other hitters in that frame would have to follow their teammate's lead. For example, if the leadoff hitter singled and ran to third instead of first, the subsequent batter would need to run to third base on a single to left, and the runner might attempt to go from third to first on the play.

Though the results from the experimental contest in Berkeley garnered considerable publicity, the innovation proved divisive: Traditionalists felt reversible baseball was radical and unnecessary, while others, like Zamloch—the son of a world-famous magician and a noted vaudeville performer in his own right—argued that the new rule would add needed excitement to a game that had grown too predictable.

Whether due to its opponents or simply to inertia, reversible baseball never caught on. Still, as organized baseball struggles to re-invigorate the game in a challenging sports and entertainment marketplace, now is perhaps an opportune time to revisit the short history of Zamloch's attempt to do exactly the same thing almost 100 years ago.

CARL ZAMLOCH: BALLPLAYER, COACH, AND MAGICIAN

Carl Eugene Zamloch was born on October 6, 1889, in Oakland, California. His father, Anton, a native Austrian, was a magician who performed throughout the western United States and by the end of the 19th century had become famous as "Zamloch the Great."[2] Carl learned sleight of hand under his father's tutelage and sometimes performed in his act, but magic was not his only talent. He was also a pretty good ballplayer, and in 1912 won 36 games, including some for Missoula (Montana) of the Class D Union Association, pitching alongside his roommate, "Bullet Joe" Bush.[3]

Zamloch's fine season led the Detroit Tigers to purchase his contract, and he broke camp with the team in 1913. His shining moment in the big leagues came on May 18, when he outpitched the great Walter Johnson but lost, 2–1, when the Nationals (aka the Senators) scratched across two unearned runs.[4] Soon thereafter, he developed arm trouble and was sent to the minors—never to make it back to the majors, as it turned out.

In 1916, Zamloch was hired as the baseball coach at the University of California, winning the Pacific Coast intercollegiate baseball championship in his first year at the helm.[5] After the college season ended, still interested in playing but unable to pitch regularly due to his arm woes, Zamloch joined Spokane of the Northwest League as a utility man. He flourished in his new role, putting up a .464 batting average in 56 at-bats. Over the next decade, he repeated this pattern often, leaving Berkeley once the collegiate schedule was completed and catching on with such minor league clubs as San Francisco and Seattle in the Pacific Coast League and Calgary in the Class B Western International League. His final stop as a regular player was in 1926 as player-manager with Twin Falls of the Class C Utah-Idaho League, where he batted .391 and was awarded a shotgun as the league's Most Valuable Player.[6] All told, Zamloch batted .316 for his career in over 1,600 at-bats.

Cal baseball coach Carl Zamloch in 1929, his final season as Bears' coach.

In addition to his baseball pursuits, Zamloch had his own offseason vaudeville act.[7] Occasionally, he combined his two interests: In a September 1919 Pacific Coast League contest, he delighted fans and players alike by performing magic. "Before he went in as a pinch-hitter, Carl Zamloch pulled one of his sleight of hand stunts by yanking a yard or more of hot dogs out of the shirt of [pitcher] Cy Falkenberg. Zamloch pretended that he was searching Cy for emory or sandpaper and Cy rather resented being pawed over, but he had to laugh when Zamloch finished his trick."[8]

As the son of a showman, Zamloch had traveled extensively as a boy. As a coach, he saw many benefits of combining baseball with travel, both for his players and for the game itself. Throughout the 1920s, he organized summertime barnstorming tours of Hawaii and Japan for the Cal squad, as well as exhibition games in Berkeley against visiting Japanese teams.[9] These tours to Japan fed the growing popularity of baseball there.

In 1927, Zamloch organized the new California Intercollegiate Baseball Association, initially consisting of Cal, Stanford, St. Mary's, and Santa Clara. UCLA and other California schools would join later.[10] It was Zamloch's belief that college baseball needed a stronger organization and that focusing on intercollegiate competition would increase its popularity. His efforts proved lasting: the CIBA was the governing structure for conference play until the Pac-8 conference was created in 1967.

THE BIRTH OF REVERSIBLE BASEBALL

But helping the game grow internationally and strengthening the conference were just two of Zamloch's ideas to expand baseball's popularity. In early 1928, he announced his intention to employ reversible baseball in exhibition contests in the coming season. In Zamloch's view, reversible baseball had several selling points:

1. More excitement for fans. "Baseball has not increased in popularity in comparison with our population. Football has made wonderful strides. I think that is partially because the fans cannot anticipate the play. In baseball we all know that when a man singles…he is going to first base. If we mix that procedure up a bit it ought to increase the interest."[12]

2. Rewarding players for braininess. "By allowing a batsman to run either to first or third base, it makes for strategy and teaches the players to think."[13]

3. Eliminating the advantage of batting left-handed. "The way the game is played now, a right-handed batter is penalized for being a right-hander. He stands on the other side of the plate from first base. Then after hitting the ball his swing carries him a bit farther away from his destination—first base…. What is the result? A left-handed batter has every advantage on his side."[14]

Zamloch initially hoped to use reversible baseball rules in the Bears' annual early-season contest against the Pacific Coast League's Oakland Oaks, but Oaks manager Del Howard wasn't having any of it. "If these college boys want to play baseball with us we'll entertain 'em, but if they want to play some funny game invented by Coach Zamloch, then that is something else again," said Howard. "How do I know what they may do after running from the plate to third instead of first? Maybe the next rule calls for skipping second base, taking a cup of tea or reading a book or something. …I'm certainly not going to let the Oaks play left handed baseball."[15]

Undeterred, Zamloch secured an agreement with the aforementioned Ambrose Tailors to play an exhibition using reversible rules. In the days leading up to the game, Bay Area newspapers and the wire services devoted considerable ink to the upcoming contest. Interest was high: Among the curious fans and media representatives who attended were former major leaguer Bill Rodgers, by then the manager of Little Rock in the Southern Association; Pittsburgh Pirates scout Joe Devine; and St. Louis Cardinals outfielder Taylor Douthit, whose brother Rolly patrolled center field for the Bears.[16]

Spectators were rewarded with an afternoon that the *Oakland Tribune* described as "an uproarious success in more ways than one," and they didn't have

COURTESY UC BERKELEY ATHLETIC DEPARTMENT

Cal baseball coach Carl Zamloch with team captain Sammy Adair circa 1916.

long to wait.[17] In the bottom of the first, Cal catcher Walter Wyatt walked, went to third base rather than first; then stole second. Pitcher Gus Nemecheck came to the plate and promptly knocked the ball out of the park, "but from force of habit he started trotting toward first when the ball was hit and [he] was declared out just as the sphere sailed over the fence."[18] As noted in the *Berkeley Gazette*, Nemecheck thereby "won the honor of being the first person in baseball history to knock out a home run that wasn't even a hit."[19]

The Bears did not have a monopoly on reversible-induced misplays. "Three times during the game, [Tailors' third baseman] Bill Marriott, former Oak and third sacker for Boston, was caught napping and runners were safe at third when Marriott started to throw the ball to first."[20]

Other highlights noted in the *Oakland Tribune*'s account of the contest included watching the Tailors' infielders attempt a "reversible double play" (second to third, presumably) and the reactions of passers-by "when they saw men being run from first to home."[21]

Cal built a 9–4 lead through seven innings before the clubs agreed to revert to traditional rules. The Bears quickly blew their lead, falling behind, 10–9, before rallying in the bottom of the ninth to score two on a Rolly Douthit double for a walk-off 11–10 victory.

Both United Press International and the Associated Press carried short accounts of the contest that were picked up by newspapers nationwide, and pundits continued to debate reversible baseball's merits for weeks afterward. Reviews reflected a wide range of opinion. The *Los Angeles Evening Express* opined that "Zamloch's left-handed game would add an element of surprise, hidden thrill, genuine deception to a game that is now just one, two, three—you're out."[22] The *Oakland Tribune* noted that "the change makes players use their heads as well as their arms and legs and calls for new techniques."[23] Former New York Giants star George Van Haltren, who had finished his career as player-manager for the Oaks from 1905 to '09, was also a fan. "Reversible base-running would put more [suspense] into the diamond sport."[24]

For every observer who found the change intriguing, however, there was another who thought it was a terrible idea. From the *San Francisco Examiner*: "The effort of Coach Zamloch… to make boarding-house hash out of the baseball rules, proved just the success that was expected. It succeeded in making a farce of the game. …Baseball has been getting along fairly well for quite a few years, thank you. Let's confine "new ideas" to ping-pong or something like that."[25] The *San Francisco Chronicle*'s Harry B. Smith noted the confusion caused by the new rules and admitted, "I confess I cannot see where the pastime will gain from the new order."[26] Succinctly summing up the feelings of opponents, the *Pittsburgh Post-Gazette* stated: "Baseball has done well as it is. Let it stay the way it is."[27]

While the idea of reversible baseball continued to generate occasional commentary from pundits in 1928, what it didn't generate were actual games played under its rules. Contemporary press accounts noted that subsequent Cal exhibition games in February and March 1928 would use traditional rather than reversible rules, but provided few clues as to why. The most likely explanation is that Zamloch had difficulty getting agreement from opponents to play under different rules. By the 1920s baseball was already a sport steeped in its own tradition, and change didn't come easily.

The last extensive discussion of reversible baseball in print appeared in April 1928 in a syndicated opinion piece authored by Detroit Tigers manager George Moriarty, a former teammate of Zamloch's on the 1913 Tigers.[28] Moriarty's review of reversible baseball was more balanced than most, noting what he saw as some of the pros and cons of such a rule change. Interestingly, Moriarty credited Kid Elberfeld, shortstop for New York during the early days of the American League, for having come up with the idea of reversible baseball in 1906, although Moriarty noted that it was never tried.

AFTER REVERSIBLE BASEBALL

While Zamloch had abandoned the idea of reversible baseball by 1929, it is worth noting that he continued to promote innovation. An exhibition that spring against alumni featured what may have been the first ever field trial of "10-man baseball,"[29] a rule change promoted by National League president John Heydler at the 1928 winter meetings that would add offense to the game by allowing another player to occupy the pitcher's spot in the batting order. The idea would ultimately be adopted 44 years later by the American League and called the designated-hitter rule.[30]

Zamloch embarked on the final chapter of his baseball life late in 1930, when he became co-owner and field manager of the Oakland Oaks. After three mediocre seasons, he was fired. He eventually moved into the executive ranks for an oil company while also continuing to perform his magic act. His viewpoint that baseball needed to evolve never changed: In an interview in 1960, three years before his death, he said that games were too long. "I can remember when an average game never went more than an hour and a half. Many of them were faster. I hear lots of fans complaining," Zamloch said. "Even if the answer is to shorten the game to seven innings, baseball has to do something about it."[31]

Increasing offense, improving competition, promoting the sport internationally, shortening games. Zamloch was an early adopter of several ideas that have since gained ground with the baseball establishment as ways of enlivening the sport. As organized baseball debates potential rule changes to increase fan interest, maybe the powers that be should dust off his most radical proposal: reversible baseball. ■

Acknowledgment

The author would like to thank John Cronin for his review and helpful comments on an early version of this article.

Notes

1. "Zamloch Wins 'Goofy' Ball Contest," *Oakland Tribune*, February 16, 1928.
2. "Magician's Bees Replace Black Art," *Oakland Tribune*, April 3, 1927.
3. "California's Coaches No. 2 Carl Zamloch," *Oakland Tribune*, March 21, 1926. Bush went directly from Missoula to the major leagues, where he won almost 200 games in a 17-year career that included stints with the Philadelphia Athletics, Boston Red Sox, and New York Yankees. See also Kim Briggeman, "Missoula, ''Bullet Joe' and Baseball History," *The Missoulian*, October 23, 2008
4. "Walter Johnson Wins 9th Straight from Detroit," *San Francisco Chronicle*, May 19, 1913.
5. "Carl Zamloch will Coach U.C.," *Oakland Tribune*, February 10, 1916.
6. "Zamloch Named Best Utah-Idaho Player," *San Francisco Examiner*, September 2, 1926. He also had a handful of pinch-hit at-bats while serving as player-manager of the Oakland Oaks.
7. "Zamloch on Stage as Vaudeville Star; Has Quit Baseball," *Great Falls Tribune*, December 19, 1919.
8. "Notes About Players," *San Francisco Chronicle*, September 25, 1919.
9. The Bears traveled to Japan for exhibitions in 1921, 1927, and 1929 and to Hawaii in in 1923 and 1926. A visiting Japanese squad stopped in Berkeley for a pair of exhibition games in 1928. See, for example, "U.C. Ball Team Is Off on Trip to the Islands," *Oakland Tribune*, June 21, 1923.
10. "California Colleges Prepare for Eight Club Ball League," *Oakland Tribune*, October 5, 1926.
11. "Brief History of California Golden Bears Baseball," Cal Baseball Foundation, hdp://calbaseballfoundaPon.org/team/cal-baseball.
12. "Sports by Harry B. Smith," *San Francisco Chronicle*, February 15, 1928.
13. "New Baseball Game is Given Test by Bears," *San Francisco Chronicle*, February 16, 1928.
14. "Players Test Backward Baseball," *San Bernardino County Sun*, March 4, 1928.
15. "Outgoing Mail from Bob Shand," *Oakland Tribune*, February 2, 1928.
16. "Notables See Bears Win New Ball Game," *Berkeley Gazette*, February 16, 1928.
17. "Zamloch Wins 'Goofy' Ball Contest," *Oakland Tribune*, February 16, 1928.
18. "Zamloch Wins 'Goofy' Ball Contest."
19. "Notables See Bears Win New Ball Game."
20. "Zamloch Wins'Goofy' Ball Contest."
21. "Zamloch Wins 'Goofy' Ball Contest."
22. "The Inside Track with Sid Ziff," *Los Angeles Evening Express*, February 21, 1928.
23. "Zamloch Idea Adds Zest to Game," *Oakland Tribune*, February 21, 1928.
24. "Players Test Backward Baseball."
25. "2nd Guess," *San Francisco Examiner*, February 17, 1928.
26. "Sports by Harry B. Smith," *San Francisco Chronicle*, February 17, 1928.
27. "Sports of All Sorts," *Pittsburgh Post-Gazette*, February 22, 1928
28. George Moriarty, "Reversible Baseball Drawing Serious, Humorous Comment," *Lincoln Journal Star*, April 20, 1928.
29. "Webb Alumni Play Bears in 4 to 4 Contest," *Oakland Tribune*, February 7, 1929.
30. John Cronin: "The Historical Evolution of the Designated Hitter Rule." *The Baseball Research Journal* 46 No.2 (2016).
31. "Marathon Dodger Games Irk Fans," *Los Angeles Times*, June 10, 1960.

The One Time the "Boston Red Sox" Played a Black Team

September 14, 1918: Hilldale Club 9, "Boston Red Sox" 0,
at Hilldale Park, Darby, Pennsylvania

Bill Nowlin

"Every one of the 16 Major League franchises that operated between 1901 and 1960 faced a black team at some point in their history." So wrote Todd Peterson in his introduction to the book *The Negro Leagues Were Major Leagues*.[1]

I have written quite a lot on the Boston Red Sox, including their being the last team in the American and National Leagues to integrate.[2] I was intrigued, because I had not come across a time when the Boston Red Sox had played a Black team. I wrote Peterson to ask him what I might have overlooked. His answer proved to provide a window into a fascinating ballgame and bit of history.[3]

The game took place in Darby, Pennsylvania, on September 14, 1918. The two teams were Hilldale, the "crack colored team of Philadelphia" and the "Champion Boston Red Sox of the American League."[4] Hilldale was, per the *Philadelphia Tribune*, "the fastest colored team in the East." The game was the last of their season, and the Red Sox had wrapped up their own season and the World Series a few days earlier.[5]

Neil Lanctot wrote that in 1918, Hilldale fielded an "all-professional lineup" and "finished the season with a 41–7 record, winning nearly 20 more games than in 1917."[6] The Hilldale club was not part of any organized league at the time, but compiled this record by barnstorming and taking on other teams that came to Darby.[7]

The game in question was played on Saturday afternoon, September 14, at Hilldale Park in Darby at 3PM. General admission was 50 cents per ticket; pavilion seats set patrons back 75 cents. One could take the #13 trolley from Walnut Street, Philadelphia, directly to the park. The *Philadelphia North American* reserved a degree of skepticism and characterized the team as a "nondescript team billed as the world's champion Red Sox."[8] Apparently only four members of the world champion team took part.

Peterson did acknowledge that the visiting team was "Red Sox-ish."[9]

Each Red Sox regular had pocketed $1,108.45 after the season was over. In addition to these Series shares, their salaries were paid to them through September 15.[10] The three Red Sox players who were on this "Red Sox-ish" team were thus still on Boston salary on the day of the game at Darby.

Promoter Art Summers of Boston had booked the event and had planned to have the "war champions" go on to play elsewhere, "such teams of Steelton, Hazleton, Lebanon, Bethlehem, Hoboken, and Baltimore."[11] Among the prior games Summers had booked was one of his "All-American Club" against Hilldale on August 15. That game, nearly a shutout, was a victory for the "All-Americans," declared by Philadelphia's *Evening Public Ledger* to be "the first white club to defeat Hilldale this season."[12]

As we shall see, this barnstorming outfit playing under the name "Red Sox" did not go unnoticed by American League president Ban Johnson.

LINEUPS

Hilldale[13]	Boston Red Sox[16]
John Edward Reese, LF	Ralph Young, SS[17]
William Fuller, 2B	Amos Strunk, CF
Tom Fiall, CF	Sherwood Magee, LF, 2b
Louis Santop, C	George Burns, 1B
Dick Lundy, SS	Wally Schang, 3B
Phil Cockrell, RF[14]	Ed Lennox, 2b, LF
Napoleon "Chance" Cummings, 1B	Jones, RF[18]
Cecil Johnson, 3B[15]	Wally Mayer, C
Bunny Downs, 3B	Bullet Joe Bush, P
Tom Williams, P	

The Hilldale team was no pushover. Santop was inducted into the National Baseball Hall of Fame in 2006. His plaque calls him one of Black baseball's "most powerful batters during the first quarter of the twentieth century." Williams and Reese were both on the 1920 Chicago American Giants championship team. Lundy played Negro Leagues baseball for more than 20 years, a dozen of them with Atlantic City's Bacharach Giants. Cockrell played professional baseball for 18 years, Lundy for more than 20 years, Downs for 10, Cummings for at least eight, and Fiall for at least six.

The *Boston Globe* described the game and the competing teams in one sentence summarizing the game:

"With Strunk, Schang and Bush in the lineup and several other big league stars an All-Star club, calling itself the Red Sox, defeated Hilldale today, 4 to 3."[19]

The *Philadelphia Record* published a game story running a few hundred words. It referred to the visiting team as "a team calling themselves the Boston 'Red Sox.'"[20] The *Philadelphia North American* noted that Bush, Schang, and Strunk were the three on the visiting team who were "real honest to goodness Red Sox."[21]

In their game accounts, only one of the newspapers made any reference or allusion to race. This would have been unnecessary for the *Tribune*, being "the nation's oldest continuously published newspaper reflecting the African-American experience."[22] Its readers would have known Hilldale to be a Black ballclub. The *Globe* article was, as indicated, very brief: just one sentence of text. The *Globe* did not acknowledge any forfeit. Why the word "forfeit" is employed will soon become clear. The *Record* box score showed the runs as Boston Red Sox 4, Hilldale 3, but placed an "X" in the bottom of the ninth inning for Hilldale.

THE GAME

The Red Sox scored once in the top of the first. With two outs, Magee walked. He was picked off first and ran to second, arriving safely since no one covered the bag. Burns drove him home with a single over second.

Hilldale took a 2–1 lead in the bottom of the first. Reese singled up the middle and was sacrificed to second base and then third. Bush walked Santop intentionally, Santop stole second. Lundy tripled to left-center.

Neither team scored in the second, but the Red Sox then added two in the top of the third. Young drew a one-out walk. Strunk hit one to right field and Young

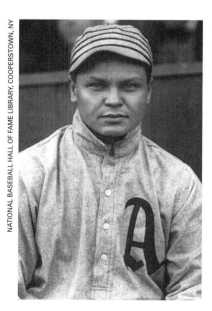

Philly native Amos Strunk played ten years with the Philadelphia A's before moving to the Red Sox for 1918–19.

NATIONAL BASEBALL HALL OF FAME LIBRARY, COOPERSTOWN, NY

tried to score but was out "by yards." But Young protested that Strunk's ball had gone beyond the ropes in right field (the game clearly attracted a sizable crowd) and should be ruled a ground-rule double. Umpire Smith agreed and the runners were positioned on second and third. Then Magee hit one "into the centre field crowd" and it was 3–2 in favor of the "Red Sox."

In the bottom of the fourth, Hilldale tied it. Santop walked, was sacrificed to second, and scored on Cockrell's hit to center field.

There was no more scoring until the top of the eighth when Williams walked Strunk and Magee. Burns grounded to second and Magee was forced. Schang hit one to Cummings at first; he threw home and erased Strunk at the plate. Lennox tapped one back to the pitcher, who fell down, resulting in the bases becoming loaded. Williams then walked Jones on four pitches, forcing home the go-ahead run. It was 4-3 "in favor of the white folks" as the *North American* put it.[23]

Bush opened the ninth with a double into the roped-off fans in left. Young sacrificed him to third. A hard-hit ball to center was handled so well by Fiall that Bush had to hold at third base. Williams got out of the inning without a run scoring.

In the bottom of the ninth, Bush tried to use a "dead ball that had previously been thrown out of the game because of a kick made by the Sox players."[24] Hilldale team captain Santop grabbed the ball and "threw the ball far out of the lot."[25] A new ball was put into play, but "Bush deliberately sat down and ripped it on his spikes and after refusing to let Umpire Smith look at it…Magee…threw the ball in the woods."

A third ball was brought forth by the umpire "and again refused by Boston."[26] After several minutes, Smith forfeited the game to Hilldale, rendering the final score 9–0.

The *Tribune* said it had been a hard-fought game: "The game was for blood, each team striving their utmost to down the other. The game bristled with inside stuff, fast fielding and sharp double plays."

OTHER GAMES FOR THE "RED SOX"

The Summers-organized team played in a few other games.

On September 21, the Baltimore Drydocks and Shipbuilding Company "defeated a team made up largely of Boston Red Sox players, 4 to 3."[27] Only three sentences described the game, and the names of Bush and Strunk were the only two Red Sox players discerned. White Sox left-hander Dave Danforth pitched for the Drydocks.

Wally Schang was one of the "real" Red Sox on the field that day, playing third base.

A game at Lebanon included Burns, Bush, Meyer, Schang, Strunk, and Young, with others, billed as "All-Stars."[28] The Lebanon team included Rogers Hornsby, Bush's former Red Sox batterymate Sam Agnew, and a player who was probably Del Pratt.

A news story that originally ran in the *Detroit Free Press* noted games in Hartford on September 22, and a game near Brooklyn.[29] The Hartford game featured Bush pitching for the Pratt & Whitney team against another local team, Poli's, which had as its pitcher none other than Babe Ruth. Bush won a 1–0 shutout when a ninth-inning error by the first baseman, mishandling Ruth's throw to first base, allowed the winning run to score from third.[30] The Brooklyn game was on September 29 in Glendale, Long Island and presented in the box score as "Boston Red Sox" versus "Farmers." The Farmers team led, 1-0, until the Red Sox tied it in the top of the ninth, and then adding five more runs in the 10th, to win, 6–1. Bush, Mayer, Schang, and Strunk were the four Red Sox on the team. The *Brooklyn Daily Eagle* news story presented the team as Boston Red Sox without any quotation marks or qualifying language.[31]

I.E. Sanborn of the *Chicago Tribune* warned, "Members of the world's champion Red Sox, who have been coining nickels and dimes out of their title [by] barnstorming in the east in defiance of the rule forbidding winners of world's series to play exhibition games afterward, will find the national commission has a long memory."[32]

DISCIPLINE AND AFTERMATH

Multiple news stories expressed concern about these postseason games. A widely-printed story datelined October 5 began: "Members of the championship Boston club, who, after the world's series, engaged in a barnstorming trip under the name of 'Red Sox,' will be severely punished by the national commission, President Johnson of the American league declares." The games had been played "in violation of the commission's orders to disband at the close of the series."[33] Bush, Mayer, Schang, and Strunk were "under investigation."[34] The article also indicated that the Boston players might be deprived of the "individual emblems usually presented to the world's series winners because of the part they played in staging the strike before the fifth game of the series."

Detroit sportswriter Joe Jackson suggested that Red Sox owner Harry Frazee should perhaps take action himself: "He should, at the very least, be able to prohibit the use of the name of his property." Jackson referred to the four players as "the alleged Red Sox."[35]

The National Commission met in Chicago on November 16. The commission "voted to impose severe fines" on Bush, Schang, and Strunk "for playing exhibition games through the East, after the World's Series, with a team advertised as the Boston Red Sox."[36]

FINAL NOTE

Peterson's book includes a listing of some 110 games between Black ball teams and either National or American League teams, covering 1885–1924. The games for each of the franchises are listed, with the following frequency: Philadelphia Athletics (40), New York Giants (15), Philadelphia Phillies (15), St. Louis Cardinals (9), Detroit Tigers (6), Cincinnati Reds (4), St. Louis Browns (4), Washington Nationals (4), Chicago Cubs (3), Brooklyn Superbas/Dodgers (2), Cleveland Indians (2), New York Yankees (2). Boston Red Sox (1), Chicago White Sox (1), Pittsburgh Pirates (1). Also listed are the Federal League's Buffalo Blues, with 1 game. The only team not represented in the listing was the Boston Braves; they are, however, represented "at some point in their history" by a May 7, 1889, game against the Cuban Giants, played in Trenton, New Jersey.

One possible fly in the ointment was found after puzzling over the material at some length. On page 209, one can find a modification of Peterson's assertion that

Joe Bush, pitching for the "Red Sox" versus Hilldale, tried to use a damaged ball in the ninth inning. When that ball was thrown (literally) out of the game, he purposefully spiked a new ball, prompting Hilldale to call for a forfeit.

opens this article. Rather than referring to "franchises that operated," the listing relates instead to "organizations advertised and/or acknowledged to be intact Major League teams." Thus, a misrepresentation by a promoter that a team was the "Boston Red Sox" when it simply had a few players who had been on that team was counted as a major-league team event.

The games listed as Cleveland Indians games were advertised as "O'Neil's All-Stars," presumably Steve O'Neill.[37] This, of course, leads one to wonder how many of the other teams may have not truly been intact, but only advertised as such. In the case of the two New York Yankees games, for instance, the table indicates that no box scores were available. One of the games was said to have been played on November 5; how many of the 1912 team were still around? (The last-place team had played the final game on its schedule a month earlier, on October 5.) No box scores have been found for the "circa October" White Sox game either, for which no actual date has been determined.

There is, as always, more research to be done. Discovering this 1918 game which Hilldale played against the "Red Sox-ish" team did indeed lead down some interesting roads. ■

Acknowledgments

The author would like to thank Todd Peterson and Neil Lanctot for comments on this article, SABR member Ed Morton, Megan E. McCall, curator of the Free Library of Philadelphia Map Collection. Thanks as well to the peer reviewers who read this article for the *Baseball Research Journal*.

Notes

1. Todd Peterson, *The Negro Leagues Were Major Leagues* (Jefferson, North Carolina: McFarland, 2020), 2.
2. See, for instance, *Pumpsie and Progress; The Red Sox, Race, and Redemption*, ed. Bill Nowlin (Burlington, Massachusetts: Rounder Books, 2010), and Bill Nowlin's *Tom Yawkey: Patriarch of the Boston Red Sox* (Lincoln and London: University of Nebraska Press, 2018).
3. In further correspondence with Todd Peterson via email during January 2021, Peterson provided details regarding "franchises that operated" during the years in question which played against Black teams. There was a pair of games between the Brooklyn Superbas on June 5 and 6, 1905, against the Cuban X-Giants and a series of six games in the second half of September in 1906 between the "home guard" Philadelphia Athletics and Brooklyn Royal Giants. After concluding a homestand on September 15, Connie Mack's Athletics went to Chicago, but many of the regular players stayed home, including Bender, Coakley, Cross, Plank, and Seybold. This "home guard" team played a series of games in Atlantic City. On the latter, see for instance, "Has Connie Mack Given Up Hope," *Washington Evening Star*, September 16, 1906: 55.
4. "Hilldale to Play the Boston Red Sox," *Philadelphia Tribune*, September 14, 1918: 7.
5. The Red Sox had won the A.L. pennant and also the 1918 World Series against the Chicago Cubs, wrapping up the Series on September 11, a postseason championship season played a month earlier than usual due to the world war in progress. The Boston Red Sox had won four times in the seven years dating back to 1912. The Chicago Cubs had won back-to-back World Series in 1907 and 1908. Partisans of neither team could have guessed that the Red Sox would not win another one for 86 years and the Cubs would endure a drought of more than 100 years, until 2016.
6. Neil Lanctot, *Fair Dealing and Clean Playing: The Hilldale Club and the Development of Black Professional Baseball, 1910–1932* (Syracuse: Syracuse University Press, 2007) 52.
7. For an overview of baseball barnstorming, see Thomas Barthel, *Baseball Barnstorming and Exhibition Games, 1901–1962* (Jefferson, North Carolina: McFarland, 2007).
8. "'Red Sox' Forfeit Game to Negro Team," *Philadelphia North American*, September 15, 1918. The paper noted wryly that the team had "in their line-up three players who actually represented Boston in the recent world's series."
9. Todd Peterson, e-mail to author, November 17, 2020.
10. "Each Sox Regular Receives $1108.45," *Boston Globe*, September 13, 1918: 8.
11. "Red Sox to Play Hilldale," *Washington Herald*, September 13, 1918: 9. They were called the "war champions" because the world war was still in progress. Summers had been promoting games in the region during the course of the 1918 season featuring the All-Star Internationals, described as "an aggregation that mainly is built up of former players who have had major and minor league experience." See "Notes of the Amateurs," *Philadelphia Evening Public Ledger*, June 29, 1918: 14.
12. "All-American Defeats Hilldale," *Philadelphia Evening Public Ledger*, August 16, 1918: 3.
13. The only box score found was in the *Record* and it only provided surnames and positions. The game story provided a couple of clues as to given names of participant, e.g., Hilldale pitcher Tom Williams. Working with the Seamheads database and other sources, we feel pretty confident about the identities of all the players.
14. Listed in both the box score and game story as "Cochrall," this is almost certainly Phil Cockrell, normally a pitcher for Hilldale.
15. Hilldale had three players named Johnson on the team. The player was likely Cecil Johnson. One was starting pitcher Daniel Spencer "Shang" Johnson. There were two infielders, both of whom are listed on Seamheads as playing third base. They were Cecil Johnson and future Hall of Famer Judy Johnson, 18 years old at the time, but not a regular on the team. Thanks to Neil Lanctot for weighing in as well with his best guess in an e-mail to author, November 29, 2020. Downs apparently replaced Johnson at some point during the game.
16. This is the way the team was listed in the *Philadelphia Record* box score.
17. Young played second base for the Detroit Tigers in 1918. Guesswork makes us believe that Lennox is former Federal League third baseman Ed Lennox.
18. We are not sure who Jones was. One would be tempted to guess Sam Jones, pitcher for the 1918 Red Sox, but he was not listed as one of the Red Sox players in the *Tribune* article, nor was he one of the Red Sox disciplined

later in the year. It's possible that another person entirely was playing under the name "Jones."

19. "Red Sox All-Stars Win, 4 to 3," *Boston Globe*, September 15, 1918: 13. The other Boston newspapers appear not to have devoted attention to the game.

20. "Patched Up Red Sox Forfeit to Hilldale," *Philadelphia Record*, September 15, 1918: 5. In the box score, there were no quotation marks around the name Boston Red Sox.

21. "'Red Sox' Forfeit Game to Negro Team." It may be of some interest that all three (Bush, Schang, and Strunk) came to the Red Sox from Philadelphia in a trade on December 14, 1917.

22. https://www.phillytrib.com/site/about.html, accessed January 30, 2021.

23. "'Red Sox' Forfeit Game to Negro Team." This was the only reference to race for either of the teams.

24. "Hilldale Holds Boston Red Sox," *Philadelphia Tribune*, September 21, 1918: 7.

25. "Patched Up Red Sox Forfeit to Hilldale."

26. "'Red Sox' Forfeit Game to Negro Team."

27. "Joe Bush Loser in Close Game," *Boston Globe*, September 22, 1918: 12.

28. "Bullet Joe Trims All-Star Club in Closing Contest," *Harrisburg Patriot*, October 14, 1918: 7.

29. "Jackson Plays Ship Baseball," *Harrisburg Patriot*, October 11, 1918: 17.

30. "Bush Shuts Out Poli's in Hard Pitcher's Battle," *Hartford Courant*, September 23, 1918: 12.

31. "Boston Red Sox Beat Farmers in the Tenth," *Brooklyn Daily Eagle*, September 30, 1918: 14. The *Brooklyn Times Union* similarly referred to the team as the "Boston Red Sox with several member of other big league teams in their line-up." See "Red Sox Go Ten Innings to Defeat the Farmers," *Brooklyn Times Union*, September 30, 1918: 8.

32. I.E. Sanborn, "Comish Keeping Tab on Red Sox Who Break Rules," *Chicago Tribune*, October 5,1918: 16.

33. See "National Commission to Discipline Red Sox," *Pittsburgh Press*, October 5, 1918: 10 and "Slicker Red Sox Who Went Out Barnstorming Are In Bad," *San Diego Evening Tribune*, October 5, 1918: 3.

34. The mention of Mayer is confusing. He was probably Wally Mayer, catcher for the Red Sox. The confusion comes from the September 21 *Philadelphia Tribune* article referring to "Meyer of the [Philadelphia] Athletics," and catcher Wally Mayer was not with the Athletics, as a Philadelphia newspaper would be likely to know. The *Christian Science Monitor* explicitly named Walter Mayer. See "Boston Men May Be Disciplined," *Christian Science Monitor*, October 7, 1918: 10. When the final discipline was meted out, it was only Bush, Schang, and Strunk who were fined. If it was Wally Mayer, we can't explain why he was not fined as well.

35. "Jackson Plays Ship Baseball."

36. "Penalize Red Sox Players," *Boston Post*, November 17, 1918: 14, and "Strunk, Schang and Bush Disciplined," *Boston Globe*, November 17, 1918: 14. The commission also reaffirmed the decision to withhold the awarding of the emblems.

37. Advertisement, *Cleveland Plain Dealer*, October 8, 1922: 4D.

Minor-League Baseball in Niagara, Canada, 1986–99

David Siegel

This paper will discuss how a conjunction of events led to the presence in or near the Niagara area of Canada of four minor-league teams for a brief period in the 1980s–90s. It will illustrate how the different cities dealt with their teams and also identify some significant changes that were occurring in minor-league baseball at this time.

Hockey and rowing are the usual sports of choice in Niagara. So how did it happen that for the period from 1989 through 1992 there were four professional baseball teams playing within or near Niagara? One was in Niagara Falls, New York; since it was not based in Canada, it will not be considered in this paper, but it was an easy drive across what was at the time a relatively open border. There were franchises in the Canadian cities of St. Catharines, Welland, and Hamilton. Hamilton is not really in the Niagara region, but it is just beyond its border so it is included in this paper.

All four teams were in the Class A (short season) New York-Pennsylvania League. A league of that name began operation in 1890. In its current incarnation, the league dates itself from 1939, and bills itself as the oldest continuously operating Class A league.[1] It currently has 14 teams located in the northeastern United States.[2] St. Catharines had a Toronto Blue Jays farm team from 1986 until 1999. Welland had a Pirates farm team from 1989 to 1994. This was the first time that either of these cities had hosted a team in Organized Baseball.[3] Hamilton had a farm team of the Cardinals from 1988 to 1992 and hosted professional baseball on several occasions before. It was a charter member of the predecessor of the New York-Penn League in 1939.[4]

ST. CATHARINES BLUE JAYS (OR BABY JAYS)/STOMPERS (1986–99)

In 1985, the Toronto Blue Jays acquired the Niagara Falls, New York, franchise which had been a farm team of the White Sox. The Blue Jays wanted to move the team to Canada, fairly close to Toronto. St. Catharines won out over the nearby cities of Niagara Falls, Ontario, Welland, and Hamilton because St. Catharines promised to upgrade significantly the existing facility.[5] The official name of the team was Blue Jays, but the

sobriquet Baby Jays was quickly adopted by most people to distinguish the local team from the parent club which operated 100 kilometers up the road and received a large amount of press in the Niagara area.

The team played in Community Park, which was an established park with much history as the home of local high-level amateur baseball teams. It had all the basic requirements of a minor-league baseball park, but there was nothing fancy about it. The playing surface was a bit rough, but new lights were installed to meet New York-Penn League standards.[6] In that first year, seating was in wooden high-school-style bleachers. It was part of a larger neighborhood park, hidden from street view by a high school building and a lawn bowling club. It wasn't exactly a luxurious setting even by minor-league standards, but it was enough for St. Catharines to be awarded the team. The city had not previously considered the idea of hosting a professional baseball team, so this request came out of the blue. Several municipal councillors were pushing the idea of sports tourism—promoting tournaments for amateur teams. There seems to have been no discussion of how this professional team could fit into a program for economic development. From the city's perspective, it was a small investment, and it had some local support, so the city provided a minimal sum to upgrade an existing facility.

In some places, there is consideration of a baseball stadium as an anchor for downtown redevelopment or economic development generally.[7] This was never on the agenda in St. Catharines. Community Park is located at the juncture of a nice, middle-class residential neighborhood and a retail area with a series of car lots and strip malls. It is in the southeast corner of the city and not easily accessible from other areas. The Dairy Queen across the street from the stadium seemed to do increased business on game nights, but beyond that there was no notion of the stadium as an anchor for economic development.

The home opener was played on June 17, 1986. It came one day after the team's first ever game, which it won in Batavia.[8] The opener was a momentous occasion. The St. Catharines Singing Saints were there to provide entertainment. The 1930–31 Niagara District Champion Merritton Alliance Baseball Club was honoured. Leo Pinckney, the revered league president, and the requisite local politicians were in attendance. Mayor Joe McCaffery, who was well known for malapropisms, threw the ceremonial first pitch after paying tribute to the fact that the city would now be the home of a professional football team. The crowd of 2,191 cheered and the game was under way. The Blue Jays won their second game in a row for an auspicious start to an inaugural season.[9]

The team and the local sportswriters recognized that this was a first for St. Catharines, so there was a conscious effort to educate local fans about what to expect from a minor-league baseball team.[10] The Jays provided a pull-out section in the local newspaper that introduced the players.[11] The first few games got special coverage in the St. Catharines *Standard*. Throughout the season, the team's games were covered in stories that usually appeared on the first page of the Sports section, sometimes relegating coverage of the parent club to an inner page.

Even halfway through the season, Jack Gatecliff, the acknowledged dean of local sportswriters, deemed this first season a success. Rick Amos, the youthful general manager, expressed pleasure with the average attendance of 1,200.[12] The only cloud on the horizon was some concern about whether the team would be able to serve beer the following season.[13]

The long-term picture was less sanguine. Baseball did not have extensive roots in St. Catharines and the team never really became a fixture in the city. It was always one of the largest cities in the league, but attendance was never stellar. At the beginning, there was some community fund-raising but over the longer term business support for the team never developed. The city council took its cues from the local citizenry and businesspeople, and provided limited financial support, usually somewhat grudgingly.[14] The new "stadium"—which amounted to improved spectator seating—was completed ahead of schedule and over the years the city came up with funds for improved concession stands, washrooms, and clubhouses, but when larger amounts, particularly requests for funds for a new stadium, were on the table, the council always drew the line.

In 1994, the team was provisionally sold to a group with plans to move it to London, Ontario. The league did not approve the move because of the additional travel that would entail, so the team stayed put, but an important signal had been sent.[15]

In 1995, the Toronto Blue Jays sold the team to a group of local businesspeople for a reported $1 million. The group included marketing guru Terry O'Malley, who planned to use his acumen to turn the team's fortunes around.[16] One of the marketing innovations was to rename the team the Stompers. St. Catharines is in grape and wine country and the logo was a stylized figure who was enjoying stomping grapes.

With John Belford as the team's general manager, attendance jumped over 60%, from 31,000 in 1994 to 51,000 in 1995, and operating losses were reduced. There was a brief period of rejuvenation, but over the longer term this did not turn around the lack of interest in baseball in the city.

In 1998, the group presented a plan to city council for construction of a new stadium on an unused parcel of land in the downtown area. A member of the group felt that they were "virtually laughed out of the room."[17]

Local residents had shown a limited interest in the team. The owners were making a very large financial ask to occupy a parcel of prime land to build a baseball diamond that would be used 10 weeks of the year. This proposal was never considered seriously. (The land was later used for a multi-use spectator facility which is home to the Niagara Ice Dogs minor hockey team and has seen a succession of minor-league basketball teams pass through.)

Alas, even this group could not increase interest in the team and suffered losses each year of operation. Finally, in 1999 the owners received an offer which was reportedly in the $2–3 million range from a group that wanted to move the team to the New York City area.[18] Doubling or tripling their money in four years on an investment that had never yielded an operating profit was more than they could resist. The next season, the Queens Kings became a reality.

After 13 years, the team left St. Catharines with more of a whimper than a bang. There were a few regular attendees who lamented the demise of local professional baseball, and local sportswriters were predictably outraged.[19] But the Stompers had never built a significant base among the general populace. There was little controversy or outcry about the team leaving; many local residents were no more aware of the demise of the team than they had been of its birth.

The remaining evidence of the existence of the minor-league team is a stadium on which minimal money had been spent to make minimal improvements. It is a reasonably good community ballpark which is currently the home of the Brock University Badgers baseball team and several local recreational leagues.

HAMILTON REDBIRDS (1988–92)

Hamilton was the only one of the three cities that had previously had a professional baseball team. Canadian baseball historian Bill Humber refers to Hamilton as "one of baseball's first strongholds in Ontario."[20] It was a member of the International League in 1886–90.[21] It was also a charter member of the PONY League in 1939. PONY League stood for Pennsylvania-Ontario-New York; it became the New York-Pennsylvania League in the 1950s when Hamilton dropped out.[22] Over the years, Hamilton had been the home of several professional baseball teams.[23]

The Hamilton Redbirds franchise was owned by Jack Tracz, who has been described, somewhat affectionately, as an "old-style baseball hack."[24] He embodied an emerging trend of minor-league team owners who wanted to make money, but were also attracted by the romantic dream of being involved in professional baseball. Growing up in upstate New York, he had been a St. Louis Cardinals fan, so he relished the idea of owning a farm team of his beloved Cardinals. At the same time, he was working to have a minor-league team in the Tampa-St. Petersburg area so that a major-league team moving to that area would have to pay him to liquidate his territorial rights.[25]

Tracz was happy to move his franchise from Erie, Pennsylvania, to Hamilton because of the poor playing field and clubhouse in Erie.[26] In Hamilton, the team would be playing at Bernie Arbour Memorial Stadium in Mohawk Sports Park. This was a nice stadium which had long been used by the Hamilton Cardinals of the Intercounty Baseball League. It was upgraded for use by the Redbirds to a seating capacity of 2,700, portable clubhouse buildings were added, better lights were installed, and a paved parking area for 400 additional cars was built.[27] However, its location in the southeast section of the city was not strategic to attract large numbers of spectators. The two major highways that now encircle this area had not been built at this time.

With a population of just over 300,000 in 1986, Hamilton was by far the largest city in the New York-Penn League.[28] It became clear fairly soon that this was likely what attracted Tracz because he wanted to establish a class A team in Hamilton to be positioned to obtain one of the expansion franchises which would soon be awarded by the class AA Eastern League.[29]

The Redbirds played their first home game on June 16, 1988, in front of an apparent over-capacity crowd of 3,271 who braved a chilly night.[30] The way the game was described in the local press was a reminder of the difference between a relatively large city and the two smaller cities which are a part of this paper. The opening game in Hamilton was marked by four skydivers. Newspaper accounts do not mention any official opening ceremonies attended by civic dignitaries. Stories on the baseball team never made it beyond the sports pages to the front page of the newspaper as they did in the smaller cities in Niagara. Even in the sports pages, the training camp of the Tiger-Cats football team drew more ink than the Redbirds.

In early 1991, Tracz sold the team to a group led by Rob Hilliard.[31] Hilliard was the same type of entrepreneur-romantic dreamer as Tracz. The new owner made a speech thanking his mother, his wife, and his children for understanding "a big kid [who wanted to] realize his childhood dream." His father had signed a contract with the Phillies in 1941, but did his duty by enlisting after Pearl Harbor and never realized his dream.[32]

Hilliard made it clear from the outset that his plan was to use this team as leverage to secure an expansion franchise in the Eastern League, and he also made it clear that he would need a better stadium to accomplish this.[33]

The Centre for Canadian Baseball Research holds in its collection a manuscript titled "Double Vision: Let's See Double A Baseball in Hamilton" (dated January 9, 1991) that provides an assessment of various Hamilton locations in comparison to the standards set out for a AA stadium. It also contains an assessment, prepared by a local university professor, of the economic impact of a AA team, and numerous letters of support from local groups. The provenance of the document is unclear, but it bears the Hamilton Redbirds logo on the title page. It is also unclear how this document was used, but it seems that someone cared enough about this to spend a significant amount of money to develop this document.

The ownership group recruited former Ontario politician and well-known baseball fan, Larry Grossman, to take the lead. There were a head-spinning number of different proposals for a stadium ranging in cost—$8 million[34]/$12 million[35]/$16–18 million[36]—to a stadium to be constructed by a private developer if he was given land by the city.

These proposals need to be set in context. The relative newcomer baseball franchise was making a multi-million dollar ask at a time when the city council had just turned down a request for $300,000 from the city's long-time cherished football team, which was threatening to leave.[37] The baseball group's credibility was also not enhanced by the constantly-changing stadium plans.

Mayor Bob Morrow and members of the council's Parks and Recreation Committee were generally sympathetic to the team's proposals, but the full council seemed to have no appetite to spend millions of dollars on a facility for a new team when the existing team had not attracted the interest of large numbers of fans.

The 1992 season was a good one for the Redbirds. Their record of 56-20 was one of the best in professional baseball, and put them into the playoffs.[38,39] To their surprise, they lost the first sudden-death game to the wild-card team and were eliminated.[40] Their season ended in sadness on September 4, 1992, but not many realized that this would be the team's last game in Hamilton.

At a reception on September 22, 1992, Mayor Morrow was discussing sports highlights in the city and referred to the Redbirds as leaders in the city moving forward. Immediately after the reception, the team owner informed Mayor Morrow that the team would be moving to Glens Falls, New York, for the 1993 season.[41]

Bernie Arbour Memorial Stadium is still there in Mohawk Sports Park, serving as the home of Hamilton's entry in the Intercounty Baseball League.

WELLAND PIRATES (1989–94)

The City of Welland finished second in the fight to land the Blue Jays' short-season A franchise. This whetted the city's appetite to search for another NY-P franchise. Its goal was to increase the entertainment value available to local residents as well as to increase the number of baseball and softball diamonds that were available for recreational use.

George Marshall, the city councillor who was chair of the council's Parks and Recreation Committee, remembers preliminary discussions with a number of interested franchises, but eventually the courting became serious with Dr. Eric Margenau and Jay Acton, the principal owners of United Baseball.[42] This group also owned the South Bend, Indiana, franchise in the Midwest League and was in the process of acquiring a franchise in the Carolina League.[43] United Baseball exemplified the same ownership approach mentioned above in Hamilton. The purpose was to make money from the resurgence of interest in minor-league baseball while also allowing grown men to pursue their boyhood dreams of being involved in professional baseball. If you weren't good enough to play, but had a few million dollars to invest, you could still live the dream.

United Baseball had operated a franchise in Watertown, New York, for three years, but had decided to move the franchise because of poor attendance and a lack of community support demonstrated by the refusal to upgrade the existing stadium.[44] United was excited to move to Welland because it was a larger city supposedly with a baseball tradition, and the city had demonstrated a willingness to invest in a new stadium.[45]

The Welland Sports Complex was a brand new facility which included the stadium built for the team, two additional diamonds built for recreational use, and a large parking area. It was built in the north end of the city to satisfy local residents who had been complaining about a lack of recreational venues.

There was some local hyperbole about it being "the finest facility in the province next to the SkyDome" in Toronto and being the best facility in the minor leagues.[46] The truth was that this was a new, good facility by Class A standards. It accommodated more than 2,500 patrons in a concrete grandstand with a nice concourse hosting concession stands.[47] The large parking lot easily accommodated all patrons. It was clearly the nicest of the four stadiums in the area.

It also came with a total price tag in excess of $3 million.[48] However, Marshall remembers the stadium being a fairly easy sell to the council for several reasons. The economy was weak and very little construction was taking place; this facility would provide construction jobs and be a stimulus to the local economy. There was general agreement that the city needed additional sports facilities, particularly in this area. There was considerable local support from sports associations and the local business improvement area.

One of the major selling points was that the $3 million total cost of the complex was covered in part by grants from the federal and provincial governments, and donations of land and cash. Marshall estimates the net cost to the city at less than $500,000. In exchange, the city obtained a new recreational facility, which was badly needed in the north end, and city services extended to an area of the city that eventually led to a significant housing development, which served as an anchor for further development. This followed a model used by Harrisburg, Pennsylvania, when it built a stadium which served as a catalyst to attract people to a previously under-used area of the city.[49]

The complex was located near a busy intersection between a major highway serving the Niagara area and a major street providing entrance to the city. The sports complex was touted as the driver that had stimulated the expansion of an existing hotel and the construction of a new hotel.[50] Honestly, it was obvious that this area of the city was ripe for development with or without the baseball stadium, but the new stadium certainly didn't hurt.

The city had the foresight to design the stadium as a multi-purpose facility. It has a large moveable stage and an oversize kitchen to accommodate various civic activities in addition to baseball.[51]

When the Welland Pirates played their home opener on June 17, 1989, everything was in place and ready to go—except the grass. The structural part of the stadium had been completed, but a very rainy spring had prevented the installation of sod on the field[52]. For the first month, the team had to play at a somewhat upgraded Burgar Park.[53] The team played its home opener at Burgar Park with all the usual dignitaries in attendance. The result was a 9–3 win over the Niagara Falls Rapids. The opening-day crowd of 613 was disappointing, but this was attributed to the temporary venue and the cloudy weather.[54] The team played its first game at the Welland Sports Complex on July 17, 1989. It was an exciting event which the home team won by a score of 5–1 before 3,162 fans.[55]

Though the Welland Pirates would be the city's first professional sports franchise, the city does have a strong baseball tradition.[56,57] However, there was an attempt to educate local residents about baseball including providing the information that the Pirates' parent team was located in Pittsburg [sic].[58]

The relationship started out well with all sorts of kind words from both team management and the city. However, the relationship did not blossom well over the years. Between 1989 and 1993, the Pirates never had a winning season. Fans responded by staying away. In every year after the first, attendance for the season was in the bottom third in the league.[59]

By the beginning of the 1994 season everyone could see where this relationship was headed. The team's five-year lease on the stadium expired at the end of the season. Even before the first hopeful pitch of the new season was thrown, the rumor was spreading that the team would be moving for next season into a brand new $8 million stadium in Erie, Pennsylvania.[60]

The rumor was confirmed at the New York-Penn League meeting shortly after the end of the season.[61] All that remained were parting shots on both sides. The team owner opined that Welland was not a good baseball town and likely never would be. The mayor of Welland and others countered that the owners had delivered a sub-standard product in spite of city efforts to provide an excellent place to play.[62]

The situation of Erie, Pennsylvania, reveals a great deal about what minor-league baseball had become in

the 1990s. Erie lost its NY-P franchise to Hamilton in 1988, in part, because of the quality of its stadium. Therefore, it set about building a new state-of-the-art facility, which attracted the Welland franchise in 1994. A perfect illustration of the musical chairs that baseball had become.

The demise of the Welland Pirates was similar to the story in the other two cities, with one significant difference: the stadium. The city was able to leverage federal, provincial, and private funds to construct a sports complex which included a high-quality multi-purpose stadium and two recreational diamonds at a limited cost to the city. After the demise of professional baseball in Welland, the stadium continues to be home to baseball teams such as the Welland Jackfish of the Intercounty League, as well as a number of civic activities.

CONCLUSION

The saga of these few years says something about both team owners and the host cities with which they have a symbiotic, but sometimes troubled, relationship. City councillors and cynical residents see franchise owners as trying to sell empty dreams, with a clear intention to pass through town, bilking the local yokels and moving on to the next town, accumulating millions as they move around. The story told in this paper would suggest this characterization gives the owners way too much credit.

A better characterization of the owners in this paper would see them as vagabond carpetbaggers wandering from town to town attempting to peddle their wares with no understanding of their market. In St. Catharines, owners paid a significant amount for a franchise that had always had weak attendance and

In 1995, St. Catharines rebranded their team as the Stompers, a nod to the area's wine-making.

89

little local support. They did some small marketing fixes, and then made a major ask of a council that had always only grudgingly parted with small amounts of money, and were surprised when they were unsuccessful.

The story in Hamilton is similar. The owners took their baseball team into a football and hockey town and ultimately made a pitch for a larger amount of money than the council had just refused to give the city's cherished football team. Again, no success.

The Welland story was a bit different. There, the city gave the owners exactly what they wanted in the form of a good stadium in a good location. The owners then made a lackluster marketing effort to sell an inferior product and blamed the local residents for not buying their product.

The owners in this story seemed to be like little boys with romantic dreams who had too much money and time on their hands, but no clear plan. Their only salvation was the fact that despite these franchises never turning a profit, as they moved around the country they continued to increase in value whenever they were sold. Maybe there was a method in these people's madness, but it is a rather unintuitive way of making money.

The other part of this symbiotic relationship was host cities that seemed willing to accept, with more or less enthusiasm, the wares these vagabonds were peddling.

In an environment where cities would fight desperately for the right to host a professional baseball team, teams fell into the laps of these three semi-interested cities. None of these cities had a strategic plan with regard to professional sport that involved minor-league baseball. To the extent that any of them considered professional sport at all, their dreams were focused on hockey.

Welland was the only city that fit the opportunity into a broader plan for development of an area of the city. In Hamilton and St. Catharines, the stadiums were located in outlying areas with no real plans for development. There was discussion of a downtown stadium in St. Catharines, but it was deemed unworkable, and there was no real effort to make it work or to find a location that would benefit the city.

This kind of laconic involvement was acceptable in the early years of this story, when minor-league baseball was coming back from its collapse in the 1950s and franchises sometimes changed hands for nominal amounts.[63] However, as franchises increased in value during this renaissance, parent teams or romantic investors could no longer hold onto teams on a whim. The local group that purchased the Baby Jays

from the parent club for $1 million was confronted with the opportunity to sell the team for double that amount five years later. How could they turn down an offer like that for a team that had never turned a profit? In Welland the team was not sold, but the owner was given the opportunity to move from a city where attendance was relatively flat to a city which had just built a shiny new stadium. Teams that now had a value measured in the millions needed to turn a profit, and teams located in Niagara were not going to do that.

The story of these three cities indicates that Welland benefited because it was systematic in its approach and had a clear and well-considered goal. It was realistic in understanding that a minor-league team would provide enjoyment and a potential source of pride to local residents; it would not provide a major economic stimulus. Fans from all over North America flock to the shrines of Wrigley Field or Chavez Ravine. Fewer fans travel any distance to see minor-league baseball.

"If you build it, they will come" is a cute maxim inspired by a charming movie, but do not invest hard cash in it. Consider carefully the kind of stadium you want to build. In Welland's case it wanted to build additional fields for recreational use anyway. It took advantage of a minor-league team to leverage funds and land from other levels of government and local businesses to build a sports complex that included two baseball fields for recreational use and a multi-purpose stadium suitable for a variety of civic events. When the team predictably left after five years, the city had a nice multi-use facility, built with minimal local funds.

It is difficult to see any plan in the actions of Hamilton and St. Catharines. Both cities spent relatively small amounts of money and ended up with marginally better baseball facilities paid for in part by the departed professional team. No attempt was made to think in broader economic development terms.

The sometimes uneasy relationship between a minor-league baseball team and its host city can be very advantageous. Cities frequently feel that they are taken advantage of by team owners, and this clearly has happened. However, this paper indicates that there can be situations in which the host city comes out very well. It is a matter of the host city having a plan that it can use to its advantage. ∎

Acknowledgments

The author would like to thank the two anonymous reviewers for this Journal, as well as John Belford, Doug Herod, Bill Humber, Joseph Kushner, George Marshall, Andrew North, and Elena North for their assistance in the preparation of the paper. All errors and omissions are the responsibility of the author.

Notes

1. https://www.milb.com/new-york-penn/history (Accessed, September 28, 2019).
2. Baseball Reference, https://www.baseball-reference.com/bullpen/New_York-Penn_League(Accessed, September 11, 2019).
3. Robert Obojski indicates that St. Catherines (sic) had a professional team in the Ontario League which began play some time in 1930 and disbanded on July 22,1930. *Bush League: A History of Minor League Baseball* (New York: Macmillan Publishing Co., Inc., 1975), 376.) The Brewers are also mentioned in: Humber, *Diamonds of the North*, 208. It does not seem like too much of a stretch to exclude this short foray from consideration.
4. Steve Milton, "A League with Pizzaz," *Hamilton Spectator*, June 14, 1988, F2; "A Look Back at Minor League Happenings," *Hamilton Spectator*, June 14, 1988, F3; Humber, *Diamonds of the North*, 207; Humber, *Cheering for the Home Team*, 28; Obojski, Bush League, 377.
5. Mike Hamilton, "Promise of New Stadium Enticed Jays to Locate its Farm Team Here," *The Standard* (St. Catharines, Ontario), June 28, 1986, 7A; Mike Hamilton, "Plan for Baseball Stadium Unveiled," *The Standard*, June 4, 1986.
6. "Park Lights Go up Today," *The Standard*, June 2, 1986, 25.
7. Arthur T. Johnson, *Minor League Baseball and Local Economic Development* (Urbana: University of Illinois Press, 1995).
8. Mike Hamilton, "Baby Jays Make Successful Debut," *The Standard*, June 17, 1986, 21.
9. Peter Conradi, "Baby Jays Hatch a Win," *The Standard*, June 18, 1986, 1; Mike Hamilton, "Blue Jays Set for Season Opener," *The Standard*, June 16, 1986, 21.
10. Mike Hamilton, "Patience Needed to Baby Jays," *The Standard*, June 7, 1986, 29; Jack Gatecliff, "Every Blue Jay in St. Catharines Has a Shot at Majors, *The Standard*, June 10, 1986, 21.
11. *The Standard*, June 28, 1986.
12. Jack Gatecliff, "Baby Jays Successful First Season," *The Standard*, July 26, 1986, 27.
13. Doug Herod, "City Hall Cool to Beer at Ballpark, *The Standard*, July 8, 1986, 9.
14. Abigail Vint, "Councillors Anxious to Go to Bat for Stompers, *The Standard*, June 7, 1999, A3.
15. Bill Potrecz, "Stompers' Final At Bat?" *The Standard*, June 19, 1999, A1.
16. Bill Potrecz, "The Stompers Are Out at Home," *The Standard*, June 2, 1999, A1, A7.
17. Peter Conradi, "City Fiddles while Stompers Burn, *The Standard*, June 5, 1999, B1, B2.
18. Bill Potrecz, "The Stompers Are Out at Home," *The Standard*, June 2, 1999, A1,A7.
19. Editorial, "City Shouldn't Just Let Team Go Stomping Off," *The Standard*, June 5, 1999, A12; Peter Conradi, "Council Blew Chance to Save Stompers," *The Standard*, June 12, 1999, B1, B3.
20. Humber, *Diamonds of the North*, 24.
21. Obojski, *Bush League*, 95, 97, and 100.
22. https://www.milb.com/new-york-penn/history (Accessed, September 28, 2019).
23. Steve Milton, "A League with Pizzaz," *Hamilton Spectator*, June 14, 1988, F2.
24. Bob Andelman, *Stadium for Rent: Tampa Bay's Quest for Major League Baseball* (McFarland and Company, Inc., Publishers, 1993).
25. Andelman, *Stadium for Rent*.
26. Larry Moko, "The Redbirds Come Home to Roost," *Hamilton Spectator*, June 13, 1988, B2.
27. Larry Moko, "The Redbirds Come Home to Roost," *Hamilton Spectator*, June 13, 1988, B2.
28. https://en.wikipedia.org/wiki/List_of_largest_Canadian_cities_by_census#1986 (Accessed, October 25, 2019).
29. Steve Milton, "Franchise Fever Class AA in Birds Plan," *Hamilton Spectator*, March 4, 1989.
30. Larry Moko, "It Was the Blue Jays in a Walk," *Hamilton Spectator*, June 17, 1988, B2.
31. "Redbirds Sale OKed by League," *Hamilton Spectator*, January 23, 1991.

32. Larry Moko, "Redbirds' Dream: Affordable, Outdoor Entertainment," *Hamilton Spectator*, February 21, 1991.
33. "Redbirds Make Pitch for AA Ball," *Hamilton Spectator*, January 23, 1991.
34. Jim Poling, "Park Pitch for $588,000 on Mark …if AA Comes, *Hamilton Spectator*, August 26, 1992, B1.
35. "Committee Backs Proposal for $12m AA Ball, *Hamilton Spectator*, January 22, 1991.
36. Jim Poling, "Stadium Study Strikes Out with Morrow," *Hamilton Spectator*, August 20, 1992, B1.
37. Ken Peters, "Big Bucks for Baseball," *Hamilton Spectator*, June 24, 1992, A1,A2; Jeff Dickins and Jim Poling, "No Cash No Cats!," *Hamilton Spectator*, June 11, 1992, A1.
38. Only the Elizabethton Twins had a better winning average in 1992 (.742, 49–17, in the Appalachian League).
39. https://www.baseball-reference.com/register/league.cgi?id=408b8984 (Accessed, November 24, 2019).
40. Larry Moko, "Shocker," *Hamilton Spectator*, September 5, 1992, E1.
41. Larry Moko, "Redbirds Leave Town Blame City for Impasse on Stadium," *Hamilton Spectator*, September 23, 1992.
42. Interview, October 10, 2019.
43. Wayne Redshaw, "Welland Pirates—A New Baseball Era," *The Tribune* (Welland, Ontario), June 13, 1989, 2A; "New Partner," *The Tribune*, June 13, 1989, 8A.
44. Wayne Redshaw, "Pirates Ran out of Shots," *The Tribune*, June 13, 1989, 3A.
45. "Complex One Reason," *The Tribune*, June 13, 1989, 8A.
46. Charles Muggeridge, "Details Are Finalized for Sports Complex Opening," *The Tribune*, June 13, 1989, 1.
47. Wayne Creighton, "Sports Complex Can Be Used," *The Tribune*, June 13, 1989, 11A.
48. Wayne Redshaw, "Welland Pirates—A New Baseball Era," *The Tribune*, June 13, 1989, 2A.
49. Johnson, *Minor League Baseball and Local Economic Development*, Chapter 10.
50. "Niagara Street Spinoffs Starting—Brunner," *The Tribune*, June 21, 1989, 3.
51. Wayne Crichton, "Sports Complex Can Be Used," *The Tribune*, June 13, 1989, 11A.
52. "Field is too Wet to Lay down Sod," *The Tribune*, June 8, 1989, 1.
53. Ken Avey and Charles Muggeridge, "Batter Up at Burgar Park—For Now," *The Tribune*, June 9, 1989, 1.
54. "Pirate Opener," *The Tribune*, June 19, 1989, 5C; Wayne Redshaw, "Where Were the Fans for the Home Opener?" *The Tribune*, June 19, 1989, 14C.
55. Ken Avey, "New Stadium to Open July 17," *The Tribune*, July 11, 1989, 3; John Sherwin, "Baseball Bosses Impressed," *The Tribune*, June 18, 1989, 1; Ken Avey, "At Long Last…" *The Tribune*, July 18, 1989, 3.
56. Wayne Redshaw, "Welland Pirates—A New Baseball Era," *The Tribune*, June 13, 1989, 2A.
57. George "Udy" Blazetich, "A Welland Baseball Flashback," *The Tribune*, June 13, 1989, 17A, 18A.
58. Ken Avey and Charles Muggerridge, "Batter Up at Burgar Park—For Now," *The Tribune*, June 9, 1989, 1.
59. Bill Sawchuck, "Pirates' Future in Limbo until Season is Over," *The Tribune*, June 21, 1994, A-1.
60. Bill Sawchuck, "Pirates' Fans Say Next Year Will Take Care of Itself," *The Tribune*, June 2, 1994, B-5; Bill Sawchuck, "Pirates' Future in Limbo until Season is Over," *The Tribune*, June 21, 1994, A-1; Bill Sawchuck, "Pirates Moving to Erie, Pa." *The Tribune*, September 16, 1994, A-1.
61. Bill Sawchuck, "Pirates' Move Stirs Little Discussion at League Meeting," *The Tribune*, September 19, 1994, B-3.
62. Bill Sawchuck, "Pirates Moving to Erie, Pa." *The Tribune*, September 16, 1994, A-1: Joop Gerritsma, "Club Let Fans Down," *The Tribune*, September 21, 1994, B-1.
63. This history is told well in: Obojski, *Bush League*, chapters 1 and 2; Harold Seymour, *Baseball: The Golden Age* (New York: Oxford University Press, 1971), chapter 20; Neil J. Sullivan, *The Minors* (New York: St. Martin's Press, 1990), chapters 12–14.

Optimizing Outfield Positioning

Creating an Area-Based Alignment Using Outfielder Ability and Hitter Tendencies

Columbia University Society for Baseball Research

Anthony Montes, Anthony Argenziano, Brian O'Sullivan, Charles Orlinsky, Drew Posner, Matthew Chagares, Anna Flieder, Bennett Bookstein, Jack Chernow, and Teddy Brodsky

The shift has been a part of baseball for as long as the sport has existed. From a crisp "give me two steps back" when the cleanup hitter steps up, to analytically placing defenders in the ideal spots, defensive configurations have drastically changed over the years. As baseball has evolved toward the creative, data-driven game seen today, managers have attempted to leverage advanced batting statistics to position players to give their teams the best chances of getting outs. Defensive statistics that account for a specific fielder's tendencies have fallen behind these complex hitting statistics. Shouldn't a team consider the individual abilities of their outfielders—eg. UZR (Ultimate Zone Rating), Sprint Speed, etc.—as well as those of opposing hitters in determining how defensive alignment looks?

Although teams have had success positioning infielders to minimize the hit probability of the opponent, hitters have also continued to adapt against these tactics. There will soon be a pressing need for defenses to advance said tactics. It is incumbent upon the next generation of managers and GMs—those who have grown into a game that has welcomed the use of advanced analytics—to continue to push the game forward defensively. The next frontier for defensive metrics appears to involve teams positioning their outfielders based on personnel.

Such placement will surely have great ramifications for many decisions. Maximizing defensive value may be dependent on moving players to all parts of the field, which could result in a complete overhaul of the player development process. Organizations may be incentivized to change players' positions, alter training programs, overhaul their draft, free agent, and scouting strategy, and ask players to contribute in unorthodox ways. In extreme cases players may begin to find that their value is maximized at a position that they've never played. Optimization of outfield positioning will also help teams evaluate defensive production and compensate players more accurately, properly weighing important skills against others.

Offense is more of a priority in the valuation of players on the open market than defense (fielding, exclusive of pitching). Teams have created a variety of ways to evaluate players based on their offensive contributions, using statistics such as wRC + . In 2017, FiveThirtyEight's Rob Arthur examined the relative price teams paid in free agency for offensive and defensive contributions. Arthur's findings suggest that teams attribute only 28% of a player's total value to his fielding—teams paid an average of $84,000 per defensive run compared to $215,000 per offensive run.[1] By finding a more efficient way to place outfielders to counter offensive production and maximize the abilities of defenders, teams could more accurately evaluate defense and reduce the premium placed on offense. The below study stands on the shoulders of excellent work contributed by the baseball analyst community over the last decade-plus. In his presentation to the 2019 SABR Analytics Conference, Brian Reiff developed a formal definition for outfield shifts as any configuration where three outfielders stand at least 110 combined feet from their average reference points.[2] In that same year, Mark Simon, in a piece for Bill James Online, documented an 89% increase in outfield shifts in 2018 compared to just two years prior, underscoring the need for further investigation of novel outfield alignment strategies.[3] Recent baseball analyses have also made tangible strides towards exploring and measuring the impacts of uniquely devised outfield alignments on team defense. In his 2013 Baseball Prospectus article, Russell Carleton considered the marginal effects of outfield performance if teams were to swap their corner outfielders with one another, determining that teams would save a handful of runs per season by placing the better of the two at each hitter's opposite field.[4] Reiff, in his same 2019 SABR presentation, expanded upon Carleton's work by using batted ball tendencies of hitters via Statcast data, rather than handedness alone, to analyze recent cases in outfielder realignments (such as those deployed against Joe Mauer). Finally, Carleton's 2017 analysis, also available on Baseball Prospectus, measured the degree to which outfielders overlap while chasing fly balls, determining that the greatest overlap generally occurs between two outfielders of disparate defensive abilities.[5]

Ultimately, fielding defense in baseball will look dramatically different in twenty years, perhaps even in five years. So how can teams do better, both before the game when constructing the team, and during the game when placing defenders on the field?

In an attempt to best answer these overarching questions, a major component of the study involved the development of a data tool, the Outfield Player Positioning Optimizer (OPPO). Constructed via a series of functions in R, OPPO takes as its inputs data on three outfielders and one hitter. Each outfielder is distinguished by his "Jump," extracted from Baseball Savant's Outfielder Jump leaderboard. More specifically OPPO uses "feet covered," the distance traveled by a given outfielder in the correct direction within three seconds of contact, as a proxy of his reaction, burst, and route efficiency.[6] Upon input, each outfielder is represented by a circle, with a movable center, and a radius equal to his feet-covered metric. Each hitter, on the other hand, is represented by his 2019 spray chart of balls hit to the outfield (using Baseball Savant's Statcast Search tool), in the form of coordinates superimposed onto the image of a generic baseball diamond.[7]

Using iterative looping techniques in the programming language, the model acts to maximize the number of balls in a particular hitter's spray chart that an outfield—represented by a set of three circles—covers. The model places the fastest outfielder among the three—denoted by the largest feet covered metric—onto the field first, maximizing the amount of balls that circle can cover alone. It then follows by placing the second fastest outfielder to maximize the previously unreached balls, and the same for the third. In practice, OPPO loosens the restrictions on where outfielders play relative to one another, while also challenging the conventional positioning of outfielders denoted on the lineup card as left, center, and right field.

Once performing this iterative maximization task, the model provides two main outputs—one numerical and one visual. Numerically, it provides the total balls covered by the set of three outfielders, which is then converted to a percentage of balls reached. Furthermore, it provides a graphical representation of the coordinates at which outfielders have been placed: the fastest outfielder is represented by a solid black circle, the intermediate by a dashed one, and the slowest

with a dotted circle. Each is also overlaid onto the spray chart of the hitter in question. These two main categories of output allow us to compare quantitatively the difference in outfields' performances with different sets of fielders against original positioning practices. The model also provides visual evidence as to how outfields ought to be spaced against different types of hitters when different outfielders are playing.

Placing outfielders using OPPO will produce results different from conventional placement. It is hypothesized that the fastest outfielder for each team will not be placed in his typical position (often center field), but instead at the location where the density of batted balls is greatest for a particular hitter. Furthermore, it is predicted that players with opposite-field power profiles will yield the greatest changes in defensive positioning compared to balanced hitters and pull hitters, because teams already repositioned more often against pull hitters than others.

It is hypothesized OPPO will impact the performance of individual outfielders. The area of a circle, as seen in its mechanics, involves a squared term: Area = $\pi \times r^2$. Replacing "r" in this formula with feet covered results in a circle that represents the total theoretically reachable space of an outfielder in three seconds in all directions.

Noting this simple yet crucial principle, it is now easy to see that a one-unit increase in feet covered has more than a one-square-foot effect in total area covered. For example, George Springer achieved an average of 34.0 feet covered after three seconds in 2019, and Starling Marte's measure was 35.0 feet.[8] Assuming uniform movements in all directions, as this study does, each player covers 3632 and 3848 square feet, respectively—a difference of 216 square feet. This is a non-trivial sum, the size of a large bedroom's worth of additional coverage by Marte. Therefore, it is predicted there will be an increasingly large positive effect of outfielders with marginally better feet covered, and increasingly large negative effects of those with marginally worse measures.

METHODS

For each experiment, the following assumptions have been made given the constraints and limitations of the study:

1. Circles are created by maximizing first touch—that is, the players are placed to get to each ball faster, which helps to both reduce the total bases and increase total outs.

2. OPPO does not discriminate based on outfield position—the model places players based on speed. This assumes a fielder's ability remains constant across each outfield position.[9]

3. Spray chart data are from Baseball Savant, and coordinate points are collected by stringers. Coordinates represent the point at which the ball is touched by an outfielder.

4. Circles are used with constant time of travel for each outfielder of three seconds from when the hitter makes contact. While Russell Carleton of Baseball Prospectus has shown that the average flyball remains in the air for 4.56 seconds, it was determined to be sufficient to use three seconds, as this duration is likely lower when accounting for hard-hit line drives and ground balls. Furthermore, 77 percent of balls in Carleton's aforementioned 2017 analysis were caught by outfielders, a stark deviation from the data used in this study, which records all balls to the outfield regardless of put-out status. Both tests ignore the reality that outfielders move at different rates and abilities in certain directions.

5. The stadium space, which was constructed by Bill Petti, is arbitrary in size and shape, and not representative of any particular stadium.[10] The OPPO model does not account for park factors nor variance in outfield areas across different stadiums.

6. Home runs are excluded from the data set as they are not categorized as balls-in-play.

7. Spray charts of hitters, the basis by which outfielders are positioned, are inherently retrospective and cannot be assumed to accurately predict a hitter's future spray chart.

8. All experiments assume that the outfielder has a "first-mover advantage"—hitters do not adjust, in this analysis, to the changes in outfield configuration.

9. Each event is treated as having occurred under equal conditions, rather than under specific in-game contexts including but not limited to inning, pitcher, pitch type, outs, injury, wind, and runners on base.

10. Hitters inputted as test subjects serve as representatives of different hitter archetypes (e.g. dead-pull lefty, all-fields righty). While no one hitter is representative of these groups, assigning representatives according to strict categorization criteria proved most feasible given the computational demands of each test.

11. For the purpose of these studies, arm accuracy and strength are disregarded. This does not reflect the importance of this particular skill in determining the quality of an outfielder's fielding.

12. The model disregards the effect of hitters compensating against defensive positioning by bunting, hitting to the opposite field, or otherwise trying to nullify the effects of strategic defensive positioning.

The order of this list does not reflect the relative importance of each assumption. The dataset includes all batted ball data from the 2019 regular season. Batted Ball data and Outfield Jump data were collected from Baseball Savant (specifically, using the Statcast Search tool to download custom datasets),[11] and summary data used to categorize hitters were compiled from Fangraphs.[12]

The following eighteen hitters were selected for both experiments: Adam Eaton, Freddie Freeman, Rafael Devers, Jeff McNeil, Max Kepler, Cody Bellinger, Alex Gordon, Michael Brantley, Juan Soto, Whit Merrifield, Tim Anderson, Miguel Cabrera, Paul DeJong, Eugenio Suarez, Pete Alonso, Starling Marte, Dansby Swanson, and Anthony Rendon. These hitters were selected to represent a right-handed and a left-handed hitter from each subgroup based on exit velocity and spray. Exit velocity is broken into the bottom third, middle third, and top third of the league in 2019. Spray is broken into heavy opposite field hitters, dead pull hitters, and average spray hitters which served as the control group. Those categorized in the opposite field group were amongst league leaders in Oppo% (a FanGraphs metric) in 2019, and hit at least 28% of total balls in-play to left, center, and right field. The criterion for dead pull hitters is that they pull the ball at least two times more frequently than they go to the opposite field. Average hitters, while still leaning slightly pull-heavy, fit into neither of the above categories as they use the middle of the field and the opposite field at an intermediate rate. Hitters selected and sub-groupings are represented in Table 1.

In order to test the effect of OPPO against straight-up outfield configuration, experiment one tested eighteen hitters against the worst, average, and best outfields based on their aggregate average feet covered. The Royals outfield of Whit Merrifield, Jorge Soler, and Alex Gordon was the worst. The Angels outfield was average, consisting of Mike Trout, Brian Goodwin, and Kole Calhoun. The best were Manuel Margot, Wil Myers, and Hunter Renfroe of the Padres.

Test one determined the difference in number of plays within reach for each individual hitter against an outfield playing with conventional positioning and an outfield aligned using OPPO. These two values were then compared. Results—represented in Table 2—were recorded as a percent difference of plays covered between the conventional outfield and OPPO-modified outfield for each hitter and team outfield, respectively.

In order to test the marginal effects of OPPO on individual performance, test two determined a baseline percentage of plays covered by inputting three clones of the Major League average outfielder—Ketel Marte—in terms of feet covered into OPPO against all eighteen hitters represented in Table 1. Then, one average outfielder—Marte again—was substituted for outfielders with the 100th, 75th, 25th, and 0th percentile feet covered from 2019—Kevin Kiermaier, Jason Heyward, Alex Gordon, and Melky Cabrera respectively—against

all eighteen hitters. Data were recorded as the percent change in balls covered between the control group and each experimental group in order to measure the impact of a substitution of outfielders with different ranges.

RESULTS
Experiment One

Table 2 contains values for the percentage point improvement in balls reached for each of three 2019 sample outfields—Royals, Angels, and Padres—against eighteen different hitters. In the chart, the hitters are classified first by their 2019 spray profile (extreme pull hitters, opposite field hitters, and slight pull types—the control group). Within those groups, hitters are then sorted by their 2019 exit velocities, where High denotes the 67th percentile and above, Medium the 34th to 66th percentile, and Low the 33rd percentile and below.

Table 1. Hitters selected sorted by exit velocity, tendency, and handedness

Data from 2019	Bottom ⅓ Exit Velo	Middle ⅓ Exit Velo	Top ⅓ Exit Velo
Dead Pull	L: Jeff McNeil	L: Max Kepler	L: Cody Bellinger
	R: Paul DeJong	R: Eugenio Suarez	R: Pete Alonso
Opposite/All Fields	L: Adam Eaton	L: Freddie Freeman	L: Rafael Devers
	R: Whit Merrifield	R: Tim Anderson	R: Miguel Cabrera
Slight Pull (Control)	L: Alex Gordon	L: Michael Brantley	L: Juan Soto
	R: Starling Marte	R: Dansby Swanson	R: Anthony Rendon

Table 2. Results of OPPO placing Royals, Angels, and Padres outfields against specific hitters. Hitters sorted by tendency, exit velocity, and handedness. Team outfields sorted in ascending order in regard to the aggregate jump statistic of all three-outfielders.

HITTER CLASSIFICATIONS			% INCREASE, PWREACH		
Spray Tendency	Exit Velocity	Batter (Handedness)	KC	LAA	SD
Dead Pull	**High**	Cody Bellinger (L)	5.0%	4.6%	5.9%•
		Pete Alonso (R)	3.4%	5.1%	2.8%
	Medium	Max Kepler (L)	8.4%*	11.9%**	12.4%**
		Eugenio Suarez (R)	1.1%	2.7%	5.5%
	Low	Jeff McNeil (L)	10%*	12.7%**	8.2%*
		Paul Dejong (R)	7.9%•	2.5%	3.5%
Opposite/All Fields	**High**	Rafael Devers (L)	2.0%	2.8%	2.4%
		Miguel Cabrera (R)	5.6%	5.2%	2.3%
	Medium	Freddie Freeman (L)	12.0%**	14.5%***	11.6%**
		Tim Anderson (R)	-1.0%	-1.5%	2.0%
	Low	Adam Eaton (L)	-0.8%	4.9%	-0.4%
		Whit Merrifield (R)	2.6%	1.3%	1.0%
Slight Pull (Control)	**High**	Juan Soto (L)	7.5%•	7.5%•	9.4%*
		Anthony Rendon (R)	6.5%•	2.8%	6.5%•
	Medium	Michael Brantley (L)	4.6%	3.8%	5.3%•
		Dansby Swanson (R)	8.9%*	8.9%*	9.9%*
	Low	Alex Gordon (L)	2.6%	2.1%	3.0%
		Starling Marte (R)	11.3%**	10.8%**	5.7%

To achieve the percentage-point improvement made by OPPO compared to traditional outfield placement, the difference in proportion of balls reached by each of these outfields was found by subtracting the proportion of balls reached of the conventional outfield from the proportion of balls reached using OPPO to align outfielders. Results are reflected in Table 2.

After computing these observed differences, significance tests were conducted to determine whether or not there was substantial improvement made by OPPO. In each, the null hypothesis was that OPPO would provide no significant increase in proportion of balls within reach, compared to the control configuration. The alternative hypothesis, however, was that OPPO significantly increased the proportion of balls reached. Following a one-sided difference in proportions test for each of the 54 computed differences, it was determined that 20 different hitter and outfield combinations—37% of cases—saw significant improvement using OPPO at the 90% confidence level or greater. Furthermore, 15 of these 20 saw significant improvement at the 95% confidence level or better. Significance is denoted in Table 2 using the following key: • (90%), * (95%), **(99%), and *** (99.9%).

The results above describe the extent to which outfields of varying abilities can improve the number of balls within reach, and how those potential improvements grow or diminish depending on the type or handedness of the hitter at bat. Most notably, the data show that if one team can significantly neutralize a particular hitter, then it is likely that the other teams can also. As seen in Table 2, 15 (75%) of the statistically significant improvements are against five particular hitters—Dansby Swanson, Juan Soto, Freddie Freeman, Jeff McNeil, and Max Kepler. This means that, for each of these hitters, all three tested outfields saw statistically significant positive gains from repositioning using OPPO.

While there are not many patterns to indicate this custom alignment has varying degrees of effectiveness across different hitter classifications, the strongest example to the contrary is the relatively different impact OPPO has on pull and opposite field hitters. The opposite-field group, located in the middle of Table 2, is almost uniformly unaffected by the use of OPPO. Other than Freddie Freeman, whom outfielders cover significantly more balls against with the use of OPPO and who will be discussed further later, no significant improvements were made in the opposite-field group. In fact, OPPO yielded its only two negative effects against members of this group—Adam Eaton and Tim Anderson—albeit statistically insignificant. Via the results, it can be concluded that the opposite-field group is more difficult to successfully reposition against than the control and dead-pull groups. This does not support the original hypothesis, which asserted that pull hitters, due to already increased levels of reshuffling of opposing outfielders, would yield a lower percentage point increase than opposite-field hitters after implementing OPPO.

Using the results presented in Table 2, specific figures were extracted from OPPO's output to provide visual evidence for the varying degrees of OPPO's effects against hitters of different types and across outfields of varying range ability. In examining the differences between the Angels' and Padres' suggested positioning against Mets All-Star Jeff McNeil—which provided 12.7% and 8.2% improvement, respectively—the data showed that the OPPO suggested configurations end up looking similar to one another. Figure 1 and Figure 2 show the relative similarity of OPPO-modified alignment against McNeil for both the Angels and Padres.

As can be easily seen, there is an interesting deviation from the norm brought forth by OPPO's suggested alignment. Manuel Margot and Brian Goodwin, both team leaders in feet covered (and thus the largest circles), are situated in right field against the dead-pull oriented McNeil. Neither Margot nor Goodwin typically play right field—they usually play center and left, respectively. This observation, coupled with the incredibly large magnitude of improvement, shows that teams would be best served placing their outfielder with the best jump in right field against left-handed pull hitters like McNeil.

Furthermore, the fact that OPPO, while improving the reach of both outfields by a significant percentage, has improved the Angels more than the Padres, shows that OPPO appears to help the median outfield relatively more than it does the fastest outfield against McNeil. This conclusion is further supported by just how equal these two outfield configurations look, proving that the circles of the Padres were reaching relatively more balls than the Angels.

The examination across team outfields against McNeil shows the prowess of the OPPO model in improving the range against a hitter regardless of the speed of the outfielders. There are instances in which OPPO produces decidedly disparate levels of improvement across players of very similar profiles. The differences in spray between Anderson and Freeman raise the problem that OPPO is extremely successful against Freeman (12%, 14.5%, 11.6%), but almost categorically worse against Anderson (-1%, -1.5%, 2%).

Using the Angels outfield as constant, it appears that each of the three circles is located in different locations against both hitters. Most notably, the fastest player is again placed in a corner—not surprisingly in left field against Freeman, as he is categorized as an opposite field hitter.

Regarding the differences in efficacy, it is puzzling at first. However, a better look at the spray charts shows a potential justification for this difference. Figure 3—Freeman—shows a higher concentration of balls hit in what would traditionally be considered in the "gaps," while Anderson does not have a high concentration of his balls in any particular portion of the field. It thus

stands to reason that, for Anderson, the placement of outfielders in a tight bunch in right field is the most beneficial positioning that OPPO can provide, as the result will likely be slightly better than playing in conventional positions. Therefore, OPPO's ability to move circles into gaps without regard for these traditional configurations does better to neutralize Freeman, who can no longer utilize the deep gaps to hit balls out of the reach of outfielders. Furthermore, while Freeman qualifies for the opposite-field group—based on criteria noted in Methods—he has a stronger pull tendency than

Figure 1. Jeff McNeil 2019 batted-ball data (n = 220) are plotted against the Los Angeles Angels outfield repositioned by OPPO. Outfielders depicted: Brian Goodwin (solid black circle), Kole Calhoun (dashied circle), Mike Trout (dotted circle).

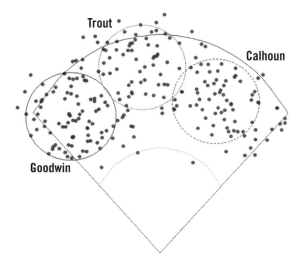

Figure 2. Jeff McNeil 2019 batted-ball data (n = 220) are plotted against the San Diego Padres outfield repositioned by OPPO. Outfielders depicted: Manuel Margot (solid black circle), Hunter Renfroe (dashed circle), Wil Myers (dotted circle).

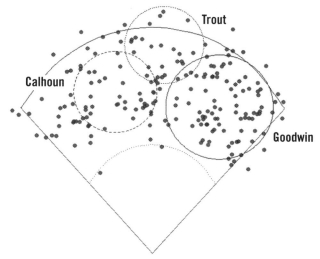

Figure 3. Freddie Freeman 2019 batted-ball data (n = 242) are plotted against the Los Angeles Angels outfield repositioned by OPPO. Outfielders depicted: Brian Goodwin (solid black circle), Kole Calhoun (dashed circle), Mike Trout (dotted circle).

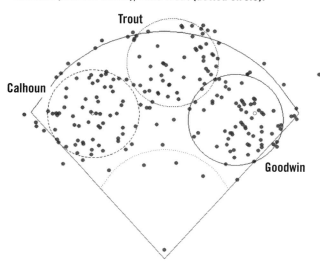

Figure 4. Tim Anderson 2019 batted-ball data (n = 201) are plotted against the Los Angeles Angels outfield repositioned by OPPO. Outfielders depicted: Brian Goodwin (solid black circle), Kole Calhoun (dashed circle), Mike Trout (dotted circle).

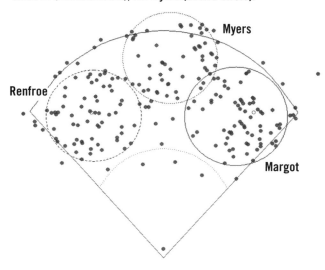

all other members of his group. This further validates OPPO's relative strength against pull profiles versus opposite-field profiles.

In some cases there were significant disparities among hitters with seemingly similar profiles in the extreme spray groups. The control spray group proved no different, in that players who lean slightly pull but hit more to the opposite field than dead-pull hitters, also yielded a disparity in balls covered after the use of OPPO. Unlike the two experimental groups, the control group found little disparity in the placement of outfielders between two similar hitters by tendency—Starling Marte and Anthony Rendon.

Again holding the Angels outfield constant, outfielders appear to be placed fairly similar to conventional outfield alignment, with the exception of the positions at which each outfielder plays. Notably, the fastest outfielder, Brian Goodwin, is in right field, Kole Calhoun is in center field, and Mike Trout is in left field against Marte—contrary to expectation. Most strikingly, the left fielder for Marte is playing closer to the foul line than a conventional left fielder would play. Rendon was expected to have a similar alignment and increase in percentage of balls within reach due to the similarity in tendency. But outfielders are placed in different portions of the field for Rendon in comparison to Marte. Goodwin, the fastest player, is placed in center field. Calhoun is placed in right field and Trout is placed in left. Most notably, both Trout and Calhoun are placed deep into the corner of the outfield.

As expected, OPPO generated similar placement for the Angels outfield for both Marte and Rendon. But OPPO produced a ten-percentage point increase in balls within reach for Marte and only a two-percentage point increase in balls within reach for Rendon. Similar to the experimental groups, in the control group there was significant variation between players despite similarity in tendencies. The discrepancy in percentage point increase in balls within reach can be explained by the disparity in exit velocity and significant clusters of plays evenly distributed throughout the outfield for Marte and lack of such clusters for Rendon.

Finally, from an exclusively visual standpoint, no OPPO realignment looks more unusual than that of the Royals against Dansby Swanson. Swanson, a very average player in terms of his pull tendency and exit velocity, is placed in the control group. Against the Royals outfield, OPPO yields an 8.9% increase, which is statistically significant at 95% confidence. This alignment is visually represented in Figure 7.

Figure 7 demonstrates that the output of OPPO suggests that teams are at times best suited to placing their outfielders in truly radical configurations. In the Swanson example, the Royals' outfielders play uniquely close to one another and tuck two outfielders in deep right field and right-center field, leaving a large portion of left field uncovered.

Ultimately, what this panoply of visuals communicates is that the effect of OPPO, while showing some similar effects against hitters of similar profiles, is unique to the player. While this may seem like a shortcoming of the model, it is in fact a strength. In reality, OPPO can be deployed against each opposing hitter—as in the experiment—and will provide a unique solution for where

Figure 5. Starling Marte 2019 batted data (n = 194) are plotted against the Los Angeles Angels outfield repositioned by OPPO. Outfielders depicted: Brian Goodwin (solid black circle), Kole Calhoun (dashed circle), Mike Trout (dotted circle).

Figure 6. Anthony Rendon 2019 batted-ball data (n = 247) are plotted against the Los Angeles Angels outfield repositioned by OPPO. Outfielders depicted: Brian Goodwin (solid black circle), Kole Calhoun (dashed circle), Mike Trout (dotted circle).

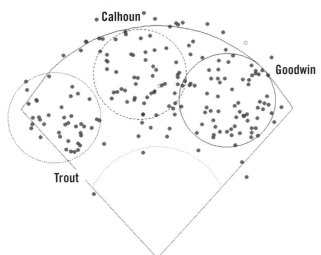

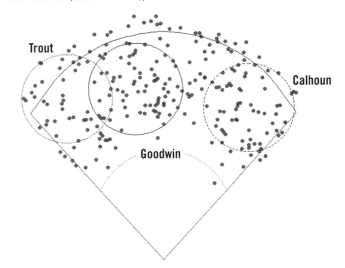

exactly teams ought to place outfielders. For example, a hitter's incremental increase in power compared to another may not require linear movements in the same previously conceived directions, but instead a unique approach catered to the density of one's batted balls across the surface of the outfield.

EXPERIMENT TWO

To determine the impact on balls reached by replacing an average outfielder with a marginally improved outfielder within OPPO, the 0th, 25th, 75th, and 100th percentile outfielders were each inserted into OPPO along with two league-average outfielders based on jump—for which this experiment was represented by clones of Ketel Marte (33.1 feet covered). It is worth noting that Marte represents the mean jump based on feet covered amongst qualified outfielders; the mean was used because it was extremely close to the median. The 0th percentile had the greatest percent decrease in plays within first touch in relation to replacement level, and 100th had the greatest percent increase of the same. Distribution of percent of plays within reach varies based on the player, and shows similar distribution by spray tendency. Table 3 (next page) represents the mean percentage of plays within reach and percent increase yielded by the replacement of one outfielder with the 0th, 25th, 75th, 100th percentile outfielders—Cabrera, Gordon, Heyward, and Kiermaier, respectively—for all eighteen hitters outlined in Table 1.

Results vary across the three spray tendencies of hitters in regard to the spread of percent increases between the 100th and 0th percentiles. Outfields against

Figure 7. Dansby Swanson 2019 batted-ball data (n = 203) are plotted against the Kansas City Royals outfield repositioned by OPPO. Outfielders depicted: Alex Gordon (solid black circle), Whit Merrifield (dashed circle), Jorge Soler (dotted circle).

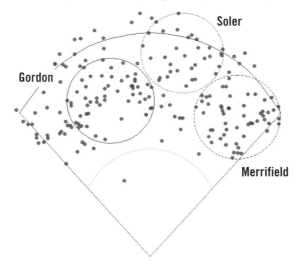

dead pull hitters have an average spread of 8.5% which is fairly similar to the average 7.9% against slight pull hitters. Outfields against opposite or all-fields hitters have a smaller average spread of 6.6%. Therefore OPPO may have similar effects against all spray tendencies on the individual player level.

In most cases, the value of adding the 75th percentile outweighs the percent decrease that is produced by adding the 25th percentile player to the outfield. The same observation can be seen with adding the 100th percentile and 0th percentile players to the outfield. Thus, it can be inferred that OPPO, consistent with the hypothesis, greatly optimizes the abilities of players whose jump statistic lies over the mean while minimizing the damage done to an outfield by adding players whose jump statistic lies below the mean.

It should be noted that there is a case in which including the 75th percentile player produces a negative improvement. This is a result of the way in which OPPO orders the placement of each player. The model focuses on optimizing each individual player, one at a time, with the assumption that it is best to optimize in regard to the jump statistic in descending order. Thus, in this example, Heyward—75th percentile—is placed first against Rendon such that his ability to be within reach of a ball is optimized. From there, the two average outfielders are sequentially placed such that their abilities are optimized based on the placement of the previous player. As illustrated in Table 3, OPPO produces an outfield with lesser improvement than a traditionally placed outfield with the same fielders in a few rare cases.

In Figure 8 (next page), the distributions of the observed percent changes in balls covered for each of the four replacement outfielders is portrayed by a series of vertical box plots. The leftmost box represents the distribution of these differences when the replacement outfielder is the league-worst in jump. The rightmost box, however, represents this distribution when the replacement outfielder is the league-best by their feet covered metric.

Looking at the two rightmost boxes, it appears that the maximum of the upper quartile of the 75th percentile outfielder—represented by the line above the second box from the right—does not even reach the uppermost portion of the 100th percentile outfielder's lower quartile. Therefore, there appears to be a clear jump in percent improvement when using the league's best outfielder compared to its 75th percentile one. In practice, this means that a player with a jump akin to Kiermaier's—the MLB leader in the statistic in 2019— provides increasing marginal returns to an

Table 3. Results of the OPPO model replacing one outfielder with different percentile jump abilities against specific hitters. Hitters sorted by tendency and handedness. Outfielders sorted by percentile in regard to their jump statistic.

HITTER CLASSIFICATIONS% INCREASE, PWFT BY PLAYER

Spray Tendency	Batter (Handedness)	0th Percentile	25th Percentile	Mean	75th Percentile	100th Percentile
Dead Pull	Cody Bellinger (L)	-2.3%	-1.3%	71.4%	1.4%	7.3%
	Pete Alonso (R)	-1.1%	0.0%	75.1%	0.6%	7.3%
	Max Kepler (L)	-4.0%	-1.0%	77.7%	2.0%	4.0%
	Eugenio Suarez (R)	-1.6%	-0.5%	75.3%	2.2%	6.7%
	Jeff McNeil (L)	-4.1%	-0.9%	80.5%	0.9%	3.6%
	Paul Dejong (R)	-2.5%	-1.0%	73.8%	2.0%	6.4%
Opposite/All Fields	Rafael Devers (L)	-2.8%	-0.4%	73.2%	3.5%	8.3%
	Miguel Cabrera (R)	-1.9%	0.0%	74.2%	1.4%	3.3%
	Freddie Freeman (L)	-3.3%	-0.8%	79.3%	1.2%	4.5%
	Tim Anderson (R)	-1.0%	-0.5%	74.1%	0.5%	2.5%
	Adam Eaton (L)	-1.3%	0.0%	70.8%	1.6%	4.5%
	Whit Merrifield (R)	-1.6%	-0.3%	71.1%	1.3%	4.5%
Slight Pull (Control)	Juan Soto (L)	-2.3%	-0.5%	75.6%	0.9%	5.2%
	Anthony Rendon (R)	-2.8%	-0.8%	70.4%	-2.0%	5.3%
	Michael Brantley (L)	-3.0%	-1.5%	81.1%	0.8%	1.9%
	Dansby Swanson (R)	-2.5%	0.0%	73.4%	3.0%	7.4%
	Alex Gordon (L)	-0.9%	0.0%	69.4%	0.4%	8.1%
	Starling Marte (R)	-1.5%	0.0%	76.8%	3.1%	6.7%

outfield's balls reached, compared to what an outfielder with an average jump provides. Meanwhile, there is no indication of a sizeable gap between other adjacent groups. Most notably, the median of percent improvement of both the 0th and 25th percentile outfielders is less than one percentage point from another—and likewise, even true between the 25th and 75th percentile outfielders. Ultimately, this shows that the change in improvement is the flattest between 25th and 75th percentile players—showing that the marginal improvement on an outfield's balls reached by replacing the former with the latter is minimally effective.

As roster evaluation adapts to new traits that make a player a strong outfielder as well as how to utilize OPPO to construct an outfield, there will be a need to compensate players for their defensive performance. As seen in Table 3, there are significant jumps throughout the data—that is, there is an exponential correlation between a player's range and the increased output on the whole outfield. This could cause a far more sectored market for defensive outfielders. Top-tier defenders were shown to increase outfield output by over 4% compared to 75th percentile defenders, which only

Figure 8. Box-plot depicts the spread of percent change in balls reached upon the replacement of the 0th, 25th, 75th, and 100th percentile outfielder in terms of feet covered.

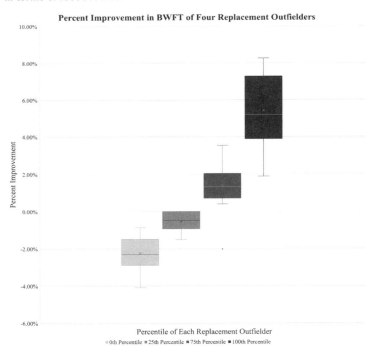

increased outfield output by about 1.4% above replacement. Thus, securing an elite defender has become even more valuable, as OPPO allows for the maximization of this player's skill set. In contrast, the discrepancy between the 75th percentile outfielder and the 0th percentile outfielder is a 3.63% increase in plays within reach. Just as OPPO allowed for maximizing the advantage of having an elite defender, it also allows teams to hide the inabilities of a weaker defender. Therefore, general managers will likely opt for a lower-graded defensive player, as it is likely not worth the financial burden to pay for an above-average defender, especially if there are tradeoffs in offensive production.

DISCUSSION

The most practical application of OPPO is as an effective advanced scouting tool used to position outfields on a game-by-game basis. Prior to a game, teams could input the lineup of the opposing team—one hitter at a time—as well as their own starting outfielders in order to maximize the odds that balls in play are reached. Where OPPO improves upon standard positioning is that it offers outfield placement that is tailored to individual hitters and outfielders. While implementing OPPO in-game, however, it may not be as simple as giving typical shift-cards to each outfielder because the outfield alignment is area-based. In addition to briefing players pregame as per usual, one way to modify these cards could be to superimpose the jersey number of each opposing hitter at the coordinate of the field OPPO suggests that one outfielder should play. Figure 9 represents a hypothetical OPPO shift-card for George Springer while he plays alongside Josh Reddick and Michael Brantley in World Series Game 7 against the Washington Nationals in 2019.

Ultimately the details of deployment and use of OPPO as an advanced scouting tool would be up to each team and what the coaches and players deem the easiest way to digest the information. Furthermore, front offices may face difficulty in convincing personnel of the benefits of a more fluid positioning system such as OPPO. To get the outfielders and pitchers to buy in, teams should explain the individual and collective improvements yielded by the new system. Thus, players will have an incentive to buy in as more front offices begin to strategize defensively in a data-driven way. Players who accommodate new tactics will increase their value on the open market.

Not limited to only in-game strategic insights, OPPO and subsequent analysis also provides the potential to evaluate outfielders on a different basis from that which they are currently assessed by front offices. Rather than using DRS and other more complex—albeit robust—proxies of defensive ability, focusing on a player's jump seems to improve the understanding of the first half of every defensive event: reaching the ball put in play. A further analysis should study the relative importance of an outfielder's ability to reach a ball, compared to other unrelated skills, such as his ability to catch, throw with power, and throw with accuracy. Perhaps if such analysis shows a large relative importance of jump alone, teams will value arm strength and other skills differently, and the conception of what defines an "elite" outfielder might be weighted in favor of a player's ability to cover ground. Furthermore, while certain aspects of jump can be taught—particularly one's route efficiency—burst and reaction are, to an extent, innate to one's body-type and athleticism. Locating players with these raw traits, even if they do not play the outfield, could indicate their future success as an outfielder, assuming they can be taught a new position.

Teaching a player to play outfield, whether entirely new to the position or adjusting to a position-fluid outfield, will require changes in player development. In all likelihood, every outfielder needs to be comfortable playing in each outfield spot—some conventional and others not. While there are some outfielders today who play multiple outfield positions, those who do not will likely face a steep learning curve. For example, the

Figure 9. Outfield shift-card for George Springer against the Washington Nationals in Game 7 of the 2019 World Series created by OPPO. Positioning is represented by placement of a hitters' uniform number. Ballpark configurations depict Minute Maid Park.

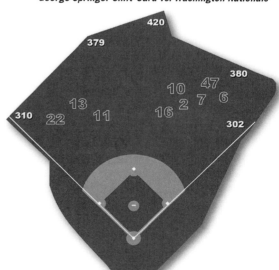

George Springer Shift-Card vs. Washington Nationals

straight trajectory of batted balls towards center field is very different compared to batted balls hit to the corners, which have a propensity to dip and dive. One would assume that center fielders, who are typically the most athletic outfielders, would adapt fairly well to changing positions. But others may initially struggle reading the path of the ball as it slices down a foul line. Teams considering using OPPO should build in additional practice time during spring training to account for the adjustment period.

Insofar as OPPO indicates the values of outfielders relative to one another, the model can form a basis by which teams assign monetary value to outfielders—in the open market and within the organization. After placing outfielders using OPPO, it was determined that the model yields the greatest jump in improvement from replacing the 75th percentile outfielder with the league's best outfielder. Therefore, it stands to reason that the largest premium between two outfielders should be placed between the "good" and "great" outfielders rather than between the "bad" and "good." Likewise, if an organization is not willing to shell out big money for an elite defensive outfielder—like Kevin Kiermaier—settling for a slightly below average defender is warranted as the gains made by improving towards the average are small.

It appears the market has begun to move towards recognizing great outfield fielding as an asset: a recent Fangraphs article by Tony Wolfe highlights trends amongst free-agent outfielders. He argues that outfielders, particularly ones with high offensive production but poor defensive statistics, have remained unsigned longer into the offseason. While this may be a sign that fielding is beginning to be valued a bit more fairly in the market, it also raises questions about how that evaluation manifests itself. One of the article's examples is Bryce Harper, who remained unsigned into February of 2019 after posting a season with -26 DRS with the Nationals in 2018. His next season with the Phillies, he posted a DRS of +10. Statistics like DRS evidently vary from year to year depending on an outfielder's teammates, pitching staff, and stadium. Jump data—with further analysis—may prove to be less variable year to year, due to its connection to players' physical tools. Utilizing OPPO, teams could begin to get a clearer picture of how players would fit into the current personnel and perhaps use their team's makeup to mask the poor defensive play of an incoming free agent.

LIMITATIONS AND AREAS OF FURTHER STUDY

Data from Baseball Savant used in this study provide the coordinates of outfield batted balls for every hitter in 2019. Hit coordinates denote where the ball is first picked up, not where it lands. Therefore, one cannot assume that a ball reached in OPPO is a ball caught. With the data available, outfielders are placed in the best possible position in order to be within reach of as many possible balls. Furthermore, even if data provided where the balls landed, there is no indication of the velocity and trajectory, thus no way of determining whether it would be caught or not. If given data that provided the coordinates of where a batted ball landed, exit velocity, and launch angle, OPPO could maximize outs in the outfield instead of merely maximizing plays within reach. In another experiment with the above variables included in the data, outfielders would be placed in the best position to create the most outs—perhaps eventually going as far as to minimize opponent xwOBA.

Another limitation caused by the data's constraints is that a player's jump is assumed to be equal in feet covered regardless of the direction he moves. In reality, while circles present the friendliest shapes to represent with code, outfielders ultimately move in different directions at different speeds and abilities. Thus, the true coverage zone of an outfielder would likely be an oblong shape that is unique to his ability. One way to achieve a more accurate portrayal would be to construct a player's coverage using his directional Outs Above Average (OAA) in each of the six directions that it is measured. By making this change, players previously treated equally by OPPO—such as Trout and Calhoun, who are virtually equal by feet covered—would be represented by shapes unique to his own skillset.

Limitations restricted the findings beyond the availability of data. The iterative placement of outfielders coded into the model maximizes balls within reach for individual players in descending order based on the number of feet covered. OPPO moves players individually with the assumption that it is best to maximize the ability of the best outfielder and then sequentially place the other two fielders in descending order to create the optimal outfield formation. This yields some overlap of outfielder coverage in the model, which could be remedied by an alternate optimization approach. A model that places all three outfielders simultaneously ensures that true maximization is achieved. While this methodology was considered in the early stages of this analysis, doing so ran the risk of producing results quite similar to a standard alignment which moves outfielders uniformly in groups. Furthermore, placing outfielders in ascending order by jump statistic could produce potentially improved but certainly different results as well. One possible justification for this tactic is that if the slowest fielder is placed first, then the fastest outfielders can make up for lack of coverage in specific areas.

Ultimately, the categorization of hitters within both tests limited the conclusions drawn from the study as a whole. A more granular and robust method of distinguishing hitters is likely required to truly understand which demographic of hitter OPPO works against best and worst. While splitting up hitters into groups of three by both exit velocity and spray tendencies proved a decent method of categorization, choosing criteria that prove to better map a hitter to his type of spray chart would allow for such categorizations to result in more accurate groups. Alternatively, if OPPO were tested against every eligible hitter, relationships between hitters previously undrawn can be parsed out. Quite possibly, hitters that were not conceived to be similar could belong to the same group or the profiles of each individual hitter could be so specific to each player that groups could even become obsolete.

Altogether, this study is the latest attempt to stay ahead of the curve in developing specific analytics-driven defensive strategies. While consequential insights were attained in this research, it marks only the start of the process of outfields reclaiming the "first-mover advantage" over constantly adapting hitters. Ultimately, the implementation of the methods detailed above in live major-league action would represent a massive leap for an already analytically driven industry. ■

Contributors' Note

The Columbia University Society for Baseball Research is an interdisciplinary undergraduate student group affiliated with Columbia University, founded by Anthony Montes and Charles Orlinsky. The mission of the club is to curate, create, and publish novel baseball research from the greater Columbia community and foster an accessible learning environment for Columbia students and faculty to grow baseball knowledge. If you have any questions or interest in collaborating feel free to contact current President Anthony Montes via email at ajm2273@columbia.edu.

Notes

1. Rob Arthur, "Do MLB Teams Undervalue Defense—Or Just Value It Differently?" FiveThirtyEight.com, April 18, 2019, accessed February 10, 2021. https://fivethirtyeight.com/features/do-mlb-teams-undervalue-defense-or-just-value-it-differently.

2. Brian Reiff , "The Effectiveness of Strategic Outfield Positioning" [Conference Presentation], SABR Analytics Conference, Phoenix, Arizona, March 8, 2019, accessed February 10, 2021. https://sabr.org/latest/2019-sabr-analytics-conference-research-presentations.

3. Mark Simon, "The Rise of Outfield Shifts," Bill James Online, February 22, 2019, accessed February 4, 2021. https://www.billjamesonline.com/the_rise_of_outfield_shifts.

4. Russell A. Carleton, "Baseball Therapy: The Corner-Outfield Inefficiency," Baseball Prospectus, November 25, 2013, accessed February 4, 2021. https://www.baseballprospectus.com/news/article/22295/baseball-therapy-the-corner-outfield-inefficiency.

5. Russell A. Carleton, "Baseball Therapy: Is the Whole the Sum of its Parts?" Baseball Prospectus, May 2, 2017, accessed January 31, 2021. https://www.baseballprospectus.com/news/article/31734/baseball-therapy-is-the-whole-the-sum-of-its-parts.

6. Statcast Jump Leaderboards, Baseball Savant, accessed May 9, 2020. https://baseballsavant.mlb.com/leaderboard/outfield_jump.

7. Statcast search, Baseball Savant, accessed May 9, 2020, https://baseballsavant.mlb.com/statcast_search.

8. Statcast Jump Leaderboards.

9. Statcast search.

10. Bill Petti, "Data Visualization Functions," baseballr, accessed May 9, 2020. http://billpetti.github.io/baseballr/articles/plotting_statcast.html.

11. Statcast Jump Leaderboards.

12. Fangraphs Leaderboards (Batted-Ball), Fangraphs, accessed May 9, 2020. https://www.fangraphs.com/leaders.aspx?pos=all&stats=bat&lg=all&qual=y&type=2&season=2019&month=0&season1=2019&ind=0&team=0&rost=0&age=0&filter=&players=0&startdate=2019-01-01&enddate=2019-12-31.

13. Minute Maid Park (Houston): Ground Rules, Major League Baseball, accessed May 9, 2020. https://www.mlb.com/groundrules/venue-2392.

14. Tony Wolfe, "Are Defensive Concerns Holding Up the Outfield Market?" Fangraphs, January 17, 2020, accessed February 10, 2021. https://blogs.fangraphs.com/are-defensive-concerns-holding-up-the-outfield-market.

The Symbiotic Relationship of Individual and Team Success

Samuel Borgemenke

Success comes in many forms—from individual exploits to team accomplishments and everything in between. Audiences watch teams and players winning titles or toppling records and live vicariously through these experiences. Baseball fans may value determination and perseverance in the face of failure, while hoping that the next at bat, pitch, or season might mark the beginning of success. But despite the many metrics that can be used to quantify it, impressions of what is considered "successful" for a player or team can be highly subjective. The degree to which fans are primed by messages of success from professional baseball raises two important questions: What constitutes success in baseball? And how interconnected are the various measures and metrics of success?

A good way to begin an analysis of this topic is by exploring the National Baseball Hall of Fame. The Hall

Ken Griffey Jr. is one of the all-time greats who never played on a championship team.

of Fame seeks to recognize personal success and now honors an elite club of 333 members who comprise some of the greatest individuals baseball has ever known.[1] These individuals range from players and managers to umpires and executives. Induction into the Hall of Fame in Cooperstown, New York, is considered by many to be the highest individual achievement in baseball. While methods have varied historically, induction is currently determined by rules of general eligibility and a voting committee. The current rules stipulate that players must have played in a minimum of ten seasons, been retired for at least five seasons, and received approval from a screening committee.[2] While it is easy for screening committees to ratify a candidate on the basis of seasons played, the voting committee undertakes the much more difficult task of evaluating a player's skill, talent, and contribution to their teams' success.[3] Individual players must have enjoyed "successful" careers in order to be inducted into the Hall of Fame. One subjective assumption that is often made is that career success is evidenced by team accomplishments such as World Series rings. In the minds of many, World Series titles are indicators of superior—potentially legendary—athletes. However, all-time greats such as Ted Williams, Ty Cobb, George Sisler, and Ken Griffey Jr. have never captured the elusive championship.[4]

This project aims to examine Hall of Fame players and World Series championships to understand how players become Hall of Famers without playing on a World Series-winning team, and conversely, how the World Series can be won with or without extraordinary players, and to determine if there is a relationship between individual success and team success. Understanding how and why World Series titles influence individual placement in the Hall of Fame is useful for recognizing what promotes success more broadly. This project will probe possible explanations for why, if Hall of Fame induction is an individual rather than team accomplishment, there are a greater number of Hall of Fame players who have won a World Series than have not. Is the subjective ideal of "success" responsible?

METHODOLOGY AND RESULTS

The initial proportion of Hall of Fame players who won a World Series was calculated from numbers given by the National Baseball Hall of Fame. As of 2020, there are 144 members in the Hall of Fame who have played on a World Series champion. There are a total of 235 players inducted in the Hall of Fame from the American and National Leagues. To ensure a fair and accurate comparison between eras, we looked at World Series that occurred from 1903 to present. Therefore, of these 235 MLB players, only 218 played in a season during this timespan. Thus, $\hat{p}$ of 144/218 ($\hat{p} \approx 0.66$) was used for statistical calculations.

The expected proportion of Hall of Fame players to win a World Series was calculated using the average career length of a Hall of Fame player and assuming World Series championships were uniformly distributed among MLB teams. The average career length for a Hall of Fame player was calculated to be 18 seasons. The average number of teams in the MLB during a World Series season was calculated to be 21 teams. (More information on how p was calculated can be found in the Appendix.)

The Binomial test was performed using values displayed in Table 1. A significance level of $\alpha = 0.05$ was used. Thus, the number of Hall of Fame players who have won a World Series is significantly greater than expected because the observed p-value of 0.0129 is less than α.

Table 1. Hall of Famers to Win World Series Binomial Test

Variable	Value
p	0.584
$\hat{p}$	0.661
Number of Trials	218
P(Z>=z) one-tail	0.0129

Variables that might explain the increase in the number of Hall of Fame players who have won a World Series were investigated. A Kendall rank correlation test was used to analyze the relationship between the number of World Series championships an MLB team had and the respective number of Hall of Fame members that correspond with that MLB team.[5,6] This correlation is displayed by Figure 1.

The Kendall rank correlation test produced a tau of 0.55. In addition, the correlation

between the two variables had a p-value of 2.2e-05. Thus, the data suggest a significant correlation between the number of Hall of Fame members that a franchise is affiliated with and the number of World Series championships a franchise has won because the observed p-value is less than the significance level set at $\alpha = 0.05$.

The number of Hall of Fame players present on each World Series championship team roster was then collected and plotted in Figure 2. Various points have been labeled to highlight teams that won the World Series with an outlying number of Hall of Fame players.

The number of Hall of Fame players on each World Series winning roster can be observed decreasing after the 1968 season. Therefore, a Student's t-test

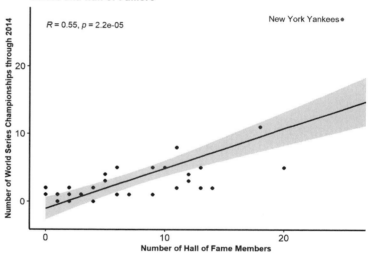

Figure 1. Kendall Rank Correlation Graph of Franchise World Series and Hall of Famers

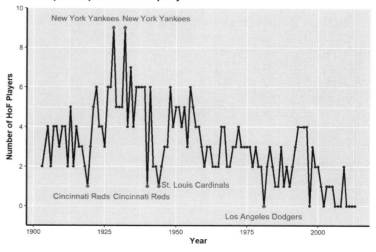

Figure 2. Number of Hall of Fame players on World Series championship team roster per year

was performed to determine whether the expansion of the playoffs in the 1969 season is associated with the decline in number of Hall of Fame players on the team that won the World Series. The t-test was calculated assuming the variances of both groups were equal. The results are displayed in Table 2.

Table 2. Number of Hall of Fame Players on Team Winning World Series Student's T-Test Comparison

Years	1903–1968	1969–2000
Average Number of Hall of Famers	3.94	2.35
Standard Deviation	1.76	1.08
Number of Observations	65	31
P(T>=t) one-tail		6.33996E-06

The total number of Hall of Fame players in each season from 1903 to 2013 was then counted and plotted in Figure 3. The number of players in each season was calculated by counting the number of active Hall of Fame players for a given season.

This total number of Hall of Fame players was divided by the number of teams in the American and National Leagues for each respective season in order to compute the expected number of Hall of Fame players on an MLB team.

Tables 3 and 4 display the average number of Hall of Fame players on the team that won the World Series and the expected number of Hall of Fame players on each team, respectively, split into groups of ten years. Years after 2002 were omitted because players are still being elected into the Hall of Fame from the period of 2003 to present.

Figure 3. Number of Hall of Fame players in MLB per year

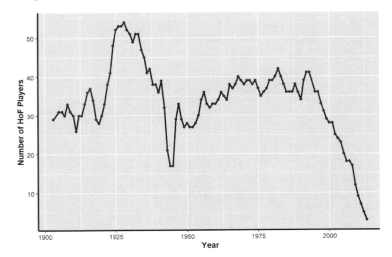

Table 3. Average Number of Hall of Fame Players on Team Winning the World Series

Years	Average HoF Players on WS Winning Roster
1903–1912	3.22
1913–1922	3.40
1923–1932	5.60
1933–1942	4.80
1943–1952	3.50
1953–1962	3.70
1963–1972	2.80
1973–1982	2.30
1983–1992	1.90
1993–2002	2.22

Table 4. Expected Number of Hall of Fame Players Per Team

Years	Expected Number of HoF per Team
1903–1912	1.88
1913–1922	2.05
1923–1932	3.15
1933–1942	2.56
1943–1952	1.59
1953–1962	1.99
1963–1972	1.76
1973–1982	1.52
1983–1992	1.44
1993–2002	1.10

A Chi-Square test of independence was performed between the observed number of Hall of Fame players on the World Series championship team roster and the expected number of Hall of Fame players per team for every season there was a World Series.

The Chi-Square test produced a p-value equal to 5.849e-08, which is less than the significance level of $\alpha = 0.05$. This p-value indicates that the observed number of Hall of Fame players on the World Series championship team roster is significantly greater than expected.

DISCUSSION

The two goals of this project were to explore the possibility for increased rates of Hall of Fame players who have won a World Series and to attempt to explain any such elevated rates. By examining Table 1, it becomes evident that the proportion of Hall of Fame players who have won a World Series is greater than expected.

In order to explain why Hall of Fame players win the World Series more often than expected, a correlation test and graph were produced in Figure 1. This figure depicts the number of Hall of Fame members associated with a franchise and the number of World Series championships a franchise has won. A significant linear relationship can be observed from this graph. Furthermore, the New York Yankees can be observed as an outlier because of their high totals in both Hall of Famers and World Series championships.

The data in Figure 2 illustrate the number of Hall of Famers present on the roster of the team that won the Fall Classic. The 1928 and 1932 Yankees teams have the most Hall of Famers on the roster with nine each. This is unsurprising as both teams are regarded as some of the best teams in the history of baseball. Nevertheless, in seasons prior to the expansion of the playoffs in 1969, teams to win the World Series with only one Hall of Fame player were the 1919 Cincinnati Reds, 1940 Cincinnati Reds, and 1944 St. Louis Cardinals. The lack of Hall of Famers on the 1944 St. Louis Cardinals team can be attributed to ballplayers leaving MLB in response to World War II. This drastic decrease in the number of Hall of Fame players in the league during World War II is shown in Figure 3.

Interestingly, a team with zero Hall of Fame players did not occur until the 1981 Los Angeles Dodgers

defeated the New York Yankees. This may be explained by 1981 being a shortened season due to the players' strike. Moreover, it is the last time a team has come back and won the World Series after losing the first two games on the road. In addition, prior to 2000, the only other team to win the World Series without Hall of Fame players on the roster is the 1997 Florida Marlins.

The decline in number of Hall of Fame players on the World Series champion roster can be explained by a few factors. Firstly, since the 1990s, a steep decline can be observed in Figure 3 for the number of Hall of Fame players present in MLB. This decline is because fewer players who played after 1990 are eligible for induction in the National Baseball Hall of Fame. Second, the expansion of the playoffs in 1969 increased the number of rounds a team must play in order to win the World Series. Thus, the likelihood that the theoretical best team, or the team with the most Hall of Famers, wins the World Series declines—as shown by Table 2. Therefore, the expansion of the playoffs increased the odds that a team with fewer Hall of Fame players will win the World Series.

This project emphasizes that a close relationship exists between individual and team success. Talented individuals contribute to the overall winning of their team, which in turn enables players who win a World Series to be seen more favorably by the Hall of Fame voting committee. Postseason baseball has the ability to transform great players into players of legendary—Hall of Fame—status in the minds of fans and voters alike. Players like Catfish Hunter have made the Hall of Fame while players like Luis Tiant have not. Both Hunter and Tiant sport similar career statistics. However, Hunter is a five-time World Series champion and Tiant failed to win a single World Series. Likewise, one of the knocks on current great Mike Trout is the fact that "he" (his team) has failed to make a deep postseason run.

Since Hall of Famers are overly represented among World Series winners, Hall of Fame players are seen to play a demonstrably vital role in a team's ability to win. So why then do such standouts as Ted Williams, Ty Cobb, George Sisler, and Ken Griffey Jr. all go down in history without ever winning a World Series? In the case of Ted Williams, a man who is widely regarded as the greatest hitter to ever live, the fact remains that he never won a World Series. This project sheds some light on ideas that might at first appear to be at odds. Williams's problem certainly was not his extraordinary talent, but may have been the talent level of those around him. In his 19-year career, Williams only played six seasons during which he had more than one Hall

George Sisler is another Hall-of-Fame great who never got a championship ring.

of Fame teammate, far below the averages of World Series teams who won during his active years, as shown in Table 3.

These data support the theory that a lack of team support inhibits players such as Ted Williams from winning the World Series. The finding that the legends we often venerate as Hall of Famers are heavily influenced by the circumstances of their team's roster should force fans (and Hall of Fame voters) to take players' career achievements into account within the context of their teams. This will ultimately produce a more complete picture of success for individual players and teams as a whole.

One way of improving this research would be to further study the teams that have included a higher-than-average number of Hall of Fame players but failed to win a World Series. This would illustrate the importance of various factors, such as time, injuries, and team chemistry, that impact a team's ability to win the World Series. ∎

Notes

1. "Hall of Famers." National Baseball Hall of Fame, 2020. https://baseballhall.org/hall-of-famers.
2. "B-R Bullpen." BR Bullpen, 2019. https://www.baseball-reference.com/bullpen/Hall_of_Fame.
3. "BBWAA Election Rules." National Baseball Hall of Fame, 2020. https://baseballhall.org/hall-of-famers/rules/bbwaa-rules-for-election.
4. "Best Players in MLB History to Never Win a World Series." MLB.com, October 25, 2012. https://www.mlb.com/news/best-players-in-mlb-history-to-never-win-a-world-series/c-40041796.
5. Gough, Christina. "Most World Series Wins." Statista, November 5, 2019. https://www.statista.com/statistics/235618/mlb--number-of-world-series-championships-by-team.
6. Baseball Almanac, Inc. "Baseball Hall of Fame Fast Facts & Frivolities." Baseball Almanac, 2019. https://www.baseball-almanac.com/hof/hofstat.shtml.

APPENDIX

The binomial probability mass function was used to calculate the expected proportion of Hall of Fame players to win a World Series. The equation used for this calculation is:

$$P(x; p,n) = \binom{n}{x} (p)^x (1-p)^{(n-x)} \quad \text{for } x = 0, 1, 2, \cdots, n$$

$$P(\textit{Winning at least 1 World Series}) = 1 - P(x=18; p=20/21, n=18) = 1 - (20/21)^{18} \approx 0.584$$

Where x is the number of seasons not winning World Series, p is the probability of not winning the World Series, and n is the number of seasons played.

A one-tailed binomial test was calculated with a predetermined significance level of $\alpha = 0.05$.

A Kendall rank correlation test was chosen because the data do not come from a bivariate normal distribution. The test was also performed with the exclusion of the New York Yankees because they might be considered an influential point—as the team greatly affected the slope of the regression line and caused the coefficient of determination, R^2, to be bigger. The resulting p-value for the adjusted correlation test was still found to be significant at the $\alpha = 0.05$ level.

Figure 4. Adjusted Correlation Graph that Does Not Include New York Yankees

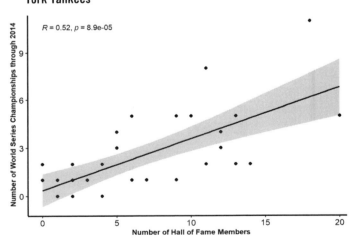

A Novel Approach for Baseball Pitch Analysis Using a Full-Body Motion Analysis System

A Descriptive Case Study

Paul K. Canavan, Bethany Suderman, Alex Sklar, and Nicholas Yang

Biomechanical analysis in sports has been used for more than 140 years, including Eadweard Muybridge's work in 1879. Muybridge created the Zoopraxiscope to analyze motion through photographs and motion pictures (Muybridge E 1882, Muybridge E. 1891, Rondinella L.F. et al.,1929). For the past 50 years, baseball coaches have used biomechanical analysis from movies of the baseball pitch to help improve pitcher performance (Bethel, 1967; Hulen, 1966; Petroff et al., 1966). High speed photography, stroboscopic photography and high-speed video cameras have been used to analyze pitching mechanics for over 40 years (Atwater, 1977; Elliott et. al, 1986; Escamilla et al., 2001; Hang et al., 1979; Pappas et al., 1985, Thurston,1984). High-speed cameras and the use of retroreflective markers worn on the major joints on the body for the baseball pitcher have been used to analyze baseball pitching for over 25 years to the present (Dillman et al., 1993; Escamilla et al., 2002; Escamilla et al., 2017; Fleisig et al., 1999, Solomito et al., 2017).

Over the past 10 years there have been several research studies that have utilized wearable sensors on the arm involving gyroscopes, accelerometers, and/or magnetometers to identify torque and other upper extremity biomechanical parameters related to baseball pitching (Camp et al., 2017; Koda et al, 2010; Makhni et al, 2018; McGinnis et al, 2012; Murray et al, 2017; Sagawa et. al, 2009). Objective testing that truly evaluates baseball ability is welcomed by professional, college, and high school coaches. Pertinent research findings and their practical applications are needed for coaches and players to help improve pitching ability (Reiff et al., 1971).

However, these sensors have only been utilized on the upper extremity and there are limitations to fixation, comfort, and practicality in the field. Coaches and analysts have requested more research advocating improved ease of use, and improved error compensation and analysis procedures to provide informative, concise, and easy-to-interpret metrics (Camomilla et al., 2018).

The XSens wearable full body motion analysis suit has been shown to reliably biomechanically analyze rehabilitation exercises, activities of daily living including walking and stair ambulation, as well as activities such as skiing and snowboarding (Karatsidis et al;, 2019; Konrath et al., 2019; Kruger et al., 2009; Slaipah et al., 2014; Supej et al., 2010). The Xsens inertial measurement suit is an acceptable unit to measure physical demand in workplace assessments such as complex lifting tasks (Poitras et al., 2019).

To date there are no known research papers that have analyzed the baseball pitch using a full body motion analysis suit such as the Xsens for kinematic analysis. This paper has two purposes: First, to present the procedures for a successful application of biomechanical motion analysis of baseball pitching utilizing a wearable sensor body suit. Second, to provide a descriptive analysis of the center-of-mass position of the pitcher's body as related to the lead foot placement and pitching accuracy.

MATERIALS AND METHODS
Participant

The volunteer participant was a male pitcher (Age 20; Height 1.96 m; Weight 102.1 kg; Throwing Arm; Right) from an NCAA Division III varsity baseball team. The research procedures were reviewed and approved by the Institutional Review Board. The participant was provided an overview of the procedures and provided written informed consent.

PROCEDURES
Set-up

A pitching mound, home plate, pitching target, and batting dummy were set-up in an indoor gymnasium at Eastern Connecticut State University. The distance of the pitching rubber to the back of home plate was placed at the NCAA regulation distance of 60 feet 6 inches (18.44 meters) from each other (Paronto and Woodward, NCAA, 2014). The participant threw from an indoor wooden pitching mound built to regulation height (10 inches/25.4 centimeters) with a gradual slope of 1 inch per foot (0.0254 centimeter per 30.48 centimeters) from a point 15.24 centimeters (6 inches) in front of the pitching rubber (all dimensions based upon NCAA regulations, see Paranto, NCAA).

A target area was designated on the canvas backstop to simulate the strike zone for a 1.75 meter (5-foot 9-inch) tall batter. The pitching target was placed behind home plate and measured 1.52 meters in height by 1.40 meters in width (Muhl Tech Pitching Target, MulTech, Wharton, Texas. See Figure 1).

A level and tape measures were utilized to ensure proper placement of the pitching target. The Designated Hitter Pro Model dummy (TAC Companies LLC, National Harbor, MD) was used to provide a more realistic pitching environment. The target area was subdivided into four equal quadrants of the strike zone. The quadrants were designated as Left Upper Quadrant (LUQ), Left Lower Quadrant (LLQ), Right Upper Quadrant (RUQ), and Right Lower Quadrant (RLQ). The pitching target area was 40.64 centimeters (16 inches) tall by 55.88 centimeters wide (22 inches) and each isolated quadrant area was 20.32 centimeters tall (8 inches) by 27.94 centimeters wide (11 inches). A 3-inch diameter circular white target was placed in the center of each quadrant, LUQ, LLQ, RUQ, RLQ. During the trials, only one of the quadrants was visible to the subject. The goal of the participant was to hit the center of the target in each quadrant.

Motion Analysis

The kinematic analysis of the body and center of mass of the subject was measured using an instrumented body suit (MVN Biomechanical Body Suit, Xsens Technologies, Enschede, Netherlands) containing 17 inertial measurement units. The sensors along with the measurements of the various limb segments created the 3-D body model.

The subject wore the Lycra body suit, with pockets allowing placement of the motion tracking sensors in the correct position on the subject's body and to hold the data logger and battery pack. A headband, gloves, and foot pads were used to secure the motion trackers to the subject's extremities. The gloves did not affect the ability of the subject to pitch normally. The sensor goes on the back side of the hand, not the palm or the fingers. According to feedback from the participants, the sensor did not affect the performance of throwing. The data from each sensor were recorded at 120 Hz and processed using the Xsens MVN Studio-Pro software package.

After the suit was put on, and the sensors, battery pack, and data logger secured in position, measurements were taken of the body height, shoe length, arm span, ankle height, hip height, hip width, knee height, shoulder width, shoulder height, and shoe sole height. These anthropometric measurements were taken as per XSens standardized protocol. A single-unit battery pack contains 3 Lithium Ion rechargeable cells, and when fully charged, the suit can be operational for continuous recording for up to 10 hours. The weight of the battery was 20.74 ounces or 1.3 lbs and placed on the posterior mid-thoracic region of the participant which had very minimal effect on the participant's center of gravity and throwing mechanics.

Prior to event recording, a complete and successful calibration phase was performed, following the Xsens calibration procedure. Connection between the recording laptop and Xsens hardware was done with the standard Bluetooth receivers provided with the Xsens system. Real time monitoring of the motion capture was also performed.

The biomechanical model consisted of 23 segments from the 17

Figure 1. Example images of pitching accuracy measurements.

(Left) Example of a strike while throwing at the Lower Left Quadrant (LLQ).

(Right) Example of a ball while throwing at the Right Upper Quadrant (RUQ). The baseball is outlined in for emphasis.

Computer generated grid squares are 2" x 2".

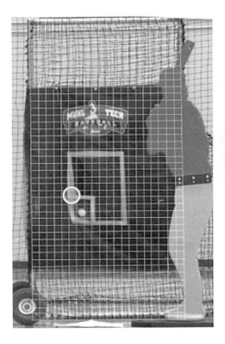

sensors which created the accurate 3-D model for each individual participant. The sensors were translated to body segment kinematics using a biomechanical model which assumes the subject's body includes body segments lined by joints. The Xsens system calculates the position, velocity, acceleration, orientation, angular velocity, and angular acceleration of each body segment and the center of gravity (COG). For each test trial, real-time standard video capture was also recorded at 29.97 frames per second at a resolution of 1920 x 1080 (Canon, EOS 7, Japan) and placement of cards that indicated quadrant and pitch number were utilized for both the high-speed camera and the standard video camera.

A midline was defined as the center of the pitching rubber to the center of home plate. MATLAB software was used to better visualize the location of the lateral distance of the center of mass related to the lead foot placement and midline.

Speed and Accuracy Measurements

A standardized and recently calibrated Stalker Sport 2 radar gun (Applied Concepts, Inc./Stalker Radar, Richardson, Texas) was used to assess pitch speed. The radar gun was placed 2.44 meters behind and 10 degrees to the right of the participant.

A high-speed camera (240 frames/sec) at a resolution of 1920 x 1080 (Sony, NEX SF700, Japan) was utilized to assess accuracy, and the x-, y-position of the ball was analyzed for each pitch relative to the center of the target and the resultant distance was calculated. The high-speed camera was placed orthogonal to the strike zone target and recorded the location of the ball when it hit the target. The camera was placed behind (1.54 meters) and 10 degrees to the left of the pitching subject. Still images of the moment of impact between the baseball and the strike zone target were taken from the high-speed camera and imported into a computer program (Adobe Illustrator, Version 23.0.3, Adobe, San Jose, California) where a 2-inch grid was placed over the strike zone target area (See Figure 1).

The grid was placed over the target area and verified by comparing the grid to physical measurements taken of the strike zone target area. Only the three most accurate and least accurate pitches were analyzed. Accuracy was determined as the resultant distance to the designated quadrant in the strike zone.

Pitching Protocol

Prior to data collection, the subject completed a 15-minute standardized warm-up throwing procedure that he typically performed before throwing off a

mound. Prior to data capture, the participant pitcher threw 3 warm-up fast balls from the indoor mound into target number 1 right upper quadrant (RUQ). The participant then threw 10 times with the goal to hit the target in the center of the quadrant. The instructions were given for the participant to throw as fast and as accurately as he could perform with emphasis on accuracy. This was followed by the same procedure for each of the other three quadrants: Left Upper Quadrant (LUQ), Left Lower Quadrant (LLQ) and Right Lower Quadrant (RLQ). All pitches were performed from the stretch position to standardize the position of the body for each trial, as shown in Figure 2.

The subject performed at least 40 pitches into the canvas backstop target, 10 pitches for each of the 4 quadrants. For each test trial, the subject was instructed to throw consecutively at one of the four defined quadrants. Pitches that completely missed the canvas backstop or hit the dummy batter did not count toward the 40-pitch total.

In addition to starting all throws from the stretch position, the participant aligned the middle of his shoe with a mark on the middle of the pitching rubber, which was itself aligned with the middle of home plate, in order to standardize the start position of each throw. The particular quadrant target circle was only visible for each of the conditions. The participant was allowed to rest as needed between pitches. The time between pitches for each quadrant was less than 60 seconds.

Figure 2. Subject in stretch position wearing the Lycra body suit and Xsens sensors.

Results

The pitching mechanics were analyzed with visual observation, use of standard video, as well as the Xsens MVN Studio-Pro software package, as shown in Figure 3.

MATLAB was utilized to observe the trace of the center of gravity during the pitching sequence (Figure 4).

Figure 4 shows top view and side view of the center of gravity and fore foot position at the initial stretch position, front foot strike, and follow through. Following ball release for each pitch, the subject's body fell towards his left side and the back, right foot came across and landed to his left side in order to maintain balance of having the center of gravity (COG) within the base of support of both feet.

The lateral distance of the center of gravity with respect to the midline and front foot at foot strike was obtained by plotting the position at foot strike, as shown in Figure 4. Table 1 shows for the three most accurate and three least accurate pitches, the pitching velocity, the lateral distance of the center of gravity to the midline, and the lateral distance of the center of gravity to the lead foot.

The participant reported that he threw 90% of his full speed for each of his pitches. The participant's least accurate pitches were low and to the outside relative to the center of the target of the respective quadrant. The combined amount of distance from the center of mass relative to the midline along with the position of the lead foot relative to the midline was 20, 22, and 25 centimeters for the most accurate pitches (Figure 4). The combined amount for the least accurate pitches were 30, 31, and 31 centimeters. The average pitching speed for the most accurate three pitches was 78.37 mph/126.12 kph. The average pitching speed for the least accurate three pitches was 78.27 mph/125.96 kph. The speeds were similar. Two of the most accurate pitches were in the right upper quadrant and two of the least accurate pitches were located in the right lower quadrant.

Figure 3. Xsens software visualization of the pitch from the stretch position to follow through.

Table 1. Most and Least Accurate Pitch Accuracy (relative to target x= inside/outside; y= low/high); Center of Gravity placement at the time of lead foot Plant.

Overall Most and Least Accurate Pitches	Quadrant	Accuracy Resultant deviation from Quadrant (cm)	Pitching Velocity (mph); (kph)	Lateral Distance Body COG related to the midline (cm) + to the right of midline— to the left of midline	Lateral Distance from Front Lead Foot placement from midline + closed position (cm)
Best Pitch # 1	RUQ	0,0; 0	77.0; 123.92	2	23
Best Pitch # 2	RUQ	0,0; 0	78.9; 126.98	0	22
Best Pitch # 3	LUQ	0,0; 0	79.2; 127.46	2	22
Worst Pitch #1	RLQ	-12, -20; 23	77.7; 125.05	3	28
Worst Pitch #2	RLQ	-8, -24; 25	77.7; 125.05	7	24
Worst Pitch #3	LUQ	-6, -30; 31	79.4; 127.78	4	26

LIMITATIONS AND BENEFITS OF THE MOTION ANALYSIS SYSTEM SUIT AND HIGH-SPEED CAMERA

- **Limitations**. Battery life on the high-speed motion camera, sampling frequency low compared to shoulder velocity, time of data processing, place and complexity of data processing (Kosa et al., 2018)

- **Benefits**: Portability—the motion analysis suit and the high-speed camera can be utilized indoors or outdoors at a pitcher's own team facility and mounds, ease of analysis—visualization of image following performance of the pitch, and convenience of set-up—the time for set-up for the pitcher may be lower than traditional motion analysis with retroreflective markers.

DISCUSSION

Many studies have investigated factors that could improve pitching accuracy and performance. A recent study (Fleisig, et al., 2017) showed that utilizing biomechanical motion analysis to identify flaws of the pitching motion, followed by instruction and a follow-up biomechanical analysis, was able to correct 44% of the flaws identified in 46 healthy baseball pitchers from high school, college, minor league, and major league levels. Studies analyzing the foot position on the pitching rubber and variable stride length did not necessarily correct pitching accuracy (Edwards et al, 1963). There also appears to be no significant relationship between shoulder proprioception and throwing accuracy (Freeston et al, 2015). To the authors' knowledge, there has been little research on the lead foot position and pitching accuracy.

There is a dearth of literature on mechanics and pitching accuracy utilizing biomechanical motion analysis of the pitching motion. Qualitative analysis of baseball pitching technique using standard 60Hz camcorders cannot provide a complete and accurate profile of the mechanics (Nicholls et al., 2003). Our study appears to be the first that has utilized a full-body wearable sensor motion analysis portable suit to analyze the pitching motion related to pitching accuracy. Coordination in pitching involves the timing of various body motions such as trunk rotation, lower limb drive, and non-throwing and throwing limb movements. The ability to drive the body forward over a stabilized front leg was characteristic of fast pitchers (Elliott et al., 1988). This current study is the first we know of that analyzes pitching accuracy using center-of-mass tracking as related to the lead foot position. This is a preliminary proof-of-concept study that in the future can be expanded and improved upon.

CONCLUSION AND PRACTICAL APPLICATIONS

The Xsens motion analysis suit, along with the described procedures within this study, could be used as an assessment process to identify flaws in the pitching motion. These identified flaws can be utilized by the pitcher and pitching coach to develop intervention to improve, reduce, or correct the flaws by being reassessed. The Xsens suit is portable and can be utilized for pitchers in the comfort and convenience of their respective pitching facilities, both indoors and outdoors, unlike many of the prior studies in which wall-mounted cameras and retroreflective markers are needed. This technology has the potential to provide

Figure 4. Top view and side view of the center of gravity and fore foot position at the initial stretch position, front foot strike, and follow through.

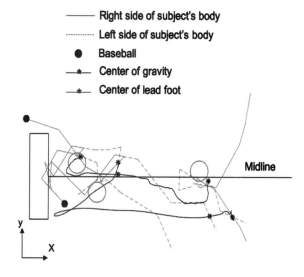

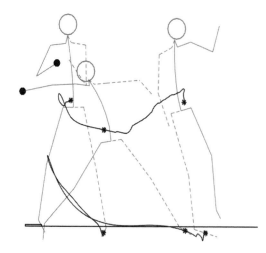

the pitching coach and player with information that is concise, easy to understand and utilize, and allow them to implement interventions to optimize mechanics and to reduce variability. Also, biomechanical reassessment could help determine the efficacy of the interventions. These interventions may improve pitching performance and reduce the risk of injury for the baseball pitcher. ∎

Acknowledgments

The authors would also like to thank Guidance Engineering for use of the High-Speed camera and Xsens™ Motion Analysis Suit. We would like to acknowledge the Head Coach Baseball Brian Hamm and Pitching Coach Chris Wojick and the volunteer pitcher participants. We would also like to express our gratitude to Christian Gosselin and Ashley Kennison for their help with data collection.

Funding

Partial funding for this project was provided by Eastern Connecticut State University and Guidance Engineering.

Declaration of Interest

The authors have no conflict of interest related to this study. The authors have no affiliations or involvement with organizations with any financial interest related to this study.

References

Atwater, A. E. 1977. "Biomechanical Analysis of Different Pitches from The Windup and Stretch Positions." *Medicine Science in Sports* no. 9: 49–50.

Bethel, D. 1967. "Mechanics of Pitching." *Scholastic Coach* 36 no.12: 86–88.

Brose D.E., Hanson D.L. 1967. "Effects of overload training on velocity and accuracy of throwing." *Research Quarterly* 38 no. 4: 528–33.

Camomilla V., Bergamini E., Fantozzi, Vannozzi G. 2018. "Trends supporting the in-field use of wearable inertial sensors for sport performance evaluation: A systematic review." *Sensors* no.18: 1–50.

Camp C.L., Tubbs T.G., Fleisig G.S., Dines J.S., Dines D.M., Altchek D.W., Dowling B. 2017. "The relationship of throwing arm mechanics and elbow varus torque." *American Journal of Sports Medicine* 45 no. 13: 3030–35.

Dillman C.J., Fleisig G.S., Andrews J.R. 1993. "Biomechanics of pitching with emphasis upon shoulder kinematics." *Journal of Orthopedic Sports Physical Therapy* 18 no. 2: 402–8.

Edwards D.K. 1963. "Effects of stride and position on the pitching rubber on control in baseball pitching." *Research Quarterly, American Association for Health, Physical Education, and Recreation*: 9–14.

Elliott B., Grove J.R., Gibson B. 1988. "Timing of the lower limb drive and throwing limb movement in baseball pitching." *International Journal of Sport Biomechanics* no. 4: 59–67.

Elliott B., Grove R., Gibson B., Thurston B. 1986. "A three dimensional cinematographic analysis of the fastball and curveball pitches in baseball." *International Journal of Sport Biomechanics* no. 2: 20–28.

Escamilla R., Fleisig G., Barrentine S., Andrews J., Moorman C. 2002. "Kinematic and kinetic comparisons between American and Korean professional baseball players." *Sports Biomechanics* no. 2: 213–16.

Escamilla R.F., Fleisig G.S., Zheng N., Barrentine S.W., Andrews J.R. 2001. "Kinematic comparisons of 1996 Olympic baseball pitchers." *Journal of Sport Science* no 19: 665–76.

Escamilla R.F., Fleisig G.S., Groeschner D., Akizuki K. 2017. "Biomechanical comparisons among fastball, slider, curveball and changeup pitch types and between balls and strikes in Professional baseball players." *American Journal of Sports Medicine* 45 no. 14: 3358–66.

Fleisig G.S., Barrentine S.W., Zheng N., Escamilla R.F., Andrews J.R. 1999. "Kinematic and kinetic comparison of baseball pitching among various levels of development." *J Biomech* no. 32: 1371–75.

Fleisig G.S., Chu Y., Weber A., Andrew J. 2009. "Variability in baseball pitching biomechanics among various levels of competition." *Sports Biomechanics* no. 1: 10–21.

Fleisig G.S., Diffendaffer A.Z., Ivey B., Aune K.T. 2018. "Do baseball pitchers improve mechanics after biomechanical evaluations?" *Sports Biomechanics* no. 3: 314–21.

Freeston J., Adams R.D., Rooney K.B. 2015. "Shoulder proprioception is not related to throwing speed or accuracy in elite adolescent male baseball players." *Journal of Strength and Conditioning Research* 29 no. 1: 181–187.

Hang Y.S., Lippert III F.G., Spolek G.A., Frankel V.H., Harrington R.M. 1979. "Biomechanical study of the pitching elbow." *International Orthopedics* 3 no. 3: 217–23.

Hulen J. 1966. "Checklist for Pitchers." *Scholastic Coach* 1966; 35.

Kawamura K. Shinya M., Kobayashi H., Obata H., Kuwata M., Nakazawa K. 2017. "Baseball pitching accuracy: an examination of various parameters when evaluating pitch locations." *Sports Biomechanics*, 16 no. 3: 399–410.

Karatsidis A., Jung M., Schepers M., Bellusci G., de Zee M., Veltink P.H., Andersen M.S. 2019. "Musculoskeletal model-based inverse dynamic analysis under ambulatory conditions using inertial motion capture." *Medical Engineering Physics* no. 65: 68–77.

Koda H., Sagawa K., Kuroshima K., Tsukamoto T., Urita K., Ishibashi Y. 2010. "3D measurement of forearm and upper arm during throwing motion using body mounted sensor." *Journal of Advanced Mechanical Design Systems Manufacturing* no. 4: 167–78.

Konrath J.M., Karatsidis A., Schpers H.M., Bellusci G., de Zee M., Andersen M.S. 2019. "Estimation of the knee adduction moment and joint contact force during daily living activities using inertial motion capture." *Sensors* no. 19: 1-12.

Kosa A., Weib Y., Tomaži a S, Umeka A. 2018. "The role of science and technology in sport." *Procedia Computer Science* no. 129: 489–95.

Kruger A., Edelmann-Nusser J. 2009. "Biomechanical analysis in freestyle snowboarding: application of a full body inertial measurement system and bilateral insole measurement system." *Sports Technology* no. 2: 17–23.

Litwhiler Dl., Hamm L. 1973. "Overload: effect on throwing velocity and accuracy." *Athletic Journal* no. 53: 64–65 1.

Marsh D.W., Richard L.A., Williams L.A., Lynch K.J. 2004. "The relationship between balance and pitching error in college baseball pitchers." *Journal of Strength and Conditioning Research* 18 no. 3: 441–46.

Makhni E.C., Lizzio V.A., Meta F. Stephens J.P., Okoroha K.R., Moutzouros V. 2018. "Assessment of elbow torque and other parameters during the pitching motion: comparison of fastball, curveball and change-up." *Journal of Arthroscopic and Related Surgery* 34 no. 3: 816–22.

McGinnis R.S., Perkins N.C. 2012. "A highly miniaturized, wireless inertial measurement unit for characterizing the dynamic of pitched baseballs and softballs," *Sensors* no. 12: 11933–45.

Murray N., Black G , Whitely R., Gahan P., Cole M. Utting A., Gabbett T.J. 2017. "Automatic detection of pitching throwing events in baseball with inertial measurement sensors." *International Journal of Sport Physiology Performance* 12 no. 4: 533–37.

Muybridge E. 1882, "The horse in motion." *Nature* no. 652: 605.

Muybridge E. 1891, "The science of animal locomotion, Zoopraxography: An electro-photographic investigation of consecutive phases of animal movements." Library of Alexandria.

Nicholls R., Fleisig G., Elliott B., Lyman S., Osinski E. 2003, "Accuracy of qualitative analysis for assessment of skilled baseball pitching technique." *Sports Biomech* 2 no. 2: 213–26.

Pappas A.M., Zawack R.M., Sullivan T.J. 1985. "Biomechanics of baseball pitching: a preliminary report." *Am J Sports Med* 13 no. 4: 316-222.

Paronto J. & Woodward B. 2014. *National Collegiate Athletic Association Baseball 2015 and 2016 Rules* — italics?, Indianapolis, IN; 12.

Petroff T.W. 1966. "Movie analysis for pitching improvement." *Scholastic Coach* 46 no. 10: 64–66.

Poitras I., Bielmann M., Campeau-Lecours A., Mercier C., Bouyer L.J., Roy J.S. 2019. "Validity of wearable sensors at the shoulder joint: Combining wireless electromyography sensors and inertial measurement units to perform physical workplace assessments." *Sensors* no. 19: 2–14.

Reiff G.G. 1971. "What research tells the coach about baseball." *American Association of Health Physical Education and Recreation*: 1–38.

Rondilla L.F. 1929, "Muybridge's motion pictures." J Franklin Institute 208 no. 3: 417–20.

Sagawa K., Abo S., Tsukamoto T., Kondo I. "Forearm trajectory measurement during pitching motion using an elbow mounted sensor." *Journal of Advanced Mechanical Design Systems Manufacturing* no. 3: 299–311.

Shinyra M., Tsuchiya S., Tamada Y., Nakazawa K., Kudo K., Oda S. 2017. "Pitching form determines probablastic structure of errors in pitching location." *Journal of Sport Science* 35 no. 21: 2142–47.

Slajpah S., Kamnik R., Munih M. 2014. "Kinematics based sensory fusion for wearable motion assessment in human walking." *Computer Methods of Program in Biomedicine* 116 no. 2: 131–44.

Solomito M.J., Ferreira J.V., Nissen C. W. 2017. "Biomechanical differences between left and right-handed baseball pitchers." *Sports Biomechanics* 16 no. 2: 143–51.

Straub W.F. 1968. "Effect of overload training procedures upon velocity and accuracy of the overarm throw." *Research Quarterly* 39 no. 2: 370–79.

Supej M., 2010. "Wearable motion analysis suits have been utilized for several activities including Alpine skiing." *Journal of Sport Science* 28 no. 7: 759–69.

Thurston B. 1984. Coaches checklist for film evaluation. Adelaide: Australian Baseball Federation.

The Henry Chadwick Award was established by SABR to honor baseball's great researchers—historians, statisticians, analysts, and archivists—for their invaluable contributions to making baseball the game that links America's present with its past.

Apart from honoring individuals for the length and breadth of their contributions to the study and enjoyment of baseball, the Chadwick Award will educate the baseball community about sometimes little known but vastly important contributions from the game's past and thus encourage the next generation of researchers.

The contributions of nominees must have had public impact. This may be demonstrated by publication of research in any of a variety of formats: books, magazine articles, websites, etc. The compilation of a significant database or archive that has facilitated the published research of others will also be considered in the realm of public impact.

GARY ASHWILL by Todd Peterson

Gary Ashwill (1966–) is a researcher and historian of Black, Cuban, and minor league baseball. His Seamheads.com Negro Leagues Database was cited by Major League Baseball as one of the contributing factors in their belated recognition of the segregated circuits in December 2020.

The Kansas City native grew up a Royals fan: his favorite player was Amos Otis and his top baseball moment was George Brett's three-run home run to beat the Yankees in Game Three of the 1980 ALCS. Ashwill's other fond Royals memories include listening on the car radio in a parking lot as John Mayberry hit a long fly ball that bounced on the top of the outfield wall and bounded over for a walk-off home run, and Dane Iorg's game-winning single in Game Six of the 1985 World Series.

As a youth, he collected baseball encyclopedias and avidly read Bill James's baseball guides and Abstracts. His interest in the Negro Leagues began in his early teens when his mother gave him a copy of Robert Peterson's seminal Blackball history *Only the Ball Was White*. He began devouring everything he could find about the subject, including works by Jim Riley, Donn Rogosin, Phil Dixon, and Larry Lester. Most intriguing for the budding scholar were the *Baseball Research Journal* issues that included Dick Clark and John Holway's statistics for the 1921 and 1930 Negro National League.

Ashwill pursued his undergraduate and graduate studies at the University of Kansas and Duke University. While at KU he won the Merrill Award for excellence in research and teaching English. His baseball research career started in earnest at Duke when he noticed microfilm rolls of the *Chicago Defender* while walking through the library stacks one day. Recalling the paper's significance from books by Holway and others, he began to read and photocopy the *Defender*'s coverage of the Negro Leagues. He soon discovered other Black newspapers, learned how to use spreadsheets, and started compiling statistics on the NNL. Ashwill also had access to the University of North Carolina at Chapel Hill's depository of twentieth century Cuban newspapers, from which he compiled Cuban League statistics as well.

After Ashwill began posting some of his results to the email forum SABR-L in the early 2000s, Blackball historian Dick Clark invited him to join the Negro Leagues Researchers and Authors Group (NLRAG), which at the time was gathering statistics for the National Baseball Hall of Fame. Gary wound up doing the research for the 1928 and 1934 Negro Leagues seasons. He also continued uploading spreadsheets of statistics online, with much of his work appearing on the Baseball Think Factory's Hall of Merit. Ashwill remembers John Holway being very supportive of his efforts at that time.

In 2006 Ashwill started the outsider baseball blog Agate Type, where he wrote posts on obscure and unknown players, tracked down the truth behind various Blackball stories and legends, and presented the statistics he had been gradually compiling, including previously unexplored data such as Negro League park factors. Taking his cue from Bill James's "Tracers" pieces and Rob Neyer's *Big Book of Baseball Legends*, Ashwill started out with two premises: 1) that it was possible to dig up more objective, empirically-based knowledge of Black baseball history than was previously thought, and 2) that readers might be interested in the research process itself and not just the results. Ashwill was among the first historians to make use of the online archival resources that were simplifying and revolutionizing research, including digitized historical newspapers and documents such as steamship passenger lists, passport applications, and draft cards. In 2010 Ashwill and fellow researcher Patrick Rock helped uncover Pete Hill's birth name and family of origin, which in turn led to the legendary outfielder's plaque being officially corrected by the Hall of Fame.

In 2011, with the aid of Dan Hirsch, Mike Lynch, Scott Simkus, and Kevin Johnson, Ashwill brought his statistical research to the baseball website Seamheads.com, and created the Negro Leagues Database. The following year, with the blessings of Larry Lester and Dick Clark, they started incorporating the old NLRAG/Hall of Fame study into the site. So far the database has collected 9,137 box scores for approximately 12,545 Negro League games (73%) for the period 1920 through 1948, garnering a SABR Baseball Research Award along the way.

Ashwill has also produced articles for *Base Ball: A Journal of the Early Game* and *Black Ball: A Journal of the Negro Leagues*, in addition to editing and writing the introduction for Summer Game Books 2014 edition of *Sol White's Official Base Ball Guide*.

After leaving graduate school with an MA, Ashwill worked as the Managing Editor for the investigative journalism magazine *Southern Exposure*. During his time there, he shepherded an award-winning series that exposed the role of big banks in subprime lending. Since 2005 Gary has worked as a freelance academic editor and currently resides in Durham with his wife and two dogs. ∎

ALAN NATHAN by Dan Raley and Dan Levitt

Alan Nathan never played in a big-league baseball game. Or in the minor leagues. Or at the collegiate level. He last grabbed a mitt and ran out on the field as a Maine high school freshman before deciding his exceptional foot speed was better suited for the track team. This lifelong Boston Red Sox and Ted Williams fan, however, would reconnect with baseball more than half a century later. Following a highly distinguished career as an experimental nuclear physicist, Nathan focused his attention on baseball—bent on finding new ways to understand it, to master it. He has been unlocking secrets from this game of never-ending nuance ever since. He has dissected the angle of the swing plane, researched the spin of a pitched ball, and analyzed the movement of a knuckleball.

His new quest began in 1997 when Nathan, invited to speak about physics to the public as part of a university community outreach program, decided to try something different. He opened a book on the physics of baseball written by Robert Adair that had been in his possession for some time, found that it piqued his interest, and shared his thoughts with the audience. That year he also published his first article on baseball in *Scientific American*.

His presentation was expected to be a one-shot deal: Nathan and this fascination with the science of baseball. However, a reporter for the *Champaign News-Gazette* (Illinois) caught his presentation and wrote about it in a front-page story in the Sunday newspaper.

A year and a half later, Nathan started conducting his own baseball research. In his first attempt—while examining bats—the results didn't make sense to him. He tried it again and his success led to an entirely new area of study for him.

In 2000 at an American Association for the Advancement of Science convention in Washington, DC, Nathan met Dave Baldwin, a former major-league pitcher who had become a genetics researcher and systems engineer after his playing career ended. They found a common bond in filtering through baseball's fine points, and wrote a paper together with two other co-authors on "Paradoxical Popups: Why Are They So Hard to Catch?"

Since then Nathan has become baseball's foremost authority on the physics of the game. He has published scores of articles—in particular on the collision between the bat and ball and the flight of the baseball—that have expanded our quantitative understanding and visualization of baseball's most fundamental interactions. Beyond the physical interactions themselves, Nathan's research examined their implications, from how a batter's swing might be optimized to what insights might be extractable from the data explosion coming out of ballpark-installed technologies.

Examples of Nathan's work include papers on the spin of a baseball, declaring in one that "All Spin is Not Alike." He has found that some pitchers are much better than others in generating spin, a concept that hasn't always been spelled out to everyone. He took a special interest in the knuckleball and its unpredictability, concluding that small, little-known factors led to big changes, some of them revolving around the use of the baseball's seams.

Nathan currently is tapping into new statistical information made available at every big-league ballpark; every pitch and batted ball is tracked now, providing a tremendous amount of new data to analyze. All baseball really needs is someone like this downstate Illinois physicist to wade through them and see where they go. His expertise is such that Major League Baseball and its teams have reached out to him for research support.

Born on September 17, 1946, in Rumford, Maine, Nathan spent his first 16 years in the New England state before moving to Maryland. After graduating from Montgomery Blair High School in Silver Spring, Maryland, Nathan earned a physics degree from the University of Maryland in 1968. He received a master's

degree and PhD in physics from Princeton University, interrupted by a two-year stint in the US Army.

Nathan joined the University of Illinois faculty in 1977 and became a full professor eight years later. Away from physics, he remains interested in politics, American history, constitutional law, mathematical puzzles, and the physics of sports that don't involve baseball. While he gave up his baseball career at an early age, Nathan didn't totally walk away from diamond games. He's played softball from that time forward, competing in assorted beer leagues and senior leagues.

Meanwhile, Nathan will continue to analyze the hardball game. He will look for new approaches, for those rare breakthroughs, something to set the game on its ear. "Had that reporter not been in the audience, listening to my talk, I never would have gotten involved with this," Nathan said. "That was not my intent. Things happen serendipitously." ■

(Adapted from "Alan Nathan," SABR Biography Project)

ROBERT W. PETERSON by Mark Armour

Robert W. Peterson (1925–2006) was a newspaper writer, a freelance journalist, and the author of several books on sports and contemporary news events. His primary contribution to baseball was the seminal *Only the Ball Was White*, a 1970 book on the Negro Leagues, which remained a foundation for the next few decades of scholarship in the field. "The seismic impact of his book shook the baseball world like the archaeological discovery  of the Lucy fossil in 1974," Larry Lester would later write. "Its aftershocks lifted Black baseball from the abyss with untold stories and unheard voices."

Born and raised in Warren, a town in northwest Pennsylvania, Peterson's childhood was filled with ballplaying of all kinds. Besides playing himself, once or twice a summer he was able to watch barnstorming Black teams take on the best local adults, even shagging balls for the visitors during batting practice. He long recalled a mammoth home run hit by Josh Gibson in Warren in 1939.

After a stint in the US Navy at the end of World War II (playing for the Navy Torpedo Shop team on his base), in 1950 he graduated from Upsala College in East Orange, New Jersey. He played college baseball, and during the summer Peterson went back to Warren and played for a semi-pro team, mainly as a

catcher. In 1948 his club took on a couple of independent Black teams, including the Indianapolis Clowns.

After college Peterson spent 16 years as a reporter and editor for several small newspapers and newspaper chains, before working as an editor at the *New York World-Telegram and The Sun* in 1962. When it folded four years later, he became a full-time freelancer, which he remained for the rest of his life. Soon after deciding on this career path, inspired by his memories of watching Black players in his youth, he turned to the research on what became his master work.

Peterson spent the summer of 1967 researching the long history of Black baseball, focusing on the sporting press and Black newspapers, covering 1885 through the early 1950s, creating league and team rosters. He spent another several months driving around the Northeast interviewing surviving ballplayers or their widows. He turned in his manuscript in late 1969, and it was published the following May. It was hardly a bestseller—he believed he sold about 8,000 copies in hardcover, and he found no interest in a paperback until 1984.

Peterson wrote thoughtfully of the two sides of the Negro Leagues' story: "Negro baseball was at once heroic and tawdry, a gladsome thing and a blot on

America's conscience." Although the leagues had been going strong only 25 years earlier, by 1970 they were hardly talked about even among famous alumni. Things slowly began to change. Satchel Paige was inducted into the National Baseball Hall of Fame in 1971, and many others have followed. Today we have many great books on the leagues and players, an accomplished and prolific SABR committee, and an annual Negro Leagues conference. Peterson's book was the start of all of it.

Peterson married Marguerite (Peggy, also a newspaper reporter) in 1954, and they raised two children, Thomas and Margaret, during a happy union that lasted until his death. Early on they moved as Bob's career required it, but eventually settled in Ramsey, New Jersey, and resided there for 40 years.

Peterson wrote several more books, about the origins of professional football and basketball, and the Boy Scouts, that relied on the same combination of newspaper research and oral history that had made *Only the Ball was White* such a critical success. He wrote for many national magazines and was a regular contributor to *Scouting* and *Boys' Life* for many years.

Although he did not do much baseball research after his book came out, Peterson was an active participant in SABR's Negro Leagues Committee, and attended several Jerry Malloy Conferences. At the very first conference—in Harrisburg in 1998—Peterson was the keynote speaker. At the time of his death, he was a member of the Special Committee on the Negro Leagues that elected 17 people to the Baseball Hall of Fame in 2006. He cast his votes in absentia but died just days before the committee votes were totaled.

Peterson died on February 11, 2006, in Lower Macungie Township, Pennsylvania. ■

Contributors

GARY BELLEVILLE is a retired Information Technology professional living in Victoria, British Columbia. He has written articles for both the SABR Games Project and the Baseball Biography Project, in addition to contributing to several SABR books. Gary grew up in Ottawa, Ontario and graduated from the University of Waterloo with a Bachelor of Mathematics (Computer Science) degree. He patiently awaits the return of his beloved Montreal Expos.

SAMUEL BORGEMENKE is a third-year undergraduate student at The Ohio State University who is studying Statistics. He is from Cincinnati, Ohio, and has been a SABR member since 2019. His interest in "ringless" Hall of Famers stems from one of his favorite players, Ken Griffey Jr., who never won a World Series.

DR. PAUL CANAVAN is an Assistant Professor at Eastern Connecticut State University (ECSU). He is a researcher and rehabilitation specialist with emphasis on injury prevention and sport performance enhancement. He is a SABR member and an accomplished scholar and has presented internationally in China, England, Turkey, Canada and recently at the 2019 National NSCA Conference. He has worked with athletes of all levels including collegiate and professional. Dr. Canavan's research has been published in many high-quality research journals including *Medicine Science in Sport and Exercise*, *Journal of Strength and Conditioning Research*, and *Archives of Physical Medicine and Rehabilitation*.

COLUMBIA UNIVERSITY SOCIETY FOR BASEBALL RESEARCH is an interdisciplinary undergraduate student group affiliated with Columbia University founded by Anthony Montes and Charles Orlinsky. The mission of the club is to curate, create, and publish novel baseball research from the greater Columbia community and foster an accessible learning environment for Columbia students and faculty to grow baseball knowledge. If you have any questions or interest in collaborating feel free to contact current President Anthony Montes via email at ajm2273@columbia.edu.

ROBERTS EHRGOTT is the author of *Mr. Wrigley's Ball Club: Chicago and the Cubs during the Jazz Age* (University of Nebraska Press, 2013). The Philip G. Spitzer Literary Agency served as the representative for the book, which placed as first runner-up in voting for the 2014 Casey Award in baseball literature. Ehrgott's career in baseball history began in the 1980s, when he reintroduced Indianapolis residents to a virtually forgotten native son, Hall of Famer Chuck Klein; as a result, the city dedicated a municipal sports complex in Klein's name. Away from squinting at microfilm and online baseball archives, Ehrgott has edited publications as diverse as *The Saturday Evening Post* and the academic journal *Educational Horizons*, founded in 1910 to serve women in education.

CAMPBELL GIBSON, PhD, is a retired Census Bureau demographer, with interests in baseball ranging from biography to statistical analysis. His first article in the *Baseball Research Journal* was "Simon Nicholls: Gentleman, Farmer, Ballplayer" published in Vol. 18 (1989). His article "WAA vs. WAR: Which is the Better Measure for Overall Performance in MLB, Wins Above Average or Wins Above Replacement?" was published in Vol. 48, No. 2 (2019).

MICHAEL HAUPERT is Professor of Economics at the University of Wisconsin-La Crosse. He is co-chair of the SABR Business of Baseball Committee, editor of the newsletter "Outside the Lines," and a 2020 recipient of the Henry Chadwick award.

MIKE HOENIGMANN has been a SABR member since 2020. He has his Masters Degree in History and is a social studies teacher on Long Island. Mike played baseball growing up and has been a lifelong Mets fan. He has a particular interest in the convergence of two of his favorite things: American history and baseball.

DOUGLAS JORDAN, PhD, is a professor at Sonoma State University in Northern California where he teaches corporate finance and investments. He's been a regular contributor to *BRJ* since 2014. He runs marathons when he is not watching or writing about baseball. You can contact him at jordand@sonoma.edu.

MIKE KASZUBA is a retired newspaper reporter, and spent 35 years at the *Minneapolis Star Tribune*. He covered local and state government, as well as sports business issues, and was the lead reporter covering the public subsidy packages used to build stadiums for the Minnesota Twins, Minnesota Vikings, and the University of Minnesota football program. He is a native of the Chicago area, currently lives in Florida and has been a SABR member since 2020. He can be reached at michaeljkaszuba@gmail.com.

BILL NOWLIN still lives in the same Cambridge, Massachusetts, house he was in when he joined SABR in the last century. He's been active both in the Boston Chapter and nationally, a member of the Board of Directors since 2004 (a good year for Red Sox fans). He has written several hundred bios and game accounts, and helped edit a good number of SABR's books.

A graduate of UC Berkeley, **DAN SCHOENHOLZ** is pleased to share the Berkeley-based story of Reversible Baseball with fans and researchers. Though this is his first *BRJ* publication, his baseball-themed poetry and fiction have appeared in *Aethlon, the Journal of Sport Literature*; his accounts of baseball roadtrips have appeared in the *San Jose Mercury News*; and his crossword puzzles, often peppered with baseball-related entries, have appeared in *The New York Times* and *Los Angeles Times*. When not rooting on his beloved Oakland A's, Dan serves as Community Development Director for the City of Fremont, California.

JOHN H. SCHWARZ is an octogenarian who has been a member of SABR for many years. He started a lifelong love of baseball with the 1945 World Series. He previously wrote for SABR in a piece on Sam "Tooth Pick" Jones, the first African American to pitch a no-hitter in the major leagues.

DAVID SIEGEL has been a member of SABR since 2006. After 40 years as a Professor of Political Science and administrator at Brock University in St. Catharines, Ontario, Canada, he has now turned his attention to doing research on baseball. Contact: dsiegel@brocku.ca.

JAY WIGLEY first joined SABR in 1999 after discovering Retrosheet in 1996. His earliest baseball memory is the scoreboard animations at the Astrodome during a game in the early 1970s. Jay lives in Knoxville, Tennessee, where he works as a Quality professional in the medical device industry.

STEVEN K. WISENSALE, PhD, is a long-time SABR member and Professor Emeritus of Public Policy in the Department of Human Development and Family Sciences at the University of Connecticut where he taught a course, "Baseball and Society: Politics, Economics, Race and Gender." He went to Japan as a Fulbright Scholar in 2017 where he taught a course, "Baseball Diplomacy in Japan-US Relations," at two universities. During his stay he also made a presentation on his research at a meeting of the Tokyo SABR chapter. He can be reached via e-mail at steven.wisensale@uconn.edu.

Society for American Baseball Research

Cronkite School at ASU
555 N. Central Ave. #416, Phoenix, AZ 85004
602.496.1460 (phone)
SABR.org

Become a SABR member today!

If you're interested in baseball — writing about it, reading about it, talking about it — there's a place for you in the Society for American Baseball Research. Our members include everyone from academics to professional sportswriters to amateur historians and statisticians to students and casual fans who enjoy reading about baseball and occasionally gathering with other members to talk baseball. What unites all SABR members is an interest in the game and joy in learning more about it.

SABR membership is open to any baseball fan; we offer 1-year and 3-year memberships. Here's a list of some of the key benefits you'll receive as a SABR member:

- Receive two editions (spring and fall) of the *Baseball Research Journal*, our flagship publication
- Receive expanded e-book edition of *The National Pastime*, our annual convention journal
- 8-10 new e-books published by the SABR Digital Library, all FREE to members
- "This Week in SABR" e-newsletter, sent to members every Friday
- Join dozens of research committees, from Statistical Analysis to Women in Baseball.
- Join one of 70+ regional chapters in the U.S., Canada, Latin America, and abroad
- Participate in online discussion groups
- Ask and answer baseball research questions on the SABR-L e-mail listserv
- Complete archives of *The Sporting News* dating back to 1886 and other research resources
- Promote your research in "This Week in SABR"
- Diamond Dollars Case Competition
- Yoseloff Scholarships

- Discounts on SABR national conferences, including the SABR National Convention, the SABR Analytics Conference, Jerry Malloy Negro League Conference, Frederick Ivor-Campbell 19th Century Conference, and the Arizona Fall League Experience
- Publish your research in peer-reviewed SABR journals
- Collaborate with SABR researchers and experts
- Contribute to Baseball Biography Project or the SABR Games Project
- List your new book in the SABR Bookshelf
- Lead a SABR research committee or chapter
- Networking opportunities at SABR Analytics Conference
- Meet baseball authors and historians at SABR events and chapter meetings
- 50% discounts on paperback versions of SABR e-books
- Discounts with other partners in the baseball community
- SABR research awards

We hope you'll join the most passionate international community of baseball fans at SABR! Check us out online at SABR.org/join.

- - - ✂ -

SABR MEMBERSHIP FORM

	Annual	3-year	Senior	3-yr Sr.	Under 30
Standard:	❑ $65	❑ $175	❑ $45	❑ $129	❑ $45
(International members wishing to be mailed the Baseball Research Journal should add $10/yr for Canada/Mexico or $19/yr for overseas locations.)					
Canada/Mexico:	❑ $75	❑ $205	❑ $55	❑ $159	❑ $55
Overseas:	❑ $84	❑ $232	❑ $64	❑ $186	❑ $55
Senior = 65 or older before Dec. 31 of the current year					

Participate in Our Donor Program!

Support the preservation of baseball research. Designate your gift toward:
❑General Fund ❑Endowment Fund ❑Research Resources ❑_____
❑ I want to maximize the impact of my gift; do not send any donor premiums
❑ I would like this gift to remain anonymous.

Note: Any donation not designated will be placed in the General Fund.
SABR is a 501 (c) (3) not-for-profit organization & donations are tax-deductible to the extent allowed by law.

Name _____

E-mail* _____

Address _____

City _____ ST_____ ZIP_____

Phone _____ Birthday _____

* Your e-mail address on file ensures you will receive the most recent SABR news.

Dues $_____

Donation $_____

Amount Enclosed $_____

Do you work for a matching grant corporation? Call (602) 496-1460 for details.

If you wish to pay by credit card, please contact the SABR office at (602) 496-1460 or sign up securely online at SABR.org/join. We accept Visa, Mastercard & Discover.

Do you wish to receive the *Baseball Research Journal* electronically? ❑ Yes   ❑ No
Our e-books are available in PDF, Kindle, or EPUB (iBooks, iPad, Nook) formats.

Mail to: SABR, Cronkite School at ASU, 555 N. Central Ave. #416, Phoenix, AZ 85004